<u>Price Guide</u>

Buying and Selling
Celebrity Dolls

Michele Karl

Portfolio Press

Dedication

To my wonderful husband Joe — his support and encouragement have given me the opportunity to do what I love, write! And to my two favorite dolls, Mathew and Angela. I love you.

The writer has made every effort to secure permission to reproduce any copyrighted material and apologizes for any errors or omissions. If we have inadvertently omitted a credit, we will be happy to acknowledge and correct this in future printings.

Barbie is a registered trademark of Mattel, Inc.
Terri Lee is a trademark of the Terri Lee Sales Corp.

This book contains information gathered from many sources. It is published as a general reference and not as a substitute for independent verification. The prices given in this book are intended as a guide only. The author and the publisher have used care and diligence in the preparation of this book and have made every effort to ensure its accuracy. We assume neither liability nor responsibility for any loss incurred by users of this book.

First edition/First printing

Copyright ©2002 Michele Karl. All rights reserved. No part of the contents of this book may be reproduced without the written permission of the publisher.

To purchase additional copies of this book, please contact:
Portfolio Press, 130 Wineow Street, Cumberland, MD 21502
877-737-1200

Library of Congress Control Number 2001-135270
ISBN 0-942620-55-0

Editors: Robert Haynes-Peterson, Virginia Ann Heyerdahl
Design and Production: Tammy S. Blank
Cover design by John Vanden-Heuvel Design
Cover photo: *Princess Diana (White House)* by Paul Crees and Peter Coe

Printed and bound in Korea

Acknowledgments

I would like to thank the following people and organizations for their help in putting this book together. Their donations of photographs, information and knowledge helped make this book complete. They include in alphabetical order: Annette's Antique Dolls, Tracy Collier, David Cox—"Wildogs," Paul Crees and Peter Coe, Robert and Jo Anne Engle—"Celebrity Splash Promotions," Rob Heroux, Marlene Grant, Jan and Ernie Jensen, Joe Karl, Ronnie Kauk, Susan Killoran, Carl Kludt, Jim Madden, Steve Malatinsky, Suellen Manning, McFarlane Toys, Jim and Shari McMasters—McMasters Doll Auctions, Sue Munsell, Ken and Sunnie Newell, Kenneth Newell, Butch Patrick, Play Along Toys, Inc., Lynnae Ramsey, Ken Reinstein, Joyce and Larry Rossiter, Jr., David Sturgeon, Toy Frantics, Billie Nelson Tyrrell, Sharon Uhr, Patricia Wood, and my Internet friends for sending me some wonderful images!

I would also like to thank Tom Farrell and Krystyna Poray Goddu of Portfolio Press for asking me to do this project. I appreciate their faith in me. When I said, "Yes! I'd love to do it!" I did not realize the amount of time it would take to add biographical information with the listings. However, I would do it all over again. There is a wealth of information in this book, not only on the dolls and figures presented, but also on the people and characters that inspired them. Some of the individuals who inspired dolls are very well known, while others you have probably never heard of. Included in this book are likenesses of Royalty and Movie Stars, Heroines and Super Heroes. Enjoy and Happy Collecting!

— *Michele Karl*

Do you have a celebrity doll not listed in this book? Send a photograph (no Polaroids, please) and complete information including size, material, maker and age to the author: Michele Karl, PO Box 1228, Seymour, TN 37865. Your doll may be a future star and featured in upcoming releases!

Introduction

Buying and Selling Celebrity Dolls is a collection of your favorite celebrities, dating from the early 1900s all the way forward to today's brightest stars, preserved forever in likenesses big enough to hold in your hand. Who says you cannot have Britney Spears, Harrison Ford and Dolly Parton in your living room at the same time? With this book, you can now have hundreds of celebrities visiting you at any one time!

Determining Value

The prices in this book reflect dolls and figures with their original clothes and, in many cases, with their original boxes. If you are evaluating a doll or figure that does not have its original clothes and box, you should deduct 50 percent of the price listed. If the dolls and figures are dirty or damaged, you should deduct an additional 25 percent. In other words, if you have a mint doll that is all original, it is worth much more than a dirty out-of-box doll in a re-dressed outfit.

If you are looking at the prices to guide you in selling your dolls and figures, there are a few things you should note. First, dealers usually only pay 50 percent of the value of an item. They need to resell it and make a profit. Second, a doll or figure is only worth what someone is willing to pay for it. I have seen dolls and figures listed for $50 that have sold for $200, and I have seen that same item sell at a different time or in a different part of the country for $25. It is all about supply and demand. Get two people who want an item and you will see the price go up. The rarer the item, the better the chance that it will sell higher than "book price." Some items, such as the original *Star Wars* figures, can go higher than the quoted prices in their original packaging. The prices listed reflect a combination of sales from different parts of the country in addition to Internet sales. They are to be used only as a guide, to help you in buying or selling a doll or figure.

How to Use This Book

The dolls are listed in alphabetical order by the last name of the person the doll was made to represent. For instance, the *I Dream of Jeannie* doll is listed under "Eden, Barbara"—the name of the actress who played Jeannie in the television series. The names are cross-referenced in the back of the book to make it easier to find a particular doll, but if you know the actual person's last name, that is the quickest way to find the doll.

A

Aaron, Hank (Henry). A professional baseball player, Aaron played for the Milwaukee Braves (later called the Atlanta Braves) from 1954 to 1974, after which he played for the Milwaukee Brewers. Aaron broke Babe Ruth's record for home runs with his 715th home run. He was inducted into the Baseball Hall of Fame in 1982.

1. Hank Aaron Nodder. Sports Spec. Corp. U.S.A. 1974. 8 inches. Composition head, painted features. Marked: "© 1974 SPORTS SPEC. CORP. LA-CAL. 90024." ......**$25-$30**

2. Henry Aaron. Ceramic bobbing head doll. S.A.M., Inc. China. Circa 1990s. 7 to 8 inches. Plastic, painted features. Limited to 1,000. ....**$20-$25**

2: This ceramic bobbing head doll represents baseball player Henry Aaron, by S.A.M. Inc.

Abbott, Bud. Comedian Abbott worked mainly with his partner, Lou Costello, and together they comprised one of the greatest comedy teams in the history of show business—Abbott & Costello. They mastered the straight man/clown relationship, while at the same time creating a magic that took them from the burlesque stage to radio, Broadway, film and television. In 1991, the United States Postal Service paid homage to the team by creating a stamp in their likeness as part of their Comedy Legends' Commemorative Stamp Booklet. (See also Costello, Lou.)

Abbott. Ideal Toy Corp. 1984-1985. 12 inches. All vinyl character, painted features; dressed in baseball uniform, with audio tape. ....**$40-$50**

Adams, Abigail. First lady of the United States, Adams was the wife of President John Adams, the second president of the United States. Her son, John Quincy Adams, went on to become the sixth president of the United States.

1. Abigail Adams. Peggy Nisbet. England. #P728. 1976. 7 inches. Plastic, painted features; dressed in long gown. ....**$25-$50**

2. Abigail Adams. Alexander Doll Company. U.S.A. 1976 to 1978. 14 inches. Plastic and vinyl; dressed in long gown. Part of the First Ladies Series. ....**$75-$125**

Adams, Don. Actor Adams is best known as the bungling Agent 86 Maxwell Smart (1965-1970) on the television series *Get Smart*. He also starred in the movie version, a remake of the series entitled *Get Smart Again—The Movie* (1989). (See also Feldon, Barbara.)

Get Smart. Exclusive Toy Products, Inc. China. 1998. 9 inches. All vinyl, painted features; wearing suit, with accessory and display stand. Sold on card. ....**$15-$20**

Adams, John. The second president of the United States, Adams was married to his wife, Abigail Adams, for more than fifty years. His son, John Quincy Adams, was elected sixth president of the United States.

John Adams. Peggy Nisbet. England. #P727. 1976. 7 inches. Plastic, painted features; dressed in suit of the times. ....**$50-$75**

Adams, Louisa. First lady of the United States, Adams was the wife of President John Quincy Adams, sixth president of the United States.

Louisa Adams. Alexander Doll Company. U.S.A. 1976 to 1978. 14 inches. Plastic and vinyl, jointed; dressed in period clothes. Part of the First Ladies Series. ....**$75-$125**

Adams, Stanley. Actor Adams played many character roles, including Tybo, the Carrot Man on the television series *Lost in Space*, which aired from 1965 to 1968 on CBS.

Carrot Man. Trendmasters, Inc. China. #09508. 1998. 11 inches. Vinyl body and face, head molded orange to look like a carrot top, orange fabric body; orange clothing, green leaf shoes, boxed with a black gun. ....**$40-$50**

Stanley Adams as Tybo, the Carrot Man, from the *Lost in Space* television series. *Courtesy of David Spurgeon.*

2: Prince Albert by Zapf Dolls.

Addams, Victoria. (See Spice Girls).

Albert, Eddie.
Actor Albert's career began in the 1938 Film *Brother Rat*. He starred in many films, but is best remembered for his television work. Albert played the role of Oliver Douglas on the hit television series *Green Acres*, which aired from September 1965 to September 1971. During the 1970s, Albert helped establish City Children's Farms in low-income areas of major cities across the country.

1. Green Acres Paper Dolls Booklet. Whitman. 1967. Cover shows Eddie Albert with co-star Eva Gabor. ....**$50-$60,** uncut

2. Green Acres Paper Dolls. Whitman. 1968. Cover shows Eddie Albert with co-star Eva Gabor. ....**$40-$50,** uncut

Albert (Prince).
Prince Albert was born near Coburg, Germany, and was known as Prince Consort, although his official title was Prince of Saxe-Coburg-Gotha. He married Queen Victoria, his first cousin, in 1840.

1. Prince Albert. Peggy Nisbet. England. #P624. Circa 1960s. 8 inches. Plastic, painted features; dressed in royal outfit. ....**$50-$60**

2. Prince Albert. Zapf Dolls. Germany. #071052. 1988. 18 inches. Vinyl, green sleep eyes, brown rooted hair; wearing white child's gown and hat; dressed in clothes styled in the fashion of the period. Signed by the artist and comes with a certificate of authenticity. Limited edition of 500. ....**$100-$150**

Alda, Alan.
Actor Alda began acting in films in the 1960s. He has appeared in more than two dozen films, including *Club Land* (2001). As a television actor, Alda is best known for his role as Captain Benjamin Franklin Pierce (aka Hawkeye) in the television series *M*A*S*H*, which aired on CBS from 1972 until 1983.

Hawkeye. Tristar International, Ltd. Hong Kong. #4100. 1982. 3 inches. All vinyl, fully jointed, painted features and clothing. Sold on card with pictures of the cast. Copyright by Aspen Productions and Twentieth Century Fox Film Corporation. ....**$15-$20**

Alden, John.
Alden was a settler in the colony of Plymouth during the time of the Pilgrims. He was written about by the poet Henry Wadsworth Longfellow in "The Courtship of Miles Standish."

John Alden. Vogue Doll Company. U.S.A. 1953. 7 inches. Hard plastic, fully jointed, sleep eyes, blonde wig; wearing black hat, gray pilgrim outfit with white collar and cuffs with black belt and black shoes. This is a Ginny doll with wig. ....**$200-$300**

Alden, Priscilla Mullens.
Alden was a settler in the colony of Plymouth during the time of the Pilgrims. She sailed on the Mayflower and was written about by poet Henry Wadsworth Longfellow.

1. Priscilla. Alexander Doll Company. U.S.A. Circa 1930s. 8 inches. Composition "Little Betty" with movable arms and legs. ....**$200-$250**

2. Priscilla Alden. Plastic Molded Arts (PMA) U.S.A. 1951. 6 inches. Plastic, jointed arms, sleep eyes. ....**$50-$75**

3. Priscilla. Vogue Doll Company. U.S.A. 1953. 7 inches. Hard plastic, fully jointed, sleep eyes, blonde wig; wearing all-white full-length dress with white hat. This is a Ginny doll with wig. ....**$200-$300**

4. Priscilla. Alexander Doll Company. U.S.A. 1965 to 1970. 1965 version #789, later version #789. 8 inches. Hard plastic, bendable knees. ....$250-$300

Alexander, Beatrice (Behrman). The
legendary designer and businesswoman known as Madame Alexander founded the Alexander Doll Company and began producing dolls in 1923. Today, it is still one of the leading producers of dolls in the country. Madame died in 1990.

1. Madame Alexander. Self Portrait. Alexander Doll Company. U.S.A. #2295. 1984. 21 inches. Wearing one-piece skirt in pink; 1985 to 1987, pink dress with overskirt; 1988 to 1990, blue dress with full lace overskirt. ....$350-$400 each

2. Madame Alexander. Self Portrait. Alexander Doll Company. U.S.A. #79507. 1995. 21 inches. Wearing pink full-length gown with lace jacket. 100th Anniversary Doll, limited to 500. ....$600-$700

1: Madame Alexander by the Alexander Doll Company, 1988 to 1990, wears the blue dress with full lace overskirt. *Courtesy of David Spurgeon.*

Alexandra (Queen). Princess of Denmark,
Alexandra married Edward, Prince of Wales, in 1863 and assumed the title of Queen when he inherited the throne.

Queen Alexandra. Peggy Nisbet. England. #P612. 1960. 7 inches. Plastic; wearing States Robes. ....$150-$200

Alexandria (Princess). Alexandria is the sister of Edward, the Duke of Kent. Her aunt is Queen Elizabeth II.

Princess Alexandria. Chad Valley. England. 1941. 17 inches. Stiff felt with velveteen body, set-in glass eyes, mohair wig. Part of a series

of dolls including Princess Elizabeth, Princess Margaret Rose and Edward, the Duke of Ken. ....$350-$500

Ali, Muhammad. A world boxing champion
who introduced a new style to the sport, Ali, born Cassius Clay, described himself as the "greatest of all time" and, to many boxing fans, he was. He held the heavyweight title and was the first man to win the title three times. In 1990 he was inducted into the International Boxing Hall of Fame.

1. Muhammad Ali. Mego. Hong Kong. #61701. 1976. 10 inches. All vinyl, painted features; wearing white Everlast trunks, sold on card with boxing outfit of red and white robe, red boxing gloves and helmet. Box marked: "© 1976 Herbert Muhammad Enterprises, Inc.," also marked on box: "Ali Trigger Mechanism activates the Champ." Shows red, white and blue striping at bottom of box. Original price $2.20. ....$75-$100

2. Muhammad Ali Opponent. Mego. Hong Kong. 1976. 10 inches. All vinyl, painted features; wearing blue Everlast trunks, packaged with boxing outfit of blue and white robe. Shows red, white and blue striping at bottom of box. The word "Ali" is marked out in red on card. ....$50-$75

1: Muhammad Ali by Mego.

2A: Muhammad Ali Opponent by Mego.

2B: The back of the box for Muhammad Ali Opponent shows the trigger mechanism and the boxing ring.

3: Effanbee's Muhammad Ali from the Great Moments in Sports Series. *Courtesy of David Spurgeon.*

3. Muhammad Ali. Effanbee. China. 1986. 18 inches. All vinyl, painted features; wearing boxing gloves, white Everlast shorts with red trim, white boots and white cape with red trim. Part of the Great Moments in Sports Series. ....**$75-$100**

Allen, Karen. Actress Allen's first film was *The Wanderers* (1979). She has appeared in more than two dozen movies including *Raiders of the Lost Ark* (1981), in which she played the role of Marion Ravenwood. Allen also appeared in *The Perfect Storm* (2000).

Marion Ravenwood. Kenner. #46010. 1982. All vinyl, fully jointed, painted features; wearing cloth skirt (other clothing parts painted), packaged with vinyl monkey. Copyright by Lucasfilm Ltd. ....**$15-$25**

Allyson, June. Actress Allyson's film debut was in *Girl Crazy* (1943), after which she appeared in more than three dozen films. One of her best-known roles was as Jo in the movie *Little Women* (1949).

Jo. Ideal. 1984 to 1988. 12 inches. Vinyl, jointed, sleep eyes with eyelashes, rooted hair; dressed as Jo from *Little Women.* Marked on head: "©1978 MGM/CBS INC/1438 IDEAL 1982." ....**$40-$50**

Anderson, Loni. Actress Anderson is best known for her role as Jennifer Marlowe, the receptionist, on the weekly television series *WKRP in Cincinnati.* The show aired on CBS from 1978 until 1982. On film, Anderson played the role of Jayne Mansfield in a television movie. She is the ex-wife of actor Burt Reynolds.

1. Loni Anderson. Ideal. #1272-4. 1981. 11 inches. All vinyl, fully jointed, rooted blonde hair, painted brown eyes; wearing a red dress with white high heels. Was to be sold with an 11-inch by 14-inch full-color picture of Loni Anderson. Not produced. (Only a prototype of this doll was made and shown in the catalog along with the statement that: "Final sculpturing of the doll pending approval by Loni Anderson." Some sources say that 5,000 pieces were produced, but when I asked Anderson, she stated that an authorized version of a doll made in her likeness was never produced.)

2. Loni. Kenner. China. #50010. 1981. 4 inches. All vinyl, jointed, rooted long blondish red hair; wearing orange pants and top called "Totally Tangerine." Fashion doll that was sold when the television show *WKRP in Cincinnati* was running and probably named Loni to capitalize on the show's popularity. Came in the Glamour Gals collection by Kenner. Sold in window box. ....**$20-$25**

Anderson, Pamela.

Actress Anderson has appeared in various television shows. She starred in her first series, *Baywatch,* and then in her own television series *V.I.P.* Anderson is considered a sex symbol by many.

1. Pamela Anderson as C.J. Parker. Toy Island. China. 1997. #26100. 12 inches. All vinyl, jointed, rooted blonde hair, painted features; wearing a red swimsuit with red jacket and blue shorts. Box is marked: "Official Baywatch Doll. Licensed © 1997 by the Baywatch Production Company" and shows photograph of Anderson and a separate photograph of the cast from *Baywatch.* ....**$15-$25**

1: Pamela Anderson as C.J. Parker from *Baywatch.* *Author's collection.*

2A: Close-up of Pamela Anderson as C.J. Parker. *Author's collection.*

2B: Right and below: Pamela Anderson as C.J. Parker-Playset, from *Baywatch*, with accessory pieces. *Author's collection.*

3: Pamela Anderson as Vallery Irons, by Play Along Toys, 2000.

2. Pamela Anderson as C.J. Parker-Playset. Toy Island. China. 1997. 12 inches. All vinyl, jointed, rooted blonde hair, painted features; wearing a red swimsuit, red jacket and blue shorts, comes with 20 accessory pieces including Baywatch Personal Watercraft. Box shows photograph of Anderson and a separate photograph of the cast from *Baywatch*. ....$35-$50

3. Pamela Anderson as Vallery Irons. Play Along Toys, Inc. 2000. 5 inches. All vinyl, painted features, blonde painted and molded hair; blue painted and molded jumpsuit. From her *V.I.P.* television series. ....$10-$15

Anderson, Richard. Actor Anderson has played several leading and supporting roles. He is perhaps best known for his character Oscar Goldman in the television series *The Six Million Dollar Man* and *The Bionic Woman*. Both shows aired in the 1970s.

1. Oscar Goldman. Kenner. Hong Kong. 1973. 13 inches. Vinyl, jointed, molded hair, painted features; wearing tan pants with black and white plaid jacket and green turtleneck shirt. ....$30-$40, loose; $85-$110, boxed

2. Oscar Goldman. Kenner. Hong Kong. #65100. 1977. 13 inches. Vinyl, fully jointed, molded hair, painted features. ..$30-$40, loose; $75-$100, boxed

2A: Close-up of Richard Anderson as Oscar Goldman. *Courtesy of Suellen Manning.*

2B: Anderson as Oscar Goldman, the "Six Million Dollar Man's Boss" by Kenner. *Courtesy of Suellen Manning.*

Andrew (Prince). Third child of Queen Elizabeth II of England, Andrew married Sarah Margaret Ferguson, known as the Duchess of York or "Princess Fergie," in 1986. They divorced in 1996.

1. H.R.H. Prince Andrew. Peggy Nisbet. England. No. #P413. Circa 1970s. 8 inches. Plastic; dressed in royal outfit. ....$50-$75

2. H.R.H. Prince Andrew in Naval Uniform. Peggy Nisbet. England. #P427. Circa 1980s. 10 inches. Plastic. ....$40-$50

Andrews, Julie. Actress, singer and children's book author, Andrews won an Academy Award for her role as *Mary Poppins* in the Walt Disney movie of the same name (1964). One of her best-remembered roles is Maria von Trapp in *The Sound of Music* (1965), which was one of the most popular films of all time.

1. Mary Poppins. Horsman. U.S.A. 1964. 11 inches. Vinyl, rooted black hair, painted blue eyes. In 1965, the same doll was released with two outfits. ....$50-$75

2. Mary Poppins. Horsman. U.S.A. 1964. 35 inches. Plastic and vinyl walker. ....$75-$125

3. Mary Poppins. Horsman. U.S.A. 1965. Same as above, but 16 inches. ....$25-$45

4. Mary Poppins. Horsman. U.S.A. 1966. 27 inches. All vinyl. ....$125-$175

5. Mary Poppins. Gund. Japan. 1966. 11 inches. Fabric head and body, painted facial features, plastic hands; wearing hat with flowers, yellow scarf, black umbrella, cloth flower print handbag, black plastic boots, white blouse, orange bow, blue felt overcoat and purple skirt. ......$75-$100

6. Mary Poppins with Jane and Michael. Horsman. U.S.A. 1966. 11 inches (Mary). Plastic and vinyl, rooted black hair, painted blue eyes. ....$50-$75, set

7. Mary Poppins. Effanbee. China. #3392. 1985. 14 inches. All vinyl, jointed, rooted black hair, sleep eyes. Box marked: "© 1985 Effanbee Doll Corp." ....$50-$75

1: Horsman's 11-inch Mary Poppins in her original box. *Courtesy of Steve Malatinsky.*

7: Effanbee's 14-inch Mary Poppins from 1985, with her bag and umbrella. *Courtesy of David Spurgeon.*

8: Effanbee's 11-inch Mary Poppins from the 1990s. *Courtesy of David Spurgeon.*

6: Above, Julie Andrews as Mary Poppins with Jane and Michael. By Horsman.

5: Right, Julie Andrews as Mary Poppins, by Gund.

8. Mary Poppins. Effanbee. China. Circa 1990s. 11 inches. All vinyl, jointed, rooted black hair, sleep eyes. ....$50-$75

9. Mary Poppins. Mattel, Inc. 1994. #10313. 11 inches. Vinyl, jointed, with Mattel's Sleeping Beauty head; wearing long red dress over white pantaloons, navy blue coat, red scarf, white blouse with red midriff and bow, black hat and red boots. ....$30-$40

10. Maria from *The Sound of Music*. Alexander Doll Company. U.S.A. #1006. 1965. 8 inches. Hard plastic; wearing costume from the film. Part of set. ....$200-$250

11. Maria from *The Sound of Music*. Alexander Doll Company. U.S.A. #1206. 12 inches. Hard plastic and vinyl with "Nancy Drew" face. Small set produced by Alexander Doll Company from 1971 to 1973. ...$250-$300

Anne (Princess). The second child and only daughter of Queen Elizabeth II, Ann Elizabeth Alice Louise has received praise and respect as one of the most serious and hard working of the royal family.

1. Princess Anne. Alexander Doll Company. U.S.A. #396. 1957. 8 inches. Hard plastic, bending knee. ......**$600-$800**

2. Princess Anne. Chelsea Art. England. 1957. 8 inches. Bisque shoulder plate, bisque lower arms and legs, cloth body, smiling painted features, painted hair. ......**$75-$100**

3. Princess Anne. Peggy Nisbet. England. #P405. 1973. 7 inches. Plastic; wearing wedding dress. ....**$40-$60**

4. H.R.H. Princess Anne. Peggy Nisbet. England. #P412. Circa 1970s. 7 inches. Plastic; wearing formal riding dress. ....**$30-$40**

Anne (Queen). Queen of Great Britain and Ireland from 1702 to 1714.

1. Queen Anne. Ann Parker. England. 1977. 11 inches. Plastic doll affixed to wooden holder and base, red mohair wig, painted blue eyes; wearing elaborate gown of purple, white, gold and aqua blue. ....**$75-$100**

2. Queen Anne. Peggy Nisbet. England. #P450. Circa 1970s. 7 inches. Plastic, painted features, jointed at arms, mohair wig; wearing royal gown. ....**$40-$60**

Ansara, Michael. Actor Ansara, whose career began in the 1950s, is probably best known for his role as the Klingon Commander from the hit television series *Star Trek*. Ansara also played leads in earlier television shows including *Broken Arrow* (1956) and *Law of the Plainsman* (1959). He has appeared in more than two dozen movies including *Batman and Mr. Freeze: SubZero* (1997).

1. Cochise and his Pinto War Horse from the *Broken Arrow* series. Hartland Plastics, Inc. Hartland, WI. #816. 1958. 8 inches. Plastic, painted features, jointed arms. ....**$100-$150**, mint-in-box

2. Klingon Commander from the *Star Trek* television series. Mego. Hong Kong. #51200/6. 1974. 8 inches. All vinyl, fully jointed, painted features and hair; wearing Klingon uniform. ....**$50-$75**

Anthony, Susan B. A leader in the women's suffrage movement in the late 1800s, Anthony devoted her life to working against slavery. She was the first woman to be portrayed on a United States coin, a one-dollar piece first produced in 1979.

1. Susan B. Anthony. Hallmark. Taiwan. #400DT113-8. 1979. 7 inches. All cloth, printed features. ....**$10-$15**

2. Susan B. Anthony. Effanbee Doll Company. China. 1980. 15 inches. All vinyl, rooted dark brown hair, stationary brown glass eyes; dressed in taffeta gown with white lace trim, includes a Susan B. Anthony coin in a collector's case. Marked: "S.B.ANTHONY//LIMITED EDITION//EFFANBEE DOLL//LTD. EDITION//19©80." A Limited Edition Club Doll. ....**$100-$150**

2: Effanbee's 15-inch Susan B. Anthony from 1980. *Courtesy of David Spurgeon.*

Antony, Mark (Antonius, Marcus). This Roman political leader and general is usually paired with the Egyptian queen, Cleopatra. Their romance was the basis for a play by William Shakespeare and countless motion pictures.

Antony by Alexander Doll Company. U.S.A. #1310. 1980. 12 inches. Hard plastic, vinyl head; dressed in period costume. Part of "Portraits in History Series." ....**$50-$100**

Armes, Jay J. Private investigator Armes runs one of the largest private investigation agencies in the country. He is perhaps best known for successfully investigating and returning Marlon Brando's kidnapped son.

Jay J. Armes. Ideal. #4400. 1976 to 1977. 9 inches. All vinyl, poseable, molded hair with painted eyes, with interchangeable hooks for hands that were stored in a small red case; wearing light brown pants, black sweater with brown vest and brown shoes. ....**$50-$75**

Armstrong, Louis. One of the greatest jazz musicians of all time, Armstrong was a trumpet player who performed in more than a dozen films from the 1930s until the 1960s. One of his best-known roles was in the film *Hello, Dolly!* (1969).

Louis Armstrong. Effanbee. U.S.A. 1984. 17 inches. All vinyl, molded and painted features, holding a trumpet; wearing blue jacket with white shirt and black pants. Part of the Greatest Moments in Music Series. ....**$100-$150**

Louis Armstrong,
17 inches, by Effanbee.

Arness, James. Actor Arness has played the role of a cowboy in a variety of western-related shows. He is best known for his role as Marshall Matt Dillon in the television series *Gunsmoke,* which aired from 1955 to 1975. Arness also played the part of Zeb Macahan on *How the West Was Won.* Early in his career, he was cast as a monster in the 1950 movie *The Thing.*

1. Marshall Matt Dillon of Gunsmoke. Hartland Plastics, Inc. Hartland, WI. #822. 1958. 8 inches. Plastic, painted, moveable arms. Sold with plastic buckskin horse. ....**$150-$200**, mint-in-box

2. Zeb Macahan from How the West Was Won. Mattel, Inc. Hong Kong. #2367. 1978. 10 inches. All vinyl, fully jointed, painted blonde (yellow) hair, brown mustache, blue eyes. Head not marked, back marked: "© 1971 MATTEL, INC.//HONG KONG US &//FOREIGN PATENTED." Copyright by MGM, Inc. ....**$40-$60**

3. The Thing. Mego. Hong Kong. Circa 1970s. 8 inches. Vinyl, painted hair and features. ..**$20-$30**

4. Matt Dillon. Exclusive Toy Products, Inc. 1997. 9 inches. Fully poseable, plastic body, vinyl head; fully detailed cloth clothing, accessories include gun belt and display stand. Limited edition of 12,000, a Target Store exclusive. ....**$15-$25**

4: Matt Dillon, as portrayed by James Arness, from the television series *Gunsmoke.* Made by Exclusive Toy Products, Inc., the 9-inch figure was limited to an edition of 12,000.

Ashley, Karen. Actress Ashley played the role of Aisha Campbell, the Yellow Ranger in *Mighty Morphin Power Rangers,* a television series airing from 1993 to 1996. She joined the Power Rangers during the television series' second season and also starred in the movie *Mighty Morphin Power Rangers.* (See Johnson, Amy Jo for photograph.)

Aisha-Yellow Power Ranger. Bandai. China. #2369. 1995. 9 inches. All dark-brown vinyl, jointed, painted features, long dark brown hair; wearing a black and yellow flowered mini dress with yellow stockings and black shoes, boxed with Yellow Power Ranger outfit, helmet and boots. Box marked: "© 1995 Saban Entertainment." ....**$25-$35**, set; **$15-$20** individually

Karen Ashley as the Yellow Power Ranger. *Courtesy of David Spurgeon.*

Autry, Gene.

Known as the "Singing Cowboy," Autry starred and sang in countless films. He wrote and produced more than two hundred popular songs including "Here Comes Santa Claus" and "Rudolph, the Red-Nosed Reindeer." He published his autobiography, entitled *Back in the Saddle Again*, in 1978.

1. Gene Autry. Ralph A. Freundlich, Inc. U.S.A. 1939. 15 or 18 inches. Composition based with painted features. ....**$400-$500**

2. Gene Autry. Terri Lee Company. U.S.A. Circa 1950s. 16 inches. All hard plastic, painted features. Dressed in three different cowboy outfits. ....**$1,500-$2,000**

3. Gene Autry. Terri Lee Company. U.S.A. Circa 1950s. 16 inches. All hard plastic, painted features; dressed in extremely rare Gene Autry outfit. ....**$2,500-$3,500**

4. Gene Autry. Terri Lee Company. U.S.A. Circa 1950s. 16 inches. All hard plastic, painted features; dressed in blue jeans, yellow cowboy shirt with belt, boots, no hat. This doll sold for $1,700 at a November 2000 McMasters Doll Auction.

5. Gene Autry. National Mask and Puppet Corp. Circa 1950s. 10 inches. Hand puppet with rubber head and molded hat, hands and feet of rubber, cloth body. ....**$50-$75**

4: This Gene Autry by the Terri Lee Company sold for $1,700 at auction in 2000. *Courtesy of McMasters Doll Auctions.*

3: Gene Autry by the Terri Lee Company in a very rare outfit. This doll is complete right down to the Gene Autry pin on the belt buckle. *Courtesy of Jan Jensen.*

Aykroyd, Dan.

An actor, writer and singer, Aykroyd first gained popularity with the public as a member of the Not Ready for Prime Time Players on the weekly television series, *Saturday Night Live*. He combined talents with another cast member, John Belushi, to form The Blues Brothers, a singing team. He then co-starred with Belushi in the rock 'n' roll comedy *The Blues Brothers* (1980), which he wrote with director John Landis. Aykroyd went on to star in

2: Gene Autry by the Terri Lee Company in three different cowboy outfits. *Courtesy of Sue Munsell.*

a variety of films, including *Dr. Detroit* and *Ghostbusters.*

    1. Conehead from *Saturday Night Live.* Hamilton Gifts Ltd. Inc. China. Sold in different sizes, including 2 inches and 8 inches. Hard vinyl, all painted. ....2 inches, **$5-$10**; 8 inches, **$20-$25**

    2. Jake & Elwood-The Blues Brothers. Fun-4 All. China. #83002. 1997. 26 inches. All vinyl, jointed at arms, legs and neck, molded black hair, painted brown eyes and features; both dolls wore black hats, black jackets and pants, black shoes, with the Blues Brothers' signature sunglasses. Box marked: "© HOB Entertainment, Inc. All Rights Reserved. The Blues Brothers." Limited Edition. ....**$100-$150**, set (See Belushi, John for photograph.)

1: Dan Aykroyd as a Conehead from *Saturday Night Live. Author's collection.*

2C: The box for the Blues Brothers showing Dan Aykroyd as Elwood and John Belushi as Jake. *Courtesy of David Spurgeon.*

Baby Jane. (See Quigley, Juanita)

Baby Peggy. (See Montgomery, Peggy)

Baby Sandy. (See Henville, Sandra)

Baby Snooks. (See Brice, Fanny)

Bach, Barbara. Actress Bach is best known for her role as "A Bond Girl" from the James Bond film *The Spy Who Loved Me* (1977), in which she played the role of Anya Amasova, Bach also starred in *Caveman* (1981) and *Princess Daisy* (1983). She is married to singer/drummer Ringo Starr of the Beatles.

    Anya Amasova 007. Exclusive Toy Products, Inc. China. #28027. 1998. 6 inches. All vinyl, painted features. Box marked: "© 1962, © 1968, © 1989 The Spy Who Loved Me © 1977 Danjaq." ....**$20-$25**

Bach, Catherine. Actress Bach is best known for her role as sexy Daisy Duke on the hit television show *The Dukes of Hazzard*, which debuted in January of 1979 and ran until 1985. She also starred in several films, including *Nicole* (1978), and the Dukes of Hazzard movies: *The Dukes of Hazzard Reunion* (1997) and *The Dukes of Hazzard-Hazzard in Hollywood* (2000).

    1. Daisy Duke. Mego. Hong Kong. #09050/3, 1981. 7 inches. All vinyl, fully jointed, rooted brown hair, painted blue eyes. Head marked: "© WARNER BROS., //INC. 1980;" back marked: "©WARNER BROS INC 1980//MADE IN HONG KONG." ......**$30-$40**

    2. Daisy. Mego. Hong Kong. #09010/3. 1982. 3 inches. All vinyl, fully jointed, painted hair, features and clothing. Box marked: "Copyright Warner Bros., Inc. Made in Hong Kong." ....**$15-$20**

    3. Daisy with Jeep. Mego. Hong Kong. #09062. 1982. Same as above doll, except this one has with a plastic jeep. Copyright by Warner Bros., Inc. ....**$40-$50**

Bain, Barbara. Actress Bain appeared with husband Martin Landeau on the television series *Mission Impossible* from 1966 to 1969. Both stars also appeared in *Space 1999*, which debuted in 1975. Bain's work includes the films *Spirit of '76* (1991) and *Panic* (2000).

1. Space 1999 Doctor Russell. Mattel, Inc. Taiwan. #9544. 1965. 9 inches. All vinyl, fully jointed, painted blonde (yellow) hair, painted blue eyes; wearing orange uniform with shoes, came with stun gun, holster, communicator-computer that clipped to belt. Marked: "© 1975 ATV LICENSING LTD. TAIWAN" on back of head; "© 1973/MATTEL, INC./TAIWAN" on back. ....**$50-$75**

2. Eagle One Spaceship. Mattel, Inc. Taiwan. #9548. 1976. 2 feet long with living quarters. Includes 3-inch plastic figures of Professor Bergman, Doctor Russell and Commander Koenig. ......**$150-$200**, complete

Lenci's very rare 19-inch Josephine Baker in her Banana Dance outfit. *Courtesy of Billie Nelson Tyrrell.*

1A: Barbara Bain as Dr. Russell from Space 1999. *Courtesy of Suellen Manning.* 1B: The back of the package for Dr. Russell shows Professor Bergman and Commander Keonig. *Courtesy of Suellen Manning.*

Baker, Josephine. One of the first well-known black entertainers, Baker performed on stage and screen, as well as on recordings. Baker was decorated for her undercover work for the French Resistance during World War II. She was also a civil rights activist, refusing to perform for segregated audiences, thereby helping to integrate the Las Vegas nightclubs.

Josephine Baker. Lenci. Italy. 19 inches. All felt, painted features, black hair wig; dressed in her famous outfit from the Banana Dance with banana leaves and gold ring jewelry around neck, toes, ankles, knees, wrists and arms, also wearing large gold earrings. Very rare. ....**$4,000** up

Baker, Kenny. Actor Baker began his career in the 1930s with the film *Mr. Dodd Takes the Air* (1937). He starred in various roles in the 1930s and 1940s before resurfacing in films in the 1980s. He played the robot Artoo-Detoo (R2-D2) in the hit movie *Star Wars* in 1977 and *The Empire Strikes Back* in 1980. Baker also appeared in later episodes of the Star Wars saga.

1. Star Wars R2-D2. Kenner. Taiwan. 1977. #38200. 2¼ inches. Vinyl action figure. ..**$50-$60**

2. Star Wars The Empire Strikes Back R2D2. Kenner. Hong Kong. 1980. 2 inches. Vinyl action figure. ....**$25-$30**

3. Star Wars R2D2. Kenner. Hong Kong. 1977. 7 inches. Plastic robot that walked. ......**$150-$200**

4. Star Wars Radio-Controlled R2-D2. Kenner. Hong Kong. 1977. 8 inches. Battery-operated walking robot. ....**$200-$250**

5. Artoo-Detoo (R2-D2) with sensor scope. Kenner. Hong Kong. 1982. 2 inches. Vinyl and plastic figure. Copyright by Lucasfilm Ltd. ..... **$15-$25**

5: Kenner's Artoo-Detoo (R2-D2) with sensor scope, as portrayed by Kenny Baker in the film *Return of the Jedi.*

Ball, Lucille. An actress, musician, comedian, model, producer, Ball is best known for her role as Lucy in the television series *I Love Lucy*, in which she starred with her husband, Desi Arnaz. The show ran from 1951 until 1957. She won countless awards, including Emmys and the Academy of Television Arts and Sciences Governor's Award. (See also Keith, Richard.)

Lucille Ball. Effanbee Doll Company. U.S.A. 1985. 16 inches. All vinyl, painted features. The Effanbee Doll Company produced a variety of limited-edition dolls with numbered certificates. Many of the dolls could only be purchased through Effanbee's Limited Edition Doll Club or on the secondary market. Part of the Legend Series. ....$100-$125

Bara, Theda. One of the most successful and glamorous stars from 1910 to 1920, she ranked behind only Mary Pickford and Charlie Chaplin in popularity. Bara starred in a variety of productions, including *Under Two Flags* and *A Star There Was*. She was considered the "First Vamp of the Screen."

Theda Bara. Maker unknown. Circa 1900s. 25 inches. Bed doll type made of composition and cloth with unusual painted features, black mohair wig; wearing black and red dress with picture of herself on a pin back. Also came with banner that read: "FOX STAR THEDA BARA" with photograph of star. ....$1,200-$1,500

Bed doll representing Theda Bara. *Courtesy of Billie Nelson Tyrrell.*

Barnum, P.T. Circus promoter and owner Barnum called his circus "The Greatest Show on Earth."

P.T. Barnum. Hallmark. Taiwan. 1979. 6 inches. Cloth figure, printed clothing and face. Tag reads: "Copyright by Hallmark Cards, Inc. August 1979." ....$10-$15

Hallmark's 6-inch P.T. Barnum doll.

Barrymore, Drew. Actress Barrymore started her career at age seven, in the film *E.T.* She has continued to act in many feature films and opened her own production company, Flower Films, in the 1990s. One of her projects was the remake of the hit television series from the 1970s *Charlie's Angels*, which was released on the big screen in 2000.

Dylan from *Charlie's Angels*. Jakks Pacific Inc. China. 2000. 11 inches. All vinyl, fully jointed, rooted red hair with painted features; wearing black snakeskin style pants with matching jacket, blue top with black lace, also sold dressed in black pants with black midriff top and short jean jacket,

The three new Charlie's Angels—Drew Barrymore, Lucy Liu and Cameron Diaz—from the 2000 *Charlie's Angels* movie.

came boxed with stand. Box marked: "Action-Fashion Body I've got all the right poses! Charlie's Angels: TM & © 2000 Columbia Pictures Industries, Inc." ....$25-$40

Barton, Clara. Founder of the American Red Cross.

Clara Barton. Hallmark. Taiwan. #400DT114-4. 1979. All cloth, printed clothing and features. Tag reads: "Copyright by Hallmark Cards, Inc., August 1979." ....$5-$10

Clara Barton,
Hallmark, all cloth.

Bass, Lance (See N'Sync)

Beatles, The. The fabulous foursome of rock music was made up of John Lennon, Paul McCartney, George Harrison and Ringo Starr. The group appeared on *The Ed Sullivan Show* in 1964 and took the United States by storm. By the time the group broke up in 1971, they had sold more than 400 million records.

1. The Official Beatles. Remco. Hong Kong. 1964. Paul is 5 inches, all others are 4½ inches. Vinyl head, one-piece vinyl body, rooted black hair, painted eyes, open mouth with molded teeth, holds a vinyl guitar. Back marked: "THE//BEATLES//INC. Copyright 1964 by Nems Ent., Ltd. Licensed by Seltaeb Inc." ....$350-$400, set

2. The Bob'n Head Beatles. Car Mascots, Inc. Japan. 1964. Ringo is 7 inches, all others are 7¾ inches. Papier-mâché and plastic nodders. ....$250-$300, set

3. The Beatles. Pelham Puppets. England. 1965. 13 inches. Strung marionettes with composition heads and hands, wooden feet; jointed wood segmented bodies, black fur wigs for hair, painted features. Called the "Pop Singers." Marked on bar: "MADE IN ENGLAND, PELHAM PUPPETS." ....$400-$600, set

4. The Beatles. Yellow Submarine. McFarlane Toys. China. 1999. 8 inches. All vinyl, painted and molded features, jointed at arms. Showing Paul with Captain Fred. Other figures include John with Jeremy, George with Yellow Submarine and Ringo with Blue Meanie. There was also another Paul sold with Glove and Love Base. Copyright 1999 Subafilms Ltd. ....$20-$30

2: The Bob'n Head Beatles by Car Mascots, Inc.

4A: Beatle Paul shown with Captain Fred from the *Yellow Submarine*.

4B: Beatle John shown with Jeremy from the *Yellow Submarine*.

Beauharnais, Josephine. Empress of France and wife of Napoleon.

1. Josephine Beauharnais. Peggy Nisbet. England. #P461. 1970s. 7 inches. Plastic. ..$30-$40

2. Josephine. Alexander Doll Company. U.S.A. #1335. 1980. 12 inches. Plastic and vinyl; dressed in period costume. Part of the Portraits of History Series. "Nancy Drew" face. ....$50-$100

Beery, Carol Ann. Beery was a child actress who played in the film *China Seas* (1935). She was the adopted daughter of actor Walter Beery.

Carol Ann Beery. American Character Doll Co. U.S.A. 1935. Produced in a variety of sizes including 13 inches, 16 inches and 19 inches. All composition, jointed, painted hair, sleep eyes, some sold with wigs. Referred to as a "Hollywood Two-Some Doll." Marked: "PETITE" or "SALLY PETITE" on back. ....13 inches, **$250-$350**; 16 inches, **$400-$500**; 19 inches, **$500-$600**

Belushi, John. Belushi first became popular with the public as a member of the Not Ready for Prime Time Players on the weekly television series *Saturday Night Live*. He combined talents with another cast member, Dan Aykroyd, to form The Blues Brothers, a singing team. He then co-starred with Aykroyd in the rock 'n' roll comedy *The Blues Brothers* (1980). Belushi appeared in many films before his death in 1982, including *National Lampoon's Animal House* (1978).

1. Belushi as the Bee. Hamilton Gifts Ltd. Inc. China. Circa 1990s. 8 inches. All vinyl, painted. ....**$15-$20**

2. Jake & Elwood-The Blues Brothers. Fun-4-All. China. #83002. 1997. 26 inches. All vinyl, jointed at arms, legs and neck, molded black hair, painted brown eyes and features; both dolls wore black hats, black jackets and pants, black shoes, came with the Blues Brothers' signature sunglasses. Box marked: "© HOB Entertainment, Inc. All Rights Reserved. The Blues Brothers." Limited Edition. ....**$100-$150**, set

1: John Belushi as the Bee, from Hamilton Gifts.

2A: Close-up of the Blues Brothers. *Courtesy of David Spurgeon.*

2B: The box for the Blues Brothers showing Dan Aykroyd as Elwood and John Belushi as Jake. *Courtesy of David Spurgeon.*

Benedict, Dirk. Actor Benedict has appeared in nearly three dozen films. He is best known for his role as Lt. Starbuck on the ABC television series *Battlestar Galactica*, which aired in 1978.

Lt. Starbuck from Battlestar Galactica. Mattel, Inc. Hong Kong. #2871. 1978. 4 inches. All vinyl, painted clothing and hair; came with a cloth cape. Box marked: "Copyright by Universal City Studios, Inc." ....**$10-$15**

Benji. This real-life dog appeared in a dozen films, including *Benji's Very Own Christmas Story* (1983) and *Benji The Hunted* (1987).

Benji Dog. R. Dakin & Co. China. 1980. Stuffed plush. Wears cotton cap and name tag around neck marked: "BENJI." ....**$15-$20**

Berenger, Tom. Actor Berenger played a variety of roles, including Butch Cassidy in *Butch and Sundance, The Early Days*. He has appeared in more than three dozen films, of which one of the most recent is *The Hollywood Sign* (2000).

Butch Cassidy. Kenner. Hong Kong. #53010. 1979. 4 inches. All vinyl, fully jointed, painted features; painted clothing. Copyright by Twentieth Century Fox. ....**$20-$30**

Berry, Halle. Actress Berry has appeared in television and on film, starring in many productions, such as *X-Men, Bulworth* and *The Rich Man's Wife*.

Storm. Toy Biz. China. #49257. 2000. 6 inches. All vinyl, painted and molded white hair, painted features; painted and molded black jumpsuit, sold with light-up lightning bolt base. Character is from the movie *X-Men*. Copyright by Marvel Comics. ....**$5-$7** (See photo on page 20.)

Halle Berry as Storm from the movie *X-Men*. *Author's collection.*

Best, James. Best is a supporting actor both in films and on television. He is best known for his roles on *The Andy Griffith Show* and on the television series *The Dukes of Hazzard*, which aired from 1979 until 1985, where he appeared as the character Sheriff Rosco P. Coltrane.

Rosco. Mego. Hong Kong. 1982. #09010/5. 3 inches. All vinyl, fully jointed, painted features, painted hair. Copyright by Warner Bros., Inc. ....**$15-$25**

Bialik, Mayim. Bialik is a young actress who starred on the television sitcom *Blossom*, which aired from January 1991 until June 1995, in the title role of Blossom Russo.

1. Blossom. Tyco Industries. People's Republic of China. #1903. 1993. 9 inches. All vinyl, jointed, painted features, smiling mouth with teeth, rooted long brown hair; came dressed in gold shirt, black top with black hat and black boots and was packaged with two other outfits, shoes and a telephone, also came wearing a mini dress. Copyright 1993 Tyco Industries. ....**$20-$30**

1: Mayim Bialik as Blossom from the television series by the same name. *Courtesy of David Spurgeon.*

2. Blossom Paper Dolls. Golden Book. 1994. Includes three dolls: Blossom, her brother, Joey and best friend, Six; 32 outfits and accessories, plus a fashion tote. ....**$10-$15**

2: Blossom Paper Dolls from Golden Books. Shown on cover are Blossom (Mayim Bialik), her brother Joey and her friend Six.

Bionic Man. (See Majors, Lee)

Bionic Woman. (See Wagner, Lindsay)

Blake, Robert. Actor Blake started his career as a child actor in the 1930s through the 1940s with the Our Gang series. At that time, he went by his real name of Mickey Gubitosi. Blake appeared in several movies but is best known for his role as detective Baretta from the ABC television series of the same name. The show aired from 1975 to 1978.

Mickey. Mego. Hong Kong. #60600/5. 1975. 6 inches. All vinyl, fully jointed, painted features and hair; wearing bibbed overalls and short-sleeved shirt. Copyright by Metro-Goldwyn-Mayer, Inc. ....**$50-$60**

Blanchard, Rachel. Actress Blanchard starred in the 1996 weekly television series *Clueless*, playing the role of Cher. After *Clueless* went off the air, Blanchard began starring in films including *Road Trip* (2000) and *Sugar & Spice* (2001).

Cher. Mattel, Inc. China. 1997. #17036. 11 inches. Vinyl, jointed, wears blue skirt with vest, jacket, hat, stockings, white shoes and animal backpack, came packaged with feather pen, blue ring and a telephone. One of three dolls based on the television series, they are all are made with the Barbie® body. The box shows a picture of the stars of the show: Rachel Blanchard (Cher), Elisa Donovan (Amber) and Stacey Dash (Dionne). Marked on back: "© MATTEL INC. 1966/CHINA." ....**$20-$30**

Rachel Blanchard as Cher, by Mattel, from *Clueless*. *Courtesy of David Spurgeon.*

Bobek, Nicole. Professional ice skater Bobek performs with Stars on Ice, a traveling ice-skating show that visits more than sixty cities across the United States.

Nicole. Playmates. China. Asst. #52500. Stock #52505. 1998. 11 inches. All vinyl, jointed, rooted blonde hair, painted blue eyes, painted features, smiling mouth and teeth; wearing dark blue ice skating skirt, long-sleeved top with gold sparkles, white sparkle-tone hose and white ice skates, came with stand and Stars on Ice medal. Copyright 1998 Playmates Toys Inc. "STARS ON ICE" is a trademark of IMG. ....**$20-$30**

Nicole Bobek, professional ice skater. *Author's collection.*

Bolger, Ray. Actor and dancer Bolger, a dancer since the 1920s, appeared in the unforgettable role as the Scarecrow in the 1939 movie *The Wizard of Oz.* After Oz, Bolger acted in many films up until 1985. His last film was *That's Dancing!* (See Garland, Judy for photograph.)

1. Scarecrow from *The Wizard of Oz.* Mego. Hong Kong. #51500/4. 1974. 8 inches. All vinyl, fully jointed, rooted hair, painted features; dressed in scarecrow attire. Copyright by Metro-Goldwyn-Mayer, Inc. ....**$30-$40**

2. Scarecrow from *The Wizard of Oz.* Mego. Hong Kong. #59039. 1974. 15 inches. Vinyl head with cloth body. ....**$50-$75**

3. Scarecrow from *The Wizard of Oz.* Ideal. 1984-1985. 9 inches. Vinyl, six-piece poseable body; wearing scarecrow outfit from movie. ....**$50-$60**

4. Scarecrow from *The Wizard of Oz.* Mattel, Inc. China. 1995. 8 inches. All vinyl, jointed, painted features; wearing costume from movie. ....**$25-$35**

Known as Ken As the Scarecrow, this vinyl doll is 12 inches. Made by Mattel in 1996. It is valued at $20-$25.

Bonaparte, Napoleon. Bonaparte was the Emperor of France in 1802 and King of Italy in 1805.

1. Napoleon Bonaparte. Peggy Nisbet. England. #P460. Circa 1970s. 7 inches. Plastic; dressed in period clothing. ....**$50-$60**

2. Napoleon. Alexander Doll Company. U.S.A. #1330. 1980. 12 inches. Vinyl head, plastic body, rooted dark brown hair, brown sleep eyes with molded eyelashes; dressed in period clothing. Part of the Portraits in History Series. ....**$50-$100**

Bond, Ward. A great supporting actor, Bond played parts in more than 200 films. He is probably best known for his role as Major Seth Adams on the television show *Wagon Train*, which aired from 1957 to 1961.

Major Seth Adams of Wagon Train. Hartland Plastics. U.S.A. #824. 1958. 8 inches. Plastic, jointed arms; came with Action Horse. Made in Hartland, WI. ....**$100-$150**, mint-in-box

Bono, Sonny. An actor, singer and politician, Bono was one-half of a successful singing act with his wife, Cher. They had their own television series—*The Sonny and Cher Comedy Hour*, which aired from 1971 to 1974. After leaving show business, Bono entered politics. He was a United States Congressman from California at the time of his death in an accident in 1996.

Sonny. Mego. Hong Kong. #62401. 1976. 12 inches. All vinyl, fully jointed, painted brown hair and mustache, painted features; wearing blue jean bell-bottom pants with white long-sleeved shirt with blue scarf collar. Marked on neck: "©MEGO CORP. 1976;" marked on box: "Manufactured exclusively for Mego Corp. New York N.Y. 10010. The British Colony of Hong Kong." Original price $7.97. ......**$60-$70**

Sonny Bono by Mego, a 12-inch poseable doll. *Courtesy of Suellen Manning.*

The back of the box for Sonny Bono shows the different outfits that were available. *Courtesy of Suellen Manning.*

Booke, Sorrell.
Actor Booke played several characters but is best known for his role as Boss Hogg from the CBS television series *The Dukes of Hazzard*, which aired from 1979 until 1985. He also appeared in more than a dozen films from 1963 until 1992.

1. Boss Hogg. Mego. Hong Kong. #09050/4. 1981. 8 inches. All vinyl, fully jointed, painted brown hair, painted brown eyes, large belly; hat made of white vinyl. Head marked: "©WARNER BROS.//INC.1980." ....**$30-$40**

2. Boss Hogg. Kenner. Hong Kong. #09010/4. 1982. 3 inches. All vinyl, fully jointed, painted features; painted clothing, came with removable hat. Copyright by Warner Bros., Inc. ......**$10-$15**

3. Boss Hogg with Caddy. Mego. Hong Kong. #09064. 1982. 3 inches. Same doll as above except comes boxed with white Cadillac convertible. Copyright by Warner Bros., Inc. ......**$60-$75**

Boone, Daniel.
Frontiersman Boone was one of the first settlers of the American West in the late 1700s. (See also Parker, Fess)

Daniel Boone. Louis Marx & Co. U.S.A. 1964. 12 inches. Rigid vinyl, fully jointed; vinyl clothing. ....**$75-$100**

Boone, Debby.
Singer Boone is the daughter of singer Pat Boone. She is best known for her hit song "You Light Up My Life."

Debby Boone. Mattel, Inc. Taiwan. #2843. 1978. 11 inches. All vinyl, fully jointed with a twist waist, rooted blonde hair, painted green-blue eyes; wearing blue satin type top and pants with blue sparkle jacket. Head marked: "©RESI, INC. 1978//TAIWAN;" lower back marked: "©MATTEL, INC. 1966//TAIWAN." ..**$40-$60**

Mattel's 11-inch Debby Boone. *Author's collection.*

Boone, Richard.
Actor Boone appeared both in films and on television, but is best known for his roles in several television series, including *Medic, The Richard Boone Show* and *Have Gun Will Travel*, all from the 1950s.

Paladin of *Have Gun Will Travel*. Hartland Plastics. U.S.A. #766. 1958. 8 inches. All plastic, jointed at arms. Made in Hartland, WI. ....**$200-$250**, mint-in-box

Borgnine, Ernest.
Actor Borgnine appeared in more than 100 roles both in films and on television. He is best known for his role in the hit ABC television series *McHale's Navy*, which aired from 1962 to 1966. Borgnine also played the part of Harry Booth in the film *The Black Hole*.

1. Harry Booth from *The Black Hole*. Mego. Hong Kong. #95010/6. 1979. 3 inches. All vinyl, fully jointed, painted features; painted clothing. Copyright by Walt Disney Productions. ..**$10-$20**

2. Harry Booth from *The Black Hole*. Same as above except 12 inches. ....**$40-$60**

Bottoms, Joseph.
Actor Bottoms starred as First Officer Charles Pizer in the film *The Black Hole*. Other film credits include *Liar's Edge* (1992) and *Treacherous Crossing* (1992).

1. Charles Pizer from The Black Hole. Mego. Hong Kong. #95010/3. 1979. 3 inches. All vinyl, fully jointed, painted features; painted clothing. Copyright by Walt Disney Productions. ..**$10-$20**

2. Charles Pizer from *The Black Hole*. Same as above except 12 inches. Stock #95005/6.....**$40-$60**

Bowie, Jim. Bowie was a frontiersman in the early 1800s and a hero in the Texas Revolution.

Jim Bowie. Hartland Plastics. U.S.A. #817. 1958. 8 inches. Plastic, jointed arms; came with plastic horse named Braze. Made in Hartland, WI. ....**$150-$200**, mint-in-box

Boy George (George O'Dowd). The flamboyant singer and actor was also founder of the 1980s pop band, Culture Club.

Boy George. L.J.N. Toys Ltd. China. 1984. 16 inches. Wearing bright outfit of white pants and long white top with red and black numbers on it. Box shows four pictures of Boy George on cover. Box marked: "The Original Outrageous Boy of Rock." ....**$50-$75**

Box for Boy George, 16 inches, by L.J.N. Toys, Ltd.

Boyd, William (Bill). Actor and producer Boyd starred in several films and on television. He is best known for his role as Hopalong Cassidy. He starred in fifty-four Hopalong Cassidy films as well as a television show that aired on NBC from 1949 to 1951.

Hopalong Cassidy. Ideal Toy Corp. U.S.A. 1949 to 1950. Various sizes. Vinyl head and hands, stuffed body, molded gray hair, painted features including painted blue eyes; dressed in black cowboy outfit with black corduroy pants, black leatherette boots, guns and holster, black felt hat. Unmarked. The 25-inch size was produced with slightly different features. Though other Hopalong Cassidy dolls were produced, these are the only ones known made in the likeness of William Boyd. ....18 inches, **$100-$150**; 20 inches, **$100-$150**; 23 inches, **$150-$200**; 25 inches, **$250-$300**; 27 inches, **$250-$300**

Brandy. Brandy first made a name for herself as a singer with her hit albums "Brandy" and "Never Say Never." She then turned her interests to acting, and starred in Disney's *Cinderella* with her mentor, actress and singer Whitney Houston.

Brandy. Mattel, Inc. China. #24502. 1999. 11 inches. All vinyl, jointed, rooted long black hair, painted features; came dressed in a variety of outfits. ....**$10-$15**

Mattel's Brandy in an evening outfit.

Brandy, by Mattel, in her original box.

Brice, Fanny. Singer and comedienne Brice appeared in films but is best known for the radio show in which she played the role of Baby Snooks. The show aired from 1938 to 1951. A movie based on her life, entitled *Funny Girl*, starred Barbra Streisand.

1. Fanny Brice as Baby Snooks. Ideal Toy Corp. U.S.A. 1939. 12 inches. Composition head and hands, wooden torso and feet, made with flexy wire for arms and legs to make her poseable, painted brown hair and features, painted blue eyes; came dressed in different outfits. Designed by Joseph Kallus. ......**$150-$250**

1: Fanny Brice as Baby Snooks by Ideal Toy Corp. *Author's collection.*

2. Mortimer Snerd. Ideal. 1939. 12 inches. Fanny Brice's sidekick on the show. Edgar Bergen and his dummy, Charlie McCarthy, provided audiences with decades of laughter, beginning in vaudeville and then moving on to radio and television. Mortimer Snerd was another of Bergen's characters who joined the show in 1939. ....**$150-$250**

1: Another example of Fanny Brice as Baby Snooks by Ideal Toy Corp. *Author's collection.*

2: Mortimer Snerd, Fanny Brice's sidekick. *Author's collection.*

Broadway Joe Namath. (See Namath, Joe)

Brooks, Louise. A star of the silent screen, Brooks appeared in the film *Pandora's Box*.

Louise Brooks. Maker unknown. France. Circa 1900s. 30 inches. Composition and cloth, face has a peach type fuzz to it, painted hair and features; dressed in ivory wedding dress with veil with long lace. Extremely rare. ....**$3,000** up

This very rare doll representing Louise Brooks is by an unknown French maker. *Courtesy of Billie Nelson Tyrrell.*

Brown, Melanie. (See Spice Girls)

Brown, Peter. Actor Brown played the roles of Deputy Johnny McKay on the television show *The Lawman* and Chad Cooper on *Laredo*. He also appeared in several films.

John McKay from Lawman. Hartland Plastics. U.S.A. #768. 1978. 7-5/8 inches. All plastic, jointed arms. Marked on the right arm: "©HARTLAND//PLASTICS.INC." Copyright by Warner Brothers Pictures, Inc. Made in Hartland, WI. ....**$75-$100**, mint-in-box

Buck Rogers. (See Gerard, Gil)

Buddy. (See McNichol, Kristy)

Bullock, Jeremy. Actor Bullock is best known for his role as the bounty hunter Boba Fett in the Star Wars film sequel *The Empire Strikes Back*, which debuted in 1980.

1. Boba Fett. Kenner. Hong Kong. #39140. 1979. 13 inches. Fully jointed plastic action figure. ....**$150-$200**

2. Boba Fett. Kenner. Hong Kong. #38899. 1980. 3 inches. Fully jointed plastic action figure. ....**$50-$75**

Bunny, John. Bunny was an actor and well-known comic of the silent screen. Weighing more than 300 pounds, he joked mainly about his weight or about Flora Finch, his sidekick who played his wife.

1. John Bunny. Louis Amberg & Son. U.S.A. 1914. 13 inches. Composition head, painted red hair, blue eyes, open/closed mouth with painted teeth; came in both a sailor suit

and soldier outfit. Marked: "©14;" cloth label on suit marked: "JOHN BUNNY DOLL COPYRIGHT L.A. & S. 1914 TRADEMARK REGISTERED. MADE EXCLUSIVELY BY LOUIS AMBERG & SON, N.Y. WITH CONSENT OF JOHN BUNNY THE FAMOUS MOTION PICTURE HERO OF THE VITAGRAPH CO." ....**$1,000-$1,500**

2. John Bunny Vitagraph Players Card. ....**$10-$15**

Two all-original versions of John Bunny. The one on the left is biskaloid while the one on the right is composition. *Courtesy of Billie Nelson Tyrrell.*

2: John Bunny Vitagraph Players card.

Bunton, Emma. (See Spice Girls)

Burke, Billie. Actress Burke worked both on stage and in films. She is best known for her role as the Good Witch Glinda in the 1939 movie *The Wizard of Oz.* (See Garland, Judy for photograph.)

1. Glinda, The Good Witch from the *Wizard of Oz.* Mego. Hong Kong. #51500/5. 1974. 8 inches. All vinyl, fully jointed, rooted red hair, painted blue eyes; wearing Glinda outfit from the movie. ....**$40-$60**

2. Glinda, The Good Witch from *The Wizard of Oz.* Mattel, Inc. China. Circa 1990s. 11½ inches. Wearing elaborate dress from the film. ....**$30-$40**

Burnett, Carol. Actress and comedian Burnett has appeared on television and in films. She played the role of Miss Hannigan in the film *Little Orphan Annie.* From 1967 to 1979, she starred in the CBS comedy-variety program *The Carol Burnett Show,* which won twenty-two Emmys (later syndicated as *Carol Burnett and Friends*).

Miss Hannigan. Knickerbocker Toy Co., Inc. #3867. 1982. 7 inches. All vinyl, fully jointed, rooted brown hair, painted features. Copyright by Columbia Pictures Industries, Inc. ....**$25-$35**

Annie (Little Orphan Annie), played by Aileen Quinn; Molly, played by Toni Ann Gisondi; and Miss Hannigan played by Carol Burnett.

Burns, George. Comedian, actor and author Burns and his wife, Gracie Allen, comprised a comedy team, appearing on stage, in films and on television, where they hosted their own show on CBS, *The Burns and Allen Show,* which aired from 1950 to 1958. He was quoted as saying, "I can't afford to die—I'd lose too much money." Burns also wrote ten books and won an Acadamy Award for his role in *The Sunshine Boys* in 1976. He lived to the age of 100, passing away in 1996.

George Burns. Exclusive Toy Products, Inc. China. #23000. 1997. 9 inches. All vinyl, painted features; wearing checked suit with white shirt and red tie, with stand and microphone. Box marked: "TM © 1997 Hollywood Chamber of Commerce." ....**$15-$20**

George Burns by Exclusive Toy Products, Inc. *Author's collection.*

Burton, Levar. Actor Burton has starred in a variety of television shows and films, first gaining attention for his portrayal of the slave Kunte Kinte in the television mini-series *Roots.* He played the role of Lt. Commander Geordi LaForge on the television series *Star Trek: The Next Generation* and in the films *Star Trek—First Contact, Star Trek—Generations* and *Star Trek—Insurrection.*

Lt. Commander Geordi LaForge. Playmates. China. #007312. 1998. 9 inches. Vinyl, fully jointed, painted black hair, painted features; wearing black and gray uniform from the movie Star Trek-Insurrection. Box marked: "© 1998 Paramount Pictures." ....**$15-$20**

Levar Burton as Lt. Commander Geordi LaForge from *Star Trek:The Next Generation. Author's collection.*

Butler, Duke. Actor Butler played the role of Tiger Man in the NBC television series *Buck Rogers in the 25th Century.* The show aired from 1979 to 1980.

1. Tiger Man. Mego. Hong Kong. #85000/3. 1979. 3 inches. All vinyl, fully jointed, painted features; plastic white clothing. Copyright by Robert C. Dille. ....**$5-$10**

2. Tiger Man. Mego. Hong Kong. #85001/2. 1979. 12 inches. Vinyl and plastic. Copyright by Robert C. Dille. ....**$30-$40**

Byrd, Ralph. Actor Byrd is best known for his role as Dick Tracy in the movie serials. Some of his films include *Dick Tracy Returns* (1938) and *Dick Tracy* (1951). He went on to become a successful character actor.

1. Dick Tracy. Maker unknown. Circa 1940s. 13 inches. All composition, molded and painted features, mouth opens and closes. ....**$200-$250**

2. Dick Tracy. Applause. China. 1997. 10 inches. All vinyl, painted features; wearing plastic yellow hat and yellow trench coat. **$10-$15**

1: Right, Ralph Byrd as Dick Tracy, from the 1940s. *Courtesy of Carl Kludt.*

2: This 1997 version of Dick Tracy by Applause does not represent Ralph Byrd.

C

Cagney, James. Cagney began his acting career in 1930. Some of his best-known roles were in the films *Lady Killer* (1933) and *Angels With Dirty Faces* (1938). Cagney appeared in more than three dozen major motion pictures.

James Cagney. Effanbee Doll Company. U.S.A. #FB1987. 1987. 18 inches. All vinyl, jointed, painted features. Box marked: "© 1987, James & Frances Cagney Trust, Made in China, Effanbee Doll Comp." The Effanbee Doll Co. produced a variety of limited-edition dolls that came complete with numbered certificates. Many of the dolls could only be purchased through Effanbee's Limited Edition Doll Club or the secondary market. Part of the Legend Series. ....**$100-$125**

Effanbee's 18-inch James Cagney from the Legend Series. *Courtesy of Marlene Grant.*

Calamity Jane (Martha Jane Canary).

An American frontier personality, Calamity Jane was in show business in the late 1800s.

1. Calamity Jane. Azark-Hamway. Hong Kong. 1973. 11 inches. Vinyl, rooted hair. ....**$20-$40**

2. Calamity Jane. Excel Toy Corp. Hong Kong. 1974. 9 inches. Vinyl, molded hair. ....**$20-$40**

Calhoun, Rory. Actor Calhoun is best known for his role as Bill Longley in the CBS television series *The Texan*, which aired from 1958 to 1960. His acting career began in the 1940s and continued into the 1990s, including the movie *Pure Country* in 1992.

The Texan Hand Puppet. Tops in Toys. 1960. Hand Puppet. Vinyl head, cloth body. ......**$30-$50**

Cameron, JoAnna. Actress Cameron is best known for her dual roles as Andrea Thomas, a school-teacher, and Isis, the Egyptian Goddess of Fertility, in the CBS television series *Isis*, which aired in 1975.

Isis. Mego. Hong Kong. #51345. 1976. 8 inches. All vinyl, fully jointed, rooted black hair, painted blue eyes; wearing short white dress with black shoes that lace up her leg. Copyright by Filmation Assoc. ....**$40-$50**

Cantor, Eddie. Actor Cantor was well known in burlesque and vaudeville. He had his own radio show in the 1930s. Cantor also starred as himself in the film *The Eddie Cantor Story*.

1. Eddie Cantor. Licensed through A. Ponnock. U.S.A. 1938. 8 inches. All rubber; wearing a suit and tie, which is part of the molded rubber. The doll was done in the like-ness of Cantor and originally sold for 50 cents. The royalties raised from the sale of this doll were donated by Cantor to selected boys camps and the distributor, Ponnock, matched all roy-alty payments as a donation also. ......**$40-$50**

2. Eddie Cantor. Licensed through A. Ponnock. U.S.A. 1938. 20 inches. Composition head, feet and hands with molded shoes and cloth body. ....**$150-$200**

Captain James T. Kirk. (See Shatner, William)

Captain Kangaroo. (See Keeshan, Robert)

Carey, Drew. Actor Carey is the star of his own television comedy *The Drew Carey Show*, which began in 1995. He has appeared in two movies— *Coneheads* (1993) and *Geppetto* (2000).

Drew Carey portraying the title character from *The Drew Carey Show*, by Creation Entertainment.

Drew Carey. Creation Entertainment. 1998. 12 inches. All vinyl, painted features; dressed in blue suit with blue tie and white shirt, wears black plastic glasses, came with a coffee cup and briefcase. Copyright Warner Brothers. ....**$25-$35**

Caron, Leslie. Actress and dancer Caron starred in *An American in Paris* with Gene Kelly, *Lili, Gigi* and *The L-shaped Room*, and played character parts in many other films. More recently, she appeared in the 2000 film *Chocolat*.

Leslie Caron as Gigi. Old Cottage Dolls. England. Circa 1950s. 10 inches. Plastic; wearing Gigi outfit. ....**$50-$75**

Carr, Charmaine. Actress Carr is best known for her role as Liesl in *The Sound of Music* (1965).

1. Liesl. Alexander Doll Company. 1965. #1005. 8 inches. All hard plastic, rooted blonde hair, blue sleep eyes; dressed in costume from movie. Part of set. ....**$200-$250**

2. Liesl. Alexander Doll Company. 1965 to 1970. #1405. 14 inches. All hard plastic, rooted blonde hair, blue sleep eyes; dressed in costume from movie, which includes short striped dress with straw hat. Part of set. ....**$250-$300**

Carrey, Jim. Actor and comedian Carrey has starred in a variety of films, including *Ace Ventura-Pet Detective* (1994), *The Mask* (1994), *Dumb and Dumber* (1994), *Batman Forever* (1995) and *How The Grinch Stole Christmas* (2000). For his work in *How The Grinch Stole Christmas*, Carrey received a Golden Globe nomination.

1. The Mask-Stanley. Hasbro. China. #29421. 1994. 16 inches. Vinyl face, plush cloth body, poseable, eyes and tongue pop out when you push a button behind his head; dressed in yellow hat and suit. Box marked: "The Mask From Zero to Hero. © New Line Productions." ....**$15-$25**

2. The Grinch. Playmates. China. Asst. #40310. Stock #40311. 2000. 14 inches. Vinyl molded and painted face, green plush body with red heart; push on stomach for red heart to light up. Box marked "Dr. Seuss How The Grinch Stole Christmas! Heart Warming Grinch. © Universal Studios." ....**$20-$30**

Carroll, Diahann. Actress and singer Carroll is best known for her role as Julia in the hit television series *Julia*. The show aired on NBC from September 1968 to May 1971. Carroll was the first black performer to be the star of a regular television series.

1. Julia. Mattel, Inc. Japan. #1127. 1969. 11 inches. Twist'n'Turn Julia in box, vinyl head and body, dark hair with tint of red, pink lips, rooted eyelashes; wearing one-piece nurse outfit, wrist tag, also sold in two-piece nurse outfit. Box dated "1969." All Julia doll heads are marked: "© 1968 MATTEL INC JAPAN;" and are marked on the rear: "© 1966//MATTEL, INC.//U.S. PATENTED//U.S. PAT. PEND.// MADE IN//JAPAN." ....**$200-$225**

2. Julia. Mattel, Inc. Japan. 1969. 11 inches. All vinyl, jointed, painted features, red hair; wearing nurse uniform. ....**$200-$225**

3. Julia Talking Doll. Mattel, Inc. Mexico. #1128. 1969. 11 inches. All vinyl, jointed, painted features; wearing a silver and gold outfit, says several different phrases. Marked on rear: "©MATTEL, INC.//U.S. & FOREIGN// PATS.PEND//MEXICO." ....**$200-$225**

4. Julia Simply Wow Set. Mattel, Inc. Japan. #1594. 1969. 11 inches. All vinyl, jointed, painted features; comes complete with boxed doll and extra white and blue dress, which is only available with the set. Sold as an exclusive catalog item through Sears, Roebuck and Co. ....**$900-$1,000**, boxed

1: Jim Carrey in *The Mask*, by Hasbro, 1994.

1: Mattel's Twist 'N Turn Julia, as portrayed by Diahann Carroll, wearing her one-piece nurse outfit, mint-in-box. *Courtesy of McMasters Doll Auctions.*

2: Mattel's Julia with red hair. *Courtesy of McMasters Doll Auctions.*

3: Mattel's Talking Julia in a silver and gold outfit. *Courtesy of McMasters Doll Auctions.*

5. Julia. Mattel, Inc. Japan. #1127. 1970. 11 inches. All vinyl, jointed, painted features; wearing redesigned nurse outfit, a one-piece dress with shorter sleeves. All else is identical to first issue. ....**$150-$200**

6. Julia Talking Doll. Mattel, Inc. Hong Kong. #1128. 1970. 11 inches. All vinyl, jointed, painted features. Sold in brown carton through catalog stores. Sticker on box marked: "STOCK No. 1128/849-6679/ 921-2234// MADE AND PRINTED IN HONG KONG." Wrist tag is the same as Mexican-made version except marked "made in Hong Kong." Doll is marked on the rear: "Made in Hong Kong." (Mattel's Mexico factory burned in 1970) Skin tone appears darker. ....**$225-$275**

7. Julia Talking Doll. Mattel, Inc. Hong Kong. 1971. 11 inches. Similar to prior talking Julia except this version has an updated hairstyle (curly Afro style) and doll is marked: "Hong Kong." ....**$225-$250**

8. Julia Paper Doll Booklet. Saalfield. U.S.A. 1971. Shows Julia on the cover with pictures of the other characters from the television show. ....**$30-$35**, uncut

Carrott, Ric. Actor Carrott played in a variety of television series, including *Space Academy*, which aired from September 1977 to September 1978. He played the role of Chris Gentry.

1. Chris Gentry. Aviva Toy Corporation. Hong Kong. #100. 1978. 8 inches. All vinyl, jointed, painted blonde hair, painted blue eyes. Marked on back: "© 1978//FILMATION ASSOCIATES//ALL RIGHTS RESERVED// MADE IN HONG KONG//PAT.PEND." Sold through F.W. Woolworth Co. ....**$25-$40**

Carson, Kit. Carson was an American hero in the mid 1800s. He was known as an adventurer, mountain man, guide, scout, Indian fighter and Indian protector.

Kit Carson. Ali Brond. Hong Kong. #6059. 1973. 12 inches. Box marked: "© 1973 Azak-Hamway Int'l, Inc." ....**$15-$25**

Kit Carson by Ali Brond. *Courtesy of Marlene Grant.*

Carter, Amy. Daughter of the thirty-ninth president of the United States, Jimmy Carter, she spent four years of her childhood living in the White House.

Amy Carter. Lim Co. Korea. Style # S-1 and S-2. 1977. 20 inches. All cloth, painted blue eyes, yellow acrylic yarn hair; wearing a flowered blue dress sewn onto doll and white felt glasses. Called An Original Tom McPartland' Love Doll. ....**$50-$75**

A 20-inch cloth version of Amy Carter. *Courtesy of David Spurgeon.*

Carter, Jimmy. The thirty-ninth president of the United States of America, Carter was a peanut farmer from Georgia before entering politics.

1. Jimmy Carter. Kasia. 1977. 15 inches. Lithographed cloth body that was stuffed with beans. ....$25-$50

2. Jimmy the Walking Peanut. BJ Wolfe Ent. Japan. Circa 1978. 8 inches. Plastic wind-up walking toy. ....$25-$50

3. Jimmie. Hollywood Creations. Hong Kong. 1980. All plastic, painted hair and features. Sold as an adult novelty doll. ....$40-$60

Carter, Lynda. Actress and singer Carter is best known for her dual role as Diana Prince/Wonder Woman on the television series *Wonder Woman*. The show aired from March 1976 to September 1979. She is a former Miss U.S.A. and Miss World.

1. Wonder Woman. Ideal Toy Corp. U.S.A. 1967 to 1968. 12 inches. All vinyl, poseable, rooted hair, painted side-glancing eyes; dressed in Wonder Woman costume. Marked on hip: "1965//Ideal//2 M-12;" on head: "1965//Ideal Toy Corp.//W-12-3." (This doll is not made in the likeness of Lynda Carter, but does represent the character she portrayed.) ....$250-$400, loose; $800-$1,000, mint-in-box

2. Wonder Woman. Mego. U.S.A. #73500. 1978. 12 inches. Came packaged different ways including Wonder Woman with Diana Prince Outfit; Wonder Woman with Fly Away Action (with string for flying); Wonder Woman with Blue Robe. The first issue has a painted-on suit and a photograph of Lynda Carter on the box. In the later issues, Wonder Woman is wearing real clothing and the photograph is no longer on the box. ....$40-$50, loose; $100-$150, boxed

3. Wonder Woman. Mego. Hong Kong. 12 inches. 1978. Two other versions were produced in Canada and Mexico. The Mexican version used a different head mold. The words "Mujer Maravilla" are printed on the window box. ......Canadian version: $50-$75, loose; $300-$400, boxed. Mexican version: $75-$100, loose; $200-$250, boxed

Cartwright, Angela. Child actress Cartwright is best known for her role as Linda Williams on the television series *The Danny Thomas Show* and *Make Room for Daddy*. Cartwright also appeared in the television series *Lost in Space*, which aired from 1965 until 1968, and as Brigitta in the movie *The Sound of Music*.

Make Room for Daddy ran from 1957 until 1964, during which time several dolls were produced representing Angela as Linda Williams. The Angela Cartwright doll was offered as a premium by General Foods Corp. while a different version was offered by the Natural Doll Company.

1. Linda Williams. Plastic Molded Arts Corp. (PMA) for General Foods Corp. U.S.A. 1959. 14 inches. All vinyl and jointed, brown rooted hair, blue sleep eyes, open smiling mouth with teeth. Marked on head: "LINDA WILLIAMS." This doll was a premium sold through General Foods Corp. and could be purchased for $2.00 and a couple of cereal box tops. ....$50-$75

2. Linda Williams. Natural Doll Company, Inc. U.S.A. 1963. Various sizes including 14 inches and 30 inches. Plastic and vinyl, rooted hair, sleep eyes; wearing a red and white plaid dress. The 30-inch doll was advertised as a doll that "Walked and Talked." ......14-inch size, $50-$75; 30-inch size, $100-$125

3. Brigitta. Alexander Doll Company. U.S.A. #1003. 1965. 8 inches. All hard plastic, dark brown wig, blue sleep eyes with eyelashes; dressed in costume from *The Sound of Music*. Marked on back: "MME//ALEXANDER." Part of set. ....$200-$250

2: Mego's 12-inch Wonder Woman as portrayed by Lynda Carter, from the television series *Wonder Woman*.

2: Angela Cartwright as Linda Williams by the Natural Doll Company. *Author's collection.*

4. Brigitta. Alexander Doll Company. U.S.A. #1403. 1965 to 1970. 14 inches. Plastic and vinyl, dark brown wig, brown sleep eyes; dressed in costume from *The Sound of Music*. Head marked: "ALEXANDER//1964." Part of set. ..**$150-$200**

5. Brigitta. Alexander Doll Company. U.S.A. 1966. 12 inches. All hard plastic, dark brown wig; dressed in Tyrolean outfit. Part of set. **$150-$200**

6. Brigitta. Alexander Doll Company. U.S.A. 1966. 12 inches. All hard plastic, dark brown wig; dressed in sailor outfit. Part of set. ....**$150-$200**

7. Brigitta. Alexander Doll Company. U.S.A. #1103. 1971-1973. 9 inches. All hard plastic, dark brown wig; dressed in costume from *The Sound of Music*. Part of set. ....**$100-$150**

1: Linda Williams by Plastic Molded Arts Corp. (PMA) as a premium doll. *Author's collection.*

Carver, George Washington. Carver, a

chemist who worked to improve the economy, was one of the first black men to excel in this field. He elevated the scientific study of farming, improved the health and agricultural output of Southern farmers, and developed hundreds of uses for their crops.

George Washington Carver. Hallmark. Taiwan. #400DT113-7. 1979. 6 inches. Cloth doll, printed features and clothing, sewn body parts, with house for box. Part of a series of dolls sold through Hallmark stores. ....**$10-$20**

Cassidy, Shawn. Actor and singer Cassidy is

the younger brother of actor and singer David Cassidy. He is best known for his role as Joe Hardy, the young detective on the television series *The Hardy Boys*. The show appeared on ABC from January 1977 until the fall of 1978. Cassidy is the son of actor Jack Cassidy and actress and singer Shirley Jones.

Shawn Cassidy as Joe Hardy. Kenner. Hong Kong. #45000. 1978. 12 inches. The doll was sold in two versions. The first had painted yellow hair with light brown eyes and dark eyebrows. The second had painted red/brown hair, brown eyebrows and darker brown eyes. Both dolls were dressed in red T-shirts and black pants. Came with guitar with red lens to insert "secret messages." Body marked: "© G.M.F.I.G.I. 1978 KENNER PROD.//CINCINNATI, OHIO 45202//MADE IN HONG KONG;" head marked: "© 1978 U.C.S.I. Copyright by Universal City Studios, Inc." ....**$25-$40**

Cassidy, Ted. Actor Cassidy is best known for

his role as Lurch the butler on the television series *The Addams Family*, which aired from 1964 until 1966. Cassidy also played the role of Injun Joe on the television series *The New Adventures of Huck Finn*, which aired from 1968 until 1969, and Bigfoot on *The Six Million Dollar Man* television series of the 1970s. Cassidy played a variety of character parts on television and in films.

1. Lurch. Remco. Hong Kong. 1964. 5 inches. Vinyl doll, jointed head, rooted hair; painted clothing. Marked on neck: "L6." Copyright by Filmways T.V. Prod., Inc. ....**$40-$60**

2. Lurch Hand Puppet. Ideal Toy Corp. U.S.A. 1964. Approximately 10 inches. Vinyl head, painted features, cloth body. ......**$60-$80**

Chamberlain, Richard. Actor Chamberlain

has appeared on stage and television as well as in films. He played the role of Dr. Kildare in the television series Dr. Kildare, which aired from September 1961 until August 1966. He also starred in the television mini-series *The Thorn Birds* (1983) and appeared in the television movie *Too Rich-The Secret Life of Doris Duke* (1999).

1. Dr. Kildare. Unmarked. Circa 1960s. 23 inches. Vinyl head and arms, plastic legs and torso, light brown painted and molded hair, blue sleep eyes with eyelashes; dressed in white doctor outfit with pin that reads: "Dr. Kildare is a Doll." The same doll was used for the Dr. Ben Casey doll, but with a different pin. ....**$200-$300**

2. Dr. Kildare. Unmarked. Circa 1960s. 11 inches. All vinyl, jointed, painted light brown hair, painted brown eyes. Shirt on doll is marked: "DR. KILDARE//(Medical sign)// BLAIR GENERAL HOSPITAL." Box is marked: "Copyright 1962 Metro-Goldwyn-Mayer, Inc. Clothes interchangeable with all dolls of similar size." ..**$200-$250**, mint-in-box

3. Richard Chamberlain as Dr. Kildare Bobber. Unmarked. Circa 1960s. 8 inches. Molded and painted features, head bobs up and down. The words "Dr. Kildare" are on the base. ......**$40-$60**

2: Richard Chamberlain as Dr. Kildare shown with the Dr. Kildare doctor kit and the Dr. Ben Casey doll, as played by Vincent Edwards. Dr. Ben Casey is valued at $200-$250, mint-in-box. *Courtesy of Steve Malaninsky.*

Chaney, Lon. Silent film actor Chaney, known as the Man of a Thousand Faces, appeared in more than 150 movies from 1913 to 1930. He is best known for portraying the title roles in *The Hunchback of Notre Dame* (1923) and *The Phantom of the Opera* (1925).

1. Phantom of the Opera. Remco. Hong Kong. #772. 1980. 4 inches. All vinyl, jointed, painted hair and features; painted clothing and vinyl opera cape. Sold on card. Copyright by Universal City Studios, Inc. ....**$25-$35**

2. The Phantom of the Opera. Hasbro Toys. China. 1999. 12 inches. All vinyl, painted green face and black and white features, painted black

2: Hasbro's 12-inch Phantom of the Opera as portrayed by Lon Chaney. *Courtesy of David Cox.*

hair; wearing black pants, vest and long cape with white shirt. Box marked: "Universal Studios Monsters The Phantom of the Opera." Part of Hasbro's "Signature Series." ....**$45-$55**

Chaney, Jr., Lon. Actor and son of actor Lon Chaney, Chaney Jr. was born Chreighton Chaney, but changed his name at the insistence of a studio producer. He starred in several of Universal Studio's monster movies in the 1940s and '50s. He was best known for his role as Lawrence Talbot/the Wolf Man in the movie *The Wolf Man.*

1. The Wolf Man. Remco. Hong Kong. #1902. 1974. 8 inches. All vinyl, jointed; dressed in Wolf Man costume. Copyright by Universal City Studios, Inc. ....**$35-$40**

2. The Wolf Man. Remco. Hong Kong. #754. 1980. 8 inches. Same as previous doll but later issue. ....**$25-$35**

3. The Wolf Man. Remco. Hong Kong. 1980. 4 inches. All vinyl, jointed, painted features and clothing. Sold on card. Copyright by Universal City Studios, Inc. ....**$40-$50**

Channing, Carol. Actress and singer Channing is known for her large eyes and bright blonde hair. She acted on Broadway and was particularly associated with the title role in *Hello, Dolly!* She was nominated for an Academy Award for her role in the film *Thoroughly Modern Millie* (1967).

2: Carol Channing by an unknown maker with a "Hello, Dolly!" costume case, which was sold separately. *Courtesy of Steve Malatinsky.*

1. Carol Channing. Maker unknown. 1961. 11 inches. Plastic, vinyl head, rooted orange hair, blue sleep eyes with eyelashes and eye shadow, high-heeled feet; wearing full-length red dress with black choker collar. Sold as a premium. Head marked: "AE". Case marked: "Hello, Dolly!" Costume Case for my teenage doll. ......Case sold separately. Doll, **$75-$100**; case, **$50-$75** (See photo on page 32.)

2. Hello Dolly. Nasco. U.S.A. 1961. 24 inches. Plastic, vinyl head, rooted white hair, blue sleep eyes with eyelashes and eye shadow, high-heeled feet. Marked on head: "1373// K//1961." ....**$100-$150**

Channing, Stockard.
Actress Channing has appeared in nearly three dozen films. One of her first roles, with which she is still associated, was the part of Rizzo in the 1978 film *Grease*. In 1985, she won a Tony for her role in the play *A Day in the Death of Joe Egg*.

Rizzo. Exclusive Toy Products, Inc. China. #14052. 1998. 9 inches. All vinyl, painted features; wearing black and white outfit. Box marked: "TM © 1998 Paramount Pictures." ....**$15-$25**

Rizzo, portrayed by Stockard Channing, manufactured by Exclusive Toy Productions, Inc. *Courtesy of David Spurgeon.*

Chaplin, Charlie.
Actor, director, screenwriter and comedian, Chaplin performed in a multitude of roles beginning around 1914. Some of his films include *The Kid* (1921), *City Lights* (1931) and *The Great Dictator* (1940). Chaplin appeared in nearly four dozen films throughout his career. He is known for his Tramp character, who has a little black mustache and bowler hat.

1. Charlie Chaplin. Maker unknown. 11 inches wind-up figure. Composition head, feet and half arms are cloth with wire, feet have walking mechanism. Unmarked. ....**$200-$250**

2. Charlie Chaplin. Louis Amberg & Son. U.S.A. 1915. 14 inches. Composition molded head with molded mustache, straw-filled body and composition hands; dressed in tan and brown pants, jacket and shirt. Cloth label on sleeve reads: "Charlie Chaplin Doll, World's Greatest Comedian, Made Exclusively by Louis Amberg & Son, N.Y." ....**$600-$700**

3. Charlie Chaplin. Louis Amberg & Son. U.S.A. 1915. 17 inches. All cloth, painted features, dressed in tan and brown pants, jacket and shirt. Marked with tag on foot. ....**$300-$400**

4. Charlie Chaplin. Mark Hampton Company. USA. 1915. 9 inches. An early Hampton composition figure featuring Charlie, with twisted wire cane, standing on self-base marked: "CHAS. CHAPLIN;" in original box marked: "look out gloom or Chaplin will get you." ....**$400-$500**

5. Charlie Chaplin. Dean's Rag Dolls. England. Circa 1920. 11 inches. Pressed cloth face; printed clothing. ....**$250-$350**

6. Charlie Chaplin. Boucher. Switzerland. Circa 1920s. 8 inches. Tin figure, cast iron feet, wind up; features a fully dressed Chaplin carrying his cane and tipping his bowler hat as he walks forward. ....**$1,000-$1,250**

7. Charlie Chaplin. Boucher. Switzerland. Circa 1920s. 7 inches. Made of steel, lead and cloth, ball-jointed, movable head, arms, legs and feet; dressed in plaid pants, black jacket with hat. ......**$500-$600**

8. Charlie Chaplin. Maker Unknown. France. Circa 1920s. 7 inches. French composition, tin-plate and cloth walker, a wind-up toy doll featuring a hand-painted face, with Charlie holding his hat and cane in both raised hands. ..**$800-$1,000**

9: A 20½-inch composition Charlie Chaplin by an unknown French maker. *Courtesy of Billie Nelson Tyrrell.*

A number of Charlie Chaplin dolls were auctioned off by Christie's East on October 30, 1990. They are, from left: A tinplate key-wind Charlie Chaplin with a spinning cane, a Swiss Boucher Charlie Chaplin, a key-wind Boucher Charlie Chaplin walker, a German wooden Charlie Chaplin whistler toy, a German tinplate Charlie Chaplin bell ringer squeeze toy, a rare early Louis Amberg & Son Charlie Chaplin and a twin Charlie Chaplin bell ringer toy. *Courtesy Christie's East.*

9. Charlie Chaplin. Maker unknown. France. Circa 1920s. 20 inches. French composition, molded shoes and hat, painted features; wearing black jacket with white shirt, black and white plaid pants with black shoes. ......**$2,000-$2,300** (See photo on page 33.)

10. Charlie Chaplin. Whistler Toy. U.S.A. Circa 1920s. 13 inches. Hand-carved Charlie stands on platform with bowler hat and cane; when wound Charlie whistles to "How Dry I Am." ....**$1,000-$1,500**

11. Charlie Chaplin. Unmarked. Circa 1920s. 12 inches. Composition and metal wind-up doll, painted features, molded and painted hair and hat; dressed in black jacket with bow tie and plaid pants. ....**$400-$500**

11: An unmarked composition and metal wind-up Charlie Chaplin. *Courtesy of Carl Kludt.*

12. Charlie Chaplin as The Tramp in *City Lights*. Peggy Nisbet. England. #P755. Circa 1970s. 7 inches. Plastic; dressed in costume from movie. ....**$50-$75**

13. Charlie Chaplin. Kenner. Hong Kong. 1973. 14 inches. All cloth with walking mechanism; dressed in traditional Chaplin attire. ....**$50-$75**

14. Charlie Chaplin. Dean's Childplay Toys Ltd. Great Britain. #280900. 1982. All cloth doll with separate hat. Reproduction of the doll made in the 1920s. ....**$50-$75**

Charles (Prince). The 21st Prince of Wales, Prince Charles was married to Princess Diana (Lady Diana Spencer) in 1981. They were divorced before her untimely death in 1997. He is the son of Queen Elizabeth the II and heir to the British Throne.

1. Prince Charles. Chelsea Art. England. 1957. Bisque shoulder-plate head with bisque lower arms and legs, painted hair and features. Marked on back of shoulder plate: "MADE FOR//DOLL-MAKERS//CHELSEA ART//1957." ..**$100-$150**

2. Prince Charles. Alexander Doll Company. U.S.A. #395 and #397. 1957. 8 inches. All hard plastic, fully jointed, blonde wig, blue sleep eyes. ....**$600-$700**

3. Prince Charles. Dean's Rag Book Co. Ltd. England. 1981. Four-color uncut sheet of Prince Charles with Lady Diana made for their wedding in 1981. ....**$40-$60**

Charlie's Angels. (See Barrymore, Drew; Diaz, Cameron; Hack, Shelley; Ladd, Cheryl; Liu, Lucy; Fawcett, Farrah; Jackson, Kate; and Smith, Jaclyn)

Chasez, J.C. (See N'Sync)

Cher. Singer and actress Cherilyn Sarkisian, known as Cher, has enjoyed a long and successful career as a singer. First teaming up with her former husband Sonny Bono, the two hit it big with such songs as "I've Got You Babe." After a successful television series, *The Sonny and Cher Comedy Hour*, which aired from 1971 to 1974, Cher began to expand her acting talents. She has appeared in several feature films and won an Academy Award for her role in *Moon Struck* (1987).

1. Cher. Mego. Hong Kong. 1976. #62400. 12 inches. Vinyl, fully jointed (including wrists and waist), long black rooted hair, painted eyes with long eyelashes, dark skin tone; dressed in hot pink halter-top gown, removable open-toed

hot pink high-heeled shoes, came with an extensive wardrobe, sold separately. Back panel has pictures of seven other outfits seen on *The Sonny and Cher Comedy Hour.* ....$75-$100

2. Growing Hair Cher. Mego. Hong Kong. 1976. #62402. 12 inches. Vinyl, jointed, long black rooted hair with key winder in the back to make hair shorter, painted eyes with long eyelashes, dark skin tone. Marked: "MEGO CORP//19©75." ....$50-$75

3. Cher. Mego. Hong Kong. 1981. #62403. 12 inches. Vinyl head, jointed. Same description as previous doll except made on five-piece cheap plastic body wearing blue nylon swimsuit. Head marked: "3906//AF//MEGO CORP//19©76." ....$50-$75

4. Cher. Mego. Hong Kong. 12 inches. All vinyl, painted features; wearing a Native American Indian outfit, with fold-out display carrying case which included a tee-pee, chairs and accessories. ....$200-$250, complete

Bandstand beginning in the 1950s. He hosted many other shows, including The *25,000 Pyramid* and *TV's Bloopers.* His production company, Dick Clark Productions, produces television shows and movies. Clark was inducted into the Rock 'n' Roll Hall of Fame in 1993.

Dick Clark Autograph Doll. Juro Novelty Co., Inc. 1958 to 1959. 26 inches. Cloth body, molded vinyl head and hands; original clothes include suede saddle shoes, yellow vest, gray trousers, gray jacket, white shirt, red plaid tie; with an autograph pen. Marked on body: "Juro;" box marked: "Juro Novelty Co., Inc. NYC// Another Celebrity Doll." Original price was $7.98. ....$300-$450

4A: Mego's Cher in a Native American Indian outfit. *Author's collection.*

4B: The fold-out display carrying case and accessories that came with Mego's Cher wearing the Native American Indian outfit. *Author's collection.*

The Dick Clark Autograph Doll by Juro Novelty Co.

Chisholm, Melanie. (See Spice Girls)

Clark, Dick. Television personality and producer Clark hosted the weekly television show *American*

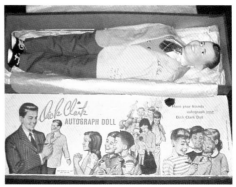

The Dick Clark Autograph Doll by Juro Novelty Co. with its original box.

Clinton, William Jefferson. The forty-second president of the United States of America. Clinton was the Governor of Arkansas before winning the presidency in 1992. His wife Hillary Rodham Clinton is now senator from the state of New York. They have one daughter, Chelsea.

Bill Clinton. Christomas Corp. China. Circa 1990s. 6 inches. Spoof doll. Box is marked: "© Celebrity Spoof Licensing Corp." ....**$10-$15**

Carlo by Trendmasters as portrayed by Kim Coates. *Author's collection.*

A 6-inch spoof doll of Bill Clinton. *Courtesy of David Spurgeon.*

Close, Glenn. Actress, singer, producer and musician, Close starred in two Disney films, *101 Dalmatians* and *102 Dalmatians*, as Cruella De Vil, and played opposite Michael Douglas in the movie *Fatal Attraction* (1987). She has been nominated for five Academy Awards and has won countless Obie, Tony and Emmy Awards.

1. Cruella De Vil-Power in Pinstripes. Mattel, Inc. China. #16295. 1996. 11 inches. All vinyl, fully jointed, rooted blonde hair, painted features; wears one-piece dress with black bodice and wrap styled white and black pin-striped skirt, black hat with veil. ....**$75-$85**

2. Cruella De Vil – Ruthless in Red. Mattel, Inc. China. #17576. 1997. 11 inches. All vinyl, fully jointed, rooted blonde hair, painted features; wears red turtleneck sweater, red leggings and red pillbox styled hat. ....**$100-$125**

Coates, Kim. Actor Coates has starred in several films, including *The Amityville Curse* (1989) and *The Client* (1994), and appeared as Carlo in John Travolta's film *Battlefield Earth* (2000).

Carlo. Trendmasters. China. 1999. 6 inches. All vinyl, molded and painted clothing and features, complete with Hunting Knife and M-16. Package marked: "© 1999 Trendmasters, Inc. St. Louis Mo. 63101 U.S.A." ....**$10-$15**

Cody, Lew. Cody was a silent film star who worked until the early 1920s and was married to actress Mabel Norman at the time of his death. Some of the films he appeared in were *The Valley of Silent Men* (1922), *Rupert of Hentzau* (1923) and *Souls for Sale* (1923).

Lew Cody. Maker unknown. Circa 1920s. 13 inches. Painted hair and features; wearing brown tweed suit with crème shirt and blue design tie. On stand bearing the words "Lew Cody." (This may be a one-of-a-kind doll, so the value is the actual price paid for this example.) **$750**

This Lew Cody doll is by an unknown maker and may be a one-of-a-kind. *Courtesy of Billie Nelson Tyrrell.*

Colbert, Claudette. Colbert was one of the most loved actresses in the 1930s. She starred in the 1934 Paramount film *Cleopatra*, as well as in many other films.

Claudette Colbert as Cleopatra. Effanbee Doll Company. China. 1990 to 1991. #FB1990. 16 inches. All vinyl, jointed, painted brown eyes, bright red lips; dressed in gold

Cleopatra outfit. Marked: "© 1934 Paramount, © 1990 Effanbee Doll." With certificate of authenticity. Limited edition. Part of the Legend Series. ....**$100-$150**

Effanbee's Claudette Colbert as Cleopatra, part of the Legend Series. *Courtesy of McMasters Doll Auctions.*

Coleman, James. Actor Coleman is best known for his role as T.J. McCabe in the television series *S.W.A.T.*, which aired from February 1975 until July 1976. (For group shot, see Perry, Rod.)

1. McCabe from S.W.A.T. L.J.N. Toys, Ltd. #6600. 1975. 7 inches. All vinyl, jointed, painted features; dressed in S.W.A.T. gear. Copyright by Spelling-Goldberg Productions. ......**$20-$30**

2. McCabe from S.W.A.T. L.J.N. Toys, Ltd. #6850. 1976. 7 inches. All vinyl, jointed, painted features; dressed in S.W.A.T. gear. A little bit better quality than the first version. Copyright by Spelling-Goldberg Productions. ......**$20-$30**

2: James Coleman as T.J. McCabe from S.W.A.T. by L.J.N. Toys, Ltd.

Collins, Joan. Actress Collins is best known for her role as Alexis Colby on the long-running television series *Dynasty*, which aired from 1981 to 1989. She has appeared in several films, including *The Flintstones in Viva Rock Vegas* (2000), in which she played Wilma Flintstone's mother.

Alexis Colby. World Doll. China. 19 inches.

All vinyl, rooted black hair, painted features; wearing full-length red gown. Box marked: "Made exclusively by World Doll 4012 Second Avenue, Brooklyn, N.Y." ....**$75-$125**

Joan Collins as Alexis Colby from *Dynasty* by World Doll, with her original box.

Collins, Stephen. Actor Collins starred in a variety of films and on television. He is best known for his role as Commodore Willard Decker in the movie *Star Trek The Motion Picture* and for his starring role in the television series *Seventh Heaven*, which debuted in 1996.

1. Decker. Mego. Hong Kong. #91200/3. 1979. 3 inches. All vinyl, painted features and clothing. Copyright by Paramount Pictures Corporation. ....**$20-$30**

2. Decker. Mego. Hong Kong. #91210/3. 1979. 12 inches. All vinyl, painted features, painted brown hair; wearing two-piece Star Trek uniform with boots. Marked on head: "© PPCo.;" marked on back: "© MEGO CORP. 1977//MADE IN HONG KONG." Copyright by Paramount Pictures Corporation. ......**$90-$125**

Connery, Sean. Actor Connery has starred on stage and in films, and is best known for his role as Agent OO7 in the James Bond movies. In 1987, he received an Academy Award for his role in *The Untouchables.*

Sean Connery as James Bond. Gilbert. Hong Kong. #16101. 1965. 12 inches. Vinyl head, painted brown hair, painted black eyes, body is plastic with vinyl arms. The mold came from the Ideal Toy Corp. Back marked: "© IDEAL TOY CORP.//B 12½//2." Copyright by Gilrose Productions, Inc. and Eon Productions, Inc. ....**$100-$125**

Cooper, Alice (Vincent Damon Furrier).

Musician, singer, songwriter and actor, Cooper has starred in a variety of films, including *Freddy's Dead, Mental Years* and *Prince of Darkness*. Known for his wild makeup, outfits and music, Cooper began his music career in 1964 in Phoenix, Arizona. He joined a rock band called Alice Cooper, named after a woman who was persecuted for being a witch in Medieval times. He went on to record seven albums during the period of 1969 to 1973 and his band was one of the most popular rock acts in the world, with hit records and sold-out concerts. When the band broke up in 1975, following a dispute over the rights to the name "Alice Cooper," the singer had his name legally changed to Alice Cooper.

Alice Cooper. McFarlane Toys. China. 2000. 6 inches. All vinyl, painted features including painted black all-around eyes; wearing black vinyl top hat, black painted-on pants and shirt with black painted-on over-the-knee boots, with basket, snake, spiders, saber, crutch, cane and guillotine with sliding blade. From the Rock & Roll Legend Figures Series. ..**$20-$25**

Alice Cooper by McFarlane Toys. *Courtesy of David Cox.*

Corby, Ellen.
Actress Corby is best known for her role as Esther "Grandma" Walton on the television series *The Waltons*, which aired from September 1972 to August 1981.

Grandma. Mego. Hong Kong. 1974. 8 inches. Vinyl, jointed, painted features; wearing a blue flowered dress with white apron. Sold as a pair with Grandpa and also sold singly. ....**$15-$20**, loose; **$25-$30**, boxed singly; **$40-$50**, boxed pair

Ellen Corby as Grandma Walton, shown with Grandpa Walton, by Mego. *Courtesy of McMasters Doll Auctions.*

Cosby, Bill.
From 1965 until 1968, comedian Cosby starred in the television series *I Spy*. In the 1980s, he returned to television with the top-rated series *The Cosby Show*. Cosby has authored several books, including a series of children's books. He brought back Art Linkletter's old series *Kids Say the Darndest Things* as a series of television specials beginning in 1997. Cosby took to animation in the 1970s with his cartoon series *Fat Albert*, which is still shown on cable stations today.

1. Lil' Bill from Fat Albert. Remco. China. 1985. 24 inches. All vinyl, molded hair, painted features; wearing a striped top with pants. Boxed with a miniature comic about Fat Albert. ....**$60-$80**

Remco's Li'l Bill from *Fat Albert*, voiced by Bill Cosby.

Costello, Lou.
Comedian Costello, together with his partner, Bud Abbott, with whom he mainly worked, comprised one of the greatest comedy teams in the history of show business—Abbott & Costello. They mastered the straight man/clown relationship, while at the same time creating a magic that took them from the burlesque stage to radio, Broadway, film and television. In 1991, the United States Postal Service paid homage to the team by creating a stamp in their likeness as part of their Comedy Legends' Commemorative Stamp Booklet. (See also Abbott, Bud.)

1. Lou Costello. Ideal. 1984 to 1985. 12 inches. All vinyl character, painted features; dressed in baseball uniform. With audio tape. ....**$40-$50**

2. Abbott & Costello. Exclusive Toy Products, Inc. China. 1999. 9 inches. All vinyl, fully poseable, painted features; wearing outfits from "Who's on First" skit including hats. From the Limited Edition Collector's Series. ....$75-$85 for the pair

2: Abbott & Costello in their "Who's on First" skit outfits by Exclusive Toy Products, Inc. *Courtesy of David Cox.*

Costner, Kevin. Actor-director Costner has played in a variety of films, including *Bull Durham* and *Field of Dreams.* Costner also played the role of Robin Hood in the film *Robin Hood-Prince of Thieves.*

1. Long Bow Robin Hood-Prince of Thieves. Kenner. Hong Kong. 1991. 4 inches. All plastic, poseable, painted hair and features; wearing fabric and vinyl clothing. Marked: "©MCP&WBI 91." Sold on card with picture of star. Copyright by Warner Brothers. ....**$15-$20**

2. Cross Bow Robin Hood-Prince of Thieves. Kenner. Hong Kong. 1991. 4 inches. All plastic, poseable, painted hair and features; wearing fabric and vinyl clothing. Marked: "©MCP&WBI 91." Sold on card with picture of star. Copyright by Warner Brothers. ....**$15-$20**

2: Kevin Costner as Cross Bow Robin Hood by Kenner.

Craig, Yvonne. Actress Craig starred as the counterpart to Batman as Barbara Gordon and Batgirl on the television series *Batman* in 1967 and 1968.

1. Batgirl. Ideal Toy Corp. U.S.A. 1967-1968. 11 inches. All vinyl, poseable, rooted hair with painted features, side-glancing painted green eyes; dressed in Batgirl outfit of black jumpsuit with blue cape, boots and mask. Marked on head: "1965//Ideal Toy Corp.//W-12-3;" marked on hip: "1965//Ideal [in oval]//2 M-12." ....**$800-$900**

2. Batgirl. Mego. Hong Kong. 8 inches. #1343. 1973. All vinyl, fully jointed; painted features; wearing Batgirl outfit. Kresge blister card style package. ....**$250-$300** (See photo on page 40.)

3. Batgirl. Mego. Hong Kong. 8 inches. 1973. All vinyl, fully jointed, painted features; wearing Batgirl outfit. Sold on card or in window box. ....**$150-$200**

4. Batgirl. Mego. Hong Kong. 5 inches. 1972. All vinyl, bendable, painted features and clothing. Part of the Super Hero Bendables Series. ..**$50-$70**

Boxes for Kenner's Robin Hood, Azeem (played by Morgan Freeman), and the Sheriff of Nottingham (played by Alan Rickman), from the film *Robin Hood-Prince of Thieves.*

2: Yvonne Craig as Batgirl, by Mego, from the 1960's television series *Batman*.

Crippen, Robert L. Crippen has been an astronaut since 1969, flying more than 506 hours in space on four space flights. Before becoming an astronaut, Crippen was a pilot in the Air Force, logging more than 6,500 hours.

GI Joe as Robert Crippen. Hasbro, Inc. Kenner. China. #81401. 1997. 12 inches. All vinyl, fully jointed, painted hair and features; dressed in orange astronaut suit with helmet and air pack. ....$25-$35

GI Joe as Robert Crippen, by Hasbro, Inc., Kenner. *Courtesy of David Spurgeon.*

Criscoula, Peter. (See KISS)

Crockett, Davy. American frontiersman Crockett died in 1836 defending the Alamo. *The Davy Crockett Show* aired on the Walt Disney television program on ABC from December 1954 until February 1955, starring actor Fess Parker. (See also Parker, Fess.)

1. Davy Crockett Puppet. Unmarked. Circa 1950s. 12 inches. All composition, painted features, mouth opens and closes; dressed in classic Davy Crockett outfit with tan clothing, orange trim and raccoon hat. ....$150-$200

2. Davy Crockett with his horse. Ideal Toy Corp. U.S.A. #3154. 1955 to 1956. 4 inches by 5-3/8 inches. All plastic, painted features; dressed in buckskin and a coonskin cap. Sits with white stallion and can be separated from horse. ....$40-$50

3. Davy Crockett. Possibly by Sun Rubber Company but unmarked. Circa 1950s. 18 inches. Magic skin body with vinyl head, all vinyl, inset eyes, painted lips, molded hair; wearing authentic Davy Crockett outfit. ....$150-$200

4. Davy Crockett Figure. Marx. U.S.A. Circa 1960. 2 inches. All rubber. ....$40-$50

5. Davy Crockett. Mattel, Inc. Malaysia. #10308. 1993. 12 inches. All vinyl, jointed, painted features; a faux buckskin two-piece fringed outfit, comes with brown bag, belt, knife and faux fur coonskin cap with tail, shoes are moccasin styled slip-ons. Disney Park and Catalog Exclusive. ....$70-$80

3: An unmarked magic skin Davy Crockett, possibly by Sun Rubber Company.

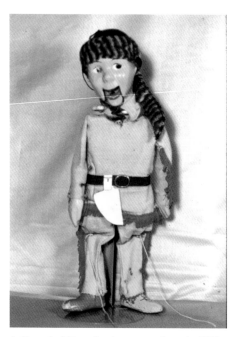

1: Unmarked Davy Crockett puppet from the 1950s. *Courtesy of Gasoline Alley.*

All vinyl, jointed, painted features; wearing blue pants with red and yellow jacket, with helmet and glasses. Box marked: "TM & © 1994 Twentieth Century//Fox Films and Turner Pictures, Inc.//All Rights Reserved// 45902// Richard Tylor Collectible Doll." ....$40-$50

1: Macauley Culkin as Kevin from the film *Home Alone. Author's collection.*

Crough, Suzanne. Actress Crough is best known for her role as Tracy Partridge on the television series *The Partridge Family*, which aired from September 1970 to August 1974.

Patti Partridge. Tracy Partridge's play doll. Ideal Toy Corp. 1971. 16 inches. Vinyl, open smiling mouth; dressed in blue jeans, white shoes and orange top. ....$75-$100, loose; $200-$250, boxed

Culkin, Macauley. A veteran in the entertainment business, Culkin began acting on stage at age four and was making commercials by age six. At ten, he starred in the film *Home Alone*, which made him a household name. Culkin also starred in other films including *Richie Rich, Pagemaster* and *Getting Even with Dad*.

1. Kevin from *Home Alone*. T-HQ, Inc. China. 1991. #7150. 6 inches. All vinyl, jointed at arms, legs and head, molded yellow hair, painted blue eyes, painted features; painted and molded clothing of blue pants and red sweater with blue and yellow design. Push button on back to hear him scream. Box marked: "© 1991 Toy Headquarters. TM & © 1991 Twentieth Century Fox Film Corporation." ....$20-$35

2. Macauley Culkin as The Pagemaster. Applause Inc. China. 1994. #45902. 11 inches.

2: Macauley Culkin as the Pagemaster from the movie by the same name, by Applause, Inc. *Author's collection.*

D

Dafoe, Allan Roy Dr. Doctor. Dafoe was the doctor who delivered and helped care for the Dionne Quintuplets in the 1930s and 1940s. (See Dionne Quintuplets for photograph.)

Dr. DaFoe. Alexander Doll Company. U.S.A. 1937 to 1939. 14 to 15 inches. All composition, fully jointed, painted eyes and features, wig. ....**$1,200** up

Dallas Cowboys Cheerleaders. These
young women cheer on the Dallas Cowboys football team. The dolls are said to have been modeled after actual cheerleaders for the team.

Dallas Cowboys Cheerleaders. Royal Doll Co. 1982. 14 inches. Plastic bodies, jointed at arms, legs and head, brown sleep eyes, painted mouth; wearing white mini shorts, blue and white long-sleeved tops with stars, white boots and blue and white pom-pons. Three versions were made, including brunette with rooted hair, blonde with rooted hair and African-American with dark plastic body and black Afro-styled rooted hair. ....**$40-$50** each

Above and below left: Dallas Cowboys Cheerleaders by Royal Doll Co. *Courtesy of David Spurgeon.*

Dash, Stacey. Actress Dash was one of the stars of the 1996 weekly television series *Clueless*, in which she appeared as Dionne.

Dionne. Mattel, Inc. China. 1997. #17037. 11 inches. Dark brown vinyl, jointed; wears light purple skirt and jacket, white blouse, hat, stockings and light purple shoes, packaged with white animal backpack, feather pen, brush and telephone. One of three dolls based on the television series, they all are made with the Barbie® body. The box shows a picture of the stars of the show: Rachel Blanchard (Cher), Elisa Donovan (Amber) and Stacey Dash (Dionne). Marked on back: "© MATTEL INC. 1966/CHINA." ....**$20-$30**

Stacy Dash as Dionne from *Clueless*, by Mattel. *Author's collection.*

Davis, Ann B. Actress Davis is best known for her role as the housekeeper Alice on the hit television series *The Brady Bunch*, which aired from September 1969 to August 1974.

Alice. Exclusive Toy Products, Inc. China. #16051. 9 inches. All vinyl, jointed, molded and painted hair and features; wearing blue dress with large white buttons, white apron and white shoes. ....**$25-$35**

Ann B. Davis as Alice from *The Brady Bunch* by Exclusive Toy Products, Inc. *Courtesy of David Spurgeon.*

Dawber, Pam. Actress Dawber is best known for her role as Mindy in the hit television series *Mork & Mindy*, also starring Robin Williams. The show aired from September 1978 to August 1982.

Mindy. Mattel, Inc. Taiwan. #1277. 1979. 9 inches. Vinyl doll, painted features; wearing red top with blue jeans. Marked on head: "© 1979 PPC TAIWAN;" marked on back: "©1973/ MATTEL INC./TAIWAN." ......**$20-$25**, loose; **$45-$50**, boxed

Dean, James. In his short career, Dean became one of the most admired screen stars of all time, achieving cult status and becoming an icon of American culture. He starred in *The Immoralist* on Broadway as well as in three feature films before his death in an auto accident in 1955: *East of Eden* (1955), *Rebel Without a Cause* (1955) and *Giant* (1956).

1. James Dean. Exclusive Toy Products, Inc. China. 1999. 11 inches. All vinyl, painted features, wearing leather jacket with jeans. Packaged in window box. A Hollywood Icon Edition. ....**$20-$30**

1: James Dean by Exclusive Toy Products, Inc., in original packaging.

2. James Dean. Headliners. Equity Marketing, Inc. China. 2000. 6 inches. All vinyl, molded and painted features; molded and painted clothing of white T-shirt, brown leather jacket and tight beige pants. Part of the Greatest Headliners-Headliners of the 20th Century Series: Limited edition of 20,000. ......**$10-$15**

3. James Dean. Mattel, Inc. China. 2000. 11 inches. All vinyl, fully jointed, painted features; wearing jeans, red jacket and white T-shirt. From the American Legend Series. ....**$20-$25**

2: James Dean Headliner by Equity Marketing, Inc. *Courtesy of David Cox.*

De Carlo, Yvonne. Actress De Carlo is best known for her role as Lily Munster on the television series *The Munsters*, which aired from 1964 until 1966.

1. Lily Munster. Ideal Toy Corp. U.S.A. 1964. 10 inches. Hand puppet. Vinyl head, painted features, cloth body. Marked on bottom of puppet: "Lily Munster;" tag marked: "© FILMWAYS PROD.INC.//1964//IDEAL TOY CORP." ....**$75-$100** each (See photo on page 44.)

2. Lily Munster. Exclusive Toy Products, Inc. China. Circa 1990s. 9 inches. All vinyl, painted features, long rooted black hair with white streak through hair; wearing full-length pink dress with purple sash and trim. ..**$15-$20**

2: Yvonne De Carlo as Lily Munster from *The Munsters* series by Exclusive Toy Products, Inc. *Courtesy of David Spurgeon.*

1: Hand puppet depicting Yvonne De Carlo as Lily Munster from *The Munsters* series. *Courtesy of Sunnie Newell.*

Ichabod Crane. Todd McFarlane Toys. China. 1999. 6 inches. Vinyl, painted and molded hair, painted features, has interchangeable snap-on head and skull; painted and molded clothing, came with satchel, two books and seven accessory pieces and instruction booklet. Package marked: "SLEEPY HOLLOW is TM Paramount Pictures and Mandalay Pictures LLC. © 1999 Todd McFarlane Productions, Inc." Part of a series of Feature Film Figures. ....$25-$35

Dempsey, Jack. Boxer William Harrison "Jack" Dempsey became a major sports figure in the 1920s. Dempsey defeated Jess Willard in 1919, winning the title and making him the new heavyweight boxing champion.

Jack Dempsey. Lenci. Italy. Circa 1930s. 18 inches. Felt with painted features. ..$1,500-$2,500

Denver, Bob. Actor Denver is best known for his role as Gilligan on the hit television series *Gilligan's Island*, which aired from September 1964 to September 1967.

Gilligan. Playskool. 1977. 3 inches. Soft rubber, painted features; from the cartoon series. Companion dolls were Skipper and Mary Ann. ....$10-$15 each

Depp, Johnny. Initially known as a teen idol, thanks to his role on the television series *21 Jump Street*, which aired from 1987 to 1992, Depp went on to be a leading film actor. He starred in hits like *Edward Scissorhands* (1990), *What's Eating Gilbert Grape* (1993) and, in 1999, played Ichabod Crane in *Sleepy Hollow*.

Dey, Susan. Actress Dey is best known for her role as Laurie Partridge on the television series *The Partridge Family*, which aired from September 1970 to August 1974. Dey also starred in the series *L.A. Law* (1986-1992) and the 1977 mini series *Love Me, Love Me Not*.

1. Susan Dey Paper Doll Booklets. Artcraft. 1971 to 1973. Two different versions were made: #4218 with a photograph on the cover (1971) and #4261 with an illustration of Susan Dey on the cover (1973). ....$20-$25, each, cut; $40-$50, each, uncut

2. Susan Dey Paper Dolls Boxed. Saalfield. 1972 to 1973. Two different versions were produced: #6024 with green background and photograph of Susan Dey (1972) and yellow background with illustration of Susan Dey (1973). ....$20-$30, each, cut; $50-$60, each, uncut

3. Laurie Partridge. Remco. Hong Kong. #3461. 1973. 19 inches. Vinyl head, rooted hair, vinyl arms and legs, plastic torso, lifelike features; dressed in white turtleneck and blue jeans frayed at the bottom. Marked on head: "© 1973//REMCO   IND.INC.//HARRISON. N.J.//ITEM No. 3461." With color poster of David and Susan in box. ......$125-$150, loose; $250-$350, boxed

Ichabod Crane as portrayed by Johnny Depp by Todd McFarlane Toys. *Author's collection.*

3A: Laurie Partridge as portrayed by Susan Dey by Remco. *Author's collection.*

3B: The original box, with poster of Susan Dey and David Cassidy, for Laurie Partridge by Remco. *Author's collection.*

1A: Princess Diana doll with wardrobe by an unknown maker. *Courtesy of David Spurgeon.*

Diana (Princess).

Princess of Wales. Born Diana Spencer, she was married to Prince Charles, future King of England, in 1981 and became known as "The People's Princess." The couple divorced before her death in an automobile accident in 1997.

1. Princess Diana. Maker unknown. China. 6 inches. Circa 1990s. All vinyl, painted features. Doll is unmarked but the box is marked: "Princess Diana Wardrobe & Doll Set. China." A complete wardrobe came in the box with the doll. ..**$50-$75**

2. Princess Diana. Peggy Nisbet Dolls. England. #3160. Circa 1990s. 16 inches. All vinyl, rooted blonde hair; wearing full-length wedding dress with flowers. ....**$125-$150**

3. Royal Diana. Wayout Toys. China. #CE #40050A. Circa 1990s. All vinyl, painted features; wearing pink dress, with crown, shoes and bag. ....**$15-$25**

4. Princess Diana. Danbury Mint. China. Circa 1990s. 18 inches. Porcelain; wearing red and white dress with red jacket and hat, with wooden stand. ....**$35-$50**

5. Princess Diana (White House). Paul Crees and Peter Coe. England. 1998. 28 inches. Poured wax; wearing replica of dark blue velvet gown, which Princess Diana wore to the White House in 1985, when she danced with John Travolta. Limited edition of 10 pieces. Sold out, not yet on secondary market. Issue price. **$2,200**

2: The tag worn by the Princess Diana doll by Peggy Nisbet.

3: Royal Diana by Wayout Toys in her box. *Courtesy of David Spurgeon.*

1B: The box for the Princess Diana doll with wardrobe by an unknown maker. *Courtesy of David Spurgeon.*

5: Princess Diana (White House) by Paul Crees and Peter Coe. *Courtesy of the artists.*

Diaz, Cameron. Actress Diaz has appeared in several films, including *My Best Friend's Wedding* and *There's Something About Mary*. She played Natalie in the 2000 film *Charlie's Angels*, which was based on the 1970s television series of the same name.

Natalie from *Charlie's Angels*. Jakks Pacific Inc. China. 2000. 11 inches. All vinyl, fully jointed, rooted blonde hair, painted features; wearing blue satin style pants with jacket, multicolored top, also came dressed in black pants with red midriff top, came boxed with stand. Box marked: "Action-Fashion Body I've got all the right poses! Charlie's Angels: TM & © 2000 Columbia Pictures Industries, Inc." (See Barrymore, Drew for photograph.) ....**$25-$40**

DiCaprio, Leonardo. Actor DiCaprio gained fame in the role of Jack in the blockbuster 1997 film *Titanic*, which made him a teen idol. He has made many other films, including *What's Eating Gilbert Grape* (1993).

Jack. Way Out Toys. China. #40304A. All vinyl, cheaply made, jointed at arms and legs with twist waist, rooted hair with painted features; wearing black tuxedo. Sold in set with Rose doll. Unauthorized versions of the characters Jack and Rose from the movie *Titanic*. ....**$10-$15**, individually; **$25-$40**, for the pair. (See Winslet, Kate for photograph.)

Dickinson, Angie. Actress Dickinson has appeared in many films and on television. She is best known for her role as Sgt. Suzanne "Pepper" Martin on the NBC television series *Police Woman*, which aired from September 1974 until August 1978.

Angie Dickinson from *Police Woman*. Horsman. U.S.A. #8000. 1976. 9 inches. All vinyl, fully jointed, rooted blonde hair, painted brown eyes; wearing pants, turtleneck and long tied jacket with boots. Head marked:

Angie Dickinson in her role as Sgt. Suzanne "Pepper" Martin from *Police Woman*. *Courtesy of Suellen Manning.*

"HORSMAN DOLLS INC//U//L CPT// 19©76." Copyright by Columbia Pictures Television. Original price $1.18. ....**$50-$75**

Dionne Quintuplets: Yvonne, Annette, Cecile, Emilie and Marie were the most famous quintuplets in the world during the 1930s. The world just could not get enough of these little girls. The five little babies were born on May 28, 1934, to Elzire Dionne. The infants' combined weight was only 10 pounds, 1 ounces. The Alexander Doll Company was

Set of 7-inch Dionne Quintuplets with furniture. Sold at a 2000 McMasters Doll Auction for $1,500. *Courtesy of McMasters Doll Auctions.*

Set of 7-inch Dionne Quintuplets in original bed. $1,200 up. *Courtesy of Lynne Ramsey.*

Set of 7-inch all original Dionne Quintuplets, with wigs, wearing their original tagged clothes, shoes, bonnets and pins. They came with extra sunsuits and bonnets. $1,500 up. *Courtesy of Susan Killoran.*

the only company authorized to produce the Dionne Quintuplet dolls, though there were many unauthorized versions.

Dionne Quintuplets. Alexander Doll Company. U.S.A. 1935 until 1938. Composition and fully jointed. The girls were dressed in a variety of outfits, but each girl had her own color: Yvonne, pink; Annette, yellow; Cecile, green; Emilie, lavender; and Marie, blue. They were made in a variety of sizes, including 7-8 inches, 10 inches, 11-12 inches, 14 inches, 16-17 inches, 20 inches and 23-24 inches.

1. 7 inches. 1935. Painted hair, painted brown eyes. Marked on head: "DIONNE// ALEXANDER." ....**$200-$250**

2. 7 inches. 1936. Mohair wig (molded straight hair under hair), painted brown eyes. Same markings as previous. ....**$200-$250**

3. 7 inches. 1936. Molded curly hair, painted brown eyes. Head and back both marked: "ALEXANDER." ....**$200-$250**

4. 10 inches. 1935. Painted straight hair, closed mouth, brown sleep eyes with eyelashes. Head marked: "DIONNE//ALEXAN-DER;" back marked: "MADAME// ALEXANDER." ....**$300-$350**

5. 11 to 12 inches. 1935. Painted curly hair, open mouth, brown sleep eyes with eyelashes, cloth body. Head marked: "DIONNE// ALEXANDER." ....**$350-$400**

Grouping of 7-inch Dionne Quints, both straight-leg and bent-knee babies. The blue outfits are original. $200-$250, each. *Courtesy of Susan Killoran.*

All-original 20-inch Dionne toddler dolls Yvonne and Annette. *Courtesy of Patricia Wood.*

A set of 11-inch Dionne Quint toddlers. They have been re-dressed. *Courtesy of Lynnae Ramsey.*

A grouping of different sizes and ages of the Dionne Quints. *Courtesy of Susan Killoran.*

Set of 8-inch Dionne Quintuplets in their original chairs and all original clothing. $800-$1,000. *Courtesy of Annette's Antique Dolls.*

6. 16 inches. 1935. Painted straight hair, closed mouth, brown sleep eyes with eyelashes, cloth body. Head marked: "DIONNE// ALEXANDER." ....$400-$500

7. 17 inches. 1936. Painted curly hair, closed mouth, brown sleep eyes with eyelashes, cloth body. Head marked: "ALEXANDER." ....$500-$600

8. 23 inches. 1935. Painted straight hair, open mouth with teeth, brown sleep eyes with eyelashes, cloth body. Marked on head: "DIONNE//ALEXANDER." ....$700-$800

Doctor Doolittle. (See Harrison, Rex)

Doherty, Shannen. Actress Doherty is best known for her bad-girl role as Brenda on the Fox hit television series *Beverly Hills 90210*. More recently, she has starred in a television series, entitled *Charmed*, about three sisters who are witches.

Brenda. Mattel, Inc. China. 1991. 11 inches. All vinyl, jointed, painted features; wearing brown shorts, white shirt with colored vest and hat, with a blue two-piece bathing suit. ....$15-$20

Mattel's 11-inch Brenda, as portrayed by Shannen Doherty, on the television series *Beverly Hills 90210*.

Dolenz, Mickey. (See Monkees, The)

Donovan, Elisa. Actress Donovan starred as Amber in the 1996 weekly television series *Clueless*.

Amber. Mattel, Inc. China. 1997. #17038. 11 inches. Vinyl, jointed; wears leathery pink pants, sweater, jacket, headband, sunglasses, yellow shoes and yellow animal backpack, came packaged with a telephone. One of three dolls based on the television series, they are all are made with the Barbie® body. The box shows a picture of the stars of the show: Rachel Blanchard (Cher), Elisa Donovan (Amber) and Stacey Dash (Dionne). Marked on back: "MATTEL INC. 1966//CHINA." ....$20-$30

Elisa Donovan as Amber, by Mattel, from *Clueless*. Author's collection.

Doohan, James. Actor Doohan is best known for his role as Commander Montgomery "Scotty" Scott on the television series *Star Trek*, which aired from 1966 until 1969. Doohan also starred in the film version of the show *Star Trek the Motion Picture*, and had small roles in hundreds of other shows.

1. Mr. Scott (Scottie). Mego. Hong Kong. #51200/5. 1974. 8 inches. All vinyl, fully jointed, painted hair and features; wearing Star Trek uniform. Copyright by Paramount Pictures Corporation. ....$75-$100

2. Mr. Scott (Scottie). Mego. Hong Kong. #91200/5. 1979. 3 inches. All vinyl, fully jointed, painted hair and features. Copyright by Paramount Pictures Corporation. ......$30-$40

Douglas, Donna. Actress Douglas is best known for her role as Elly May Clampett in the hit television series *The Beverly Hillbillies*, which aired from September 1962 to September 1971.

1. Elly May Clampett. Unique. Circa 1960s. 12 inches. Vinyl head and arms, plastic legs and torso, fully jointed, rooted blonde hair, painted blue eyes; dressed in pants or in a skirt. Head marked: "© UNIQUE." Sold as a cereal premium. ....$50-$75

1: Donna Douglas as Elly May Clampet, by Unique, from the television series *The Beverly Hillbillies*. Courtesy of David Spurgeon.

2. Elly May Paper Dolls. Watkins Strathmore Co. 1963. In booklet with likeness on cover. ....$40-$50,cut; $60-$70, uncut

3. Donna Douglas. Produced by Jim Madden. Phoenix, Arizona. U.S.A. 1991. 15 inches. Porcelain; wearing pink and white lace blouse with beautifully made Levi pants with tiny tag on back, little moccasins with rope belt like the ones worn on the show. All handmade. With accessories, which include old magazines, memorabilia, behind-the-scenes stories, special personalized photographs, and a hand-written letter from Donna Douglas. Limited edition of 250. ....$1,000-$1,200

3: Donna Douglas by Jim Madden. Limited edition of 250.

Draeger, Jason and Justin. The Draeger twins were the babies who took turns playing the role of Joey Stivic on the television series *All in the Family*. Carroll O'Connor played Archie Bunker, the main character and Joey's grandfather. The twins appeared on the show from 1975 until 1978.

Joey Stivic, Archie Bunker's Grandson. Ideal. U.S.A. #1380-5. 1976-1977. 14 inches. Vinyl head, one-piece vinyl body, rooted hair, painted eyes, open mouth, an anatomically correct boy doll who drinks and wets. Marked on body: "© 1976//TANDEM PRODS. INC//ALL RIGHTS RESERVED//IDEAL//B-58;" marked on head: "IDEAL TOY CORP//J-14-H-253." Original price $13.99. ....$75-$100

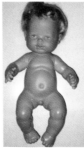

Joey Stivic, Archie Bunker's Grandson, by Ideal, an anatomically correct boy doll. *Author's collection.*

The front of the box for Joey Stivic showing Carroll O'Connor as Archie Bunker holding the real baby from the show. *Author's collection.*

Drescher, Fran. Actress Drescher starred as Fran Fine on the CBS sitcom *The Nanny*, which first aired in 1993. She is credited with creating the show idea and working to help produce it. Drescher has starred in more than a dozen films, including *The Beautician and the Beast* (1997).

The Nanny. Street Players Co. China. 1995. 11 inches. All vinyl, jointed, rooted black hair, painted features; wearing black tights and top with gold mini-skirt, boxed with coat, shoes and brush. Push button to hear Drescher's voice speaking "Nanny phrases" such as: "Sweetie, don't ever lose weight for a guy. That's what control tops are for;" "Honey, I know what I am, But trust me, you're a doll too" and "Remember, the bigger the hair, the smaller the hips look." ....$40-$50

The Nanny, as portrayed by Fran Drescher, from the television series of the same name. Made by Street Players Co.

Duke, Patty. Actress Duke has starred in a variety of television shows and films. Her television series, *The Patty Duke Show*, aired from September 1963 to August 1966. Duke played two parts—cousins Cathy and Patty Lane—on the show. She won an Academy Award for her portrayal of Helen Keller in *The Miracle Worker* in 1962.

1. Patty Duke Paper Dolls. Milton Bradley. 1963. Includes both Patty and Cathy dolls. ....**$20-$30**, cut; **$40-$50**, uncut

2. Patty Duke. Horsman. U.S.A. 1965-1966. 12 inches. Vinyl head, rooted hair, painted blue eyes, vinyl arms and legs with wire inside for posing, plastic torso. Two different versions were made. The first doll (1965) has a telephone and photo, wears a red sweater with gray flannel pants and is marked: "HORSMAN DOLL//6211." The second doll is dressed in light colored slacks with a pink and lace blouse and came in a box marked "Go-Go with Patty Duke" which included one of her 45-rpm singles. ....First doll: **$40-$60**, loose; **$150-$200**, boxed; second doll: **$50-$60**, loose; **$250-$300**, boxed.

3. Patty Duke Board Game. Milton Bradley. Circa 1960s. ....**$50-$60**

2: Patty Duke by Horsman, wearing the red sweater and gray flannel pants. *Courtesy of Steve Malatinsky.*

3: The Patty Duke board game by Milton Bradley. *Courtesy of Steve Malatinsky.*

1A: Patty Duke paper dolls by Milton Bradley. *Author's collection.*

1B: The box for the Patty Duke paper dolls. *Author's collection.*

Durbin, Deanna.

Actress and singer Durbin appeared in many films in the 1930s and 1940s, including *Every Sunday* with Judy Garland.

1. Deanna Durbin. Ideal Toy Corp. U.S.A. 1938 to 1941. 20 inches. All composition, sleep eyes, brunette wig; all original outfit of a full-length white wedding dress with veil. Shown with 20-inch Horsman groom doll. $800-$900. (Groom: $300-$400.) The Ideal Doll Company produced a wide variety of Deanna Durbin dolls including a 14- to 15-inch size, 18-inch size, 21-inch size, 24-inch size and 25-inch size. They were produced from 1938 until 1941 of composition with sleep eyes and open smiling mouth with teeth. Deanna Durbin was sold in many outfits including a full-length short-sleeved dress with yellow and red miniature flowers, a knee-length blue wool jumper with dotted swiss blouse and a selection of party and school dresses as well as costumes from her movies. The marks vary depending on size of the doll. ....14- to 15 inches, **$500-$600**;

18 inches, $650-$750; 20-21 inches, **$800-$900**; 24 inches, **$1,000-$1,300**; 25 inches, **$1,200-$1,500**

2. Deanna Durbin. Ideal Toy Corp. U.S.A. 21 inches. 1938 to 1941. All original; wearing full-length light pink gown with pink mesh overlay. Marked on head: "DEANNA DURBIN//IDEAL DOLL;" marked on body: "IDEAL DOLL//21." ....**$800-$900**

3. Deanna Durbin. Ideal Toy Corp. U.S.A. 1938 to 1941. 25 inches. All original; wearing exquisite full-length floral dress with black lace trim, large straw hat and lace gloves. ..**$1,500** up

4. Deanna Durbin. Ideal Toy Corp. U.S.A. 1938 to 1941. 25 inches. Wearing full-length white dress with yellow and orange flowers, pin on dress. ....**$800-$900**

5. Deanna Durbin. Ideal Toy Corp. U.S.A. 1938 to 1941. 25 inches. Wearing all original red and white dress. ....**$1,200-$1,500**

1: Ideal's Deanna Durbin, 20 inches, dressed as a bride, shown with a Horsman Groom. *Courtesy of McMasters Doll Auctions.*

3: Deanna Durbin, 25 inches, wearing a full-length floral dress and hat. *Courtesy of Patricia Wood.*

4: Deanna Durbin, 25 inches, wearing a full-length dress with a pin on the front. *Courtesy of Annette's Antique Dolls.*

5: Deanna Durbin, 25 inches, wearing a red and white dress. *Author's collection.*

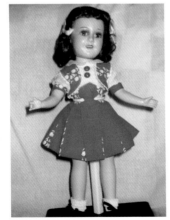

2: Deanna Durbin, 21 inches, wearing a full-length pink gown. *Courtesy of Lynnae Ramsey.*

E

Earhart, Amelia. A famous female American aviator, Earhart was the first woman to cross the Atlantic by plane, doing it solo in 1932. On a flight over the Pacific Ocean in 1937, her plane was lost and never found.

1. Amelia Earhart. Lenci. Italy. Circa 1930s. 16 inches. All felt, painted features, mohair wig. ....**$400-$500**

2. Amelia Earhart. Hallmark. Taiwan. #400DT113-6. 1979. 7 inches. All cloth, printed features; in box with airplane and airport picture on front. ....**$15-$25**

Earp, Wyatt. A famous law officer, Earp was in a gunfight with his brothers and Doc Holliday at the OK Corral in 1881.

Wyatt Earp and his horse, Tombstone. Hartland Plastics, Inc. U.S.A. #809. 1958. 8 inches. All plastic. ....**$100-$150**, mint-in-box

Eden, Barbara. Actress Eden is best known for her role as Jeannie in the hit television series *I Dream of Jeannie*, which aired from September 1965 to September 1970.

1. Jeannie. Libby Majorette Doll Corp. 1966. 20 inches. All vinyl, fully jointed, rooted blonde hair, blue sleep eyes with heavy painted eyelashes; in either a green or pink outfit. (The green outfit is rarer than the pink, and tends to bring slightly higher prices.) Head marked: "© 1966//LIBBY." Box shows photograph of

Barbara Eden on sides and bottom. ..**$300-$400**, loose; **$500-$600**, boxed

2. Jeannie Doll Accessories. Libby Majorette Doll Corp. 1966. Doll outfit in large box for the 20-inch Libby doll. ....**$200-$250**

3. Jeannie. Remco. Hong Kong. 1977. 6 inches. Vinyl, fully jointed, rooted blonde hair, painted black eyes, holes in feet for stand; dressed in blue harem outfit. Marked on back: "© REMCO TOYS INC.//MADE IN HONG KONG." ....**$20-$30**, loose; **$60-$80**, boxed

4. I Dream of Jeannie. Trendmasters. China. #60501. 1997. 11 inches. Blonde hair. Box marked: "© 1997 CPT Holdings, Inc." From episode 125. ....**$15-$20**

5. I Dream of Jeannie. Trendmasters. China. 1997. 11 inches. Brunette hair. Box marked: "© 1997 CPT Holdings, Inc." From episode 125. In total, five dolls were made in this series. ..**$15-$20**

4: I Dream of Jeannie by Trendmasters. *Author's collection.*

1: Barbara Eden as Jeannie, from Libby Majorette Doll Corp. From the television series *I Dream of Jeannie.*

5: I Dream of Jeannie by Trendmasters with brunette hair and in her original box. *Author's collection.*

Elizabeth (Princess). Princess Elizabeth ascended the throne as Queen Elizabeth II of England on February 6, 1952, upon the death of her father, King George VI. Her coronation was held on June 2, 1953.

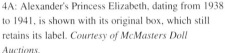

4B: Back view showing the label on the back of the dress. *Courtesy of McMasters Doll Auctions.*

3: Alexander's Princess Elizabeth dating from 1938 to 1941. *Courtesy of Susan Killoran.*

4A: Alexander's Princess Elizabeth, dating from 1938 to 1941, is shown with its original box, which still retains its label. *Courtesy of McMasters Doll Auctions.*

1. Princess Elizabeth. Alexander Doll Company. U.S.A. 1937. 8 inches. Composition, jointed, blonde mohair wig over molded hair, blue painted eyes; dressed in gown. Head marked: "DIONNE// ALEXANDER;" back marked: "ALEXANDER." The head and body of this doll came from the Dionne Quint toddler mold. Hard-to-find doll. ....**$400-$500**

2. Princess Elizabeth. Alexander Doll Company. U.S.A. 1937 to 1941. 13 inches. Composition, fully jointed, closed mouth, blonde human hair wig with blue tin sleep eyes, dimples in cheeks; wearing lavender full-length taffeta dress and metal crown with "jewels." ..**$500-$600**

3. Princess Elizabeth. Alexander Doll Company. U.S.A. 1938 to 1941. 15 inches. All composition, fully jointed; wearing full-length pink dress with tiara. ....**$500-$600**

4. Princess Elizabeth. Alexander Doll Company. U.S.A. 1938 to 1941. 16 inches. All composition, fully jointed, blonde wig, sleep eyes, open mouth; wearing peach taffeta dress with original tiara, also came in various costumes. Head marked: "PRINCESS ELIZABETH" and "ALEXANDER;" sometimes marked: "ALEXANDER DOLL CO." ....**$600-$700**

5. Princess Elizabeth. Alexander Doll Company. U.S.A. 1942. 14 inches. All composition, fully jointed; wearing all original clothes with military style hat. Marked with a circle with an "X" on the back of the head. ....**$400-$500**

6. Princess Elizabeth. Arranbee (R&B) Doll Company. U.S.A. Circa 1940s. 18 inches. All

5: An all original Princess Elizabeth by Alexander, 1942. *Courtesy of Sharron's Dolls.*

6: Princess Elizabeth by Arranbee, circa 1940s, with box.

composition, sleep eyes, brunette wig. Original box is marked "Nannette" with a line through it and "Princess Elizabeth" written in. Many times in department stores boxes would get switched and they would sell a doll with the wrong box. ....**$300-$400**

7. Princess Elizabeth. Chelsea Art. England. Circa 1950s. 14 inches. Ceramic shoulder head on cloth body, molded and painted features, brown hair, blue eyes; dressed in uniform from the Grenadier Guards. ....**$75-$125**

8. Princess Elizabeth. Alexander Doll Company. U.S.A. #2025 1953. 18 inches. All hard plastic, fully jointed, blonde wig, sleep eyes; wearing white gown with blue sash. ....**$750-$850**

Elizabeth (Queen). See biographical notes for Elizabeth, Princess, above.

Queen Elizabeth. Reliable Doll Company. Canada. 15 inches. All composition, sleep eyes, mohair wig; dressed in ceremonial gown with crown. Marked: "Reliable Doll Co. Canada 450 Her Highness Coronation Co." This doll was made in honor of the Queen's Coronation from the Barbara Ann Scott doll. Scott was a Canadian Ice Skating Champion. ....**$500-$600**

Queen Elizabeth made in honor of her coronation by the Reliable Doll Company of Canada. *Courtesy of Patricia Wood.*

Elliott, Cass (Mama Cass). Singer Elliott was part of a successful singing group, the Mamas and The Papas, who performed from 1963 until 1967. After 1967, Elliott performed solo until her death from a heart attack in 1974.

Cass of The Mamas and The Papas. Show Biz Babies. Hasbro. Hong Kong. #8809. 1967. 4 inches. All vinyl, jointed at head, wired vinyl body for posing, rooted dark blonde hair, painted green eyes, open/closed mouth with painted teeth; attached to a record cover. Copyright Hassenfeld Bros. Inc. (Hasbro). Marked on back: "© 1967//HASBRO//HONG KONG." ....**$30-$40**

Englund, Robert. Actor Englund has appeared in several films, including *Python* (2000), *The Prince and the Surfer* (1999) and *Urban Legend* (1998). He is probably best known for his role as Freddy in the film series *Nightmare on Elm Street.*

Feddy. China. Circa 1990s. 12 inches. Vinyl, molded and painted features with golden right hand; wearing black pants with red and green sweater, came boxed with hat. This doll is an unauthorized version of the character Freddy from the film *Nightmare on Elm Street.* Therefore, it is unmarked and the name is not spelled the same. The only marking on the box is "CHINA." ....**$40-$50**

Feddy, an unauthorized version of Robert Englund as Freddy from *Nightmare on Elm Street. Courtesy of David Spurgeon.*

Erving, Julius. Basketball player Erving led the American Basketball Association in scoring in 1973, 1974 and 1976. He was an all-star player for the National Basketball Association in 1977 and 1978.

Julius (Dr. J.) Erving. Shindana. Hong Kong. #9025. 1977. 9 inches. All vinyl, fully jointed (including wrists), painted black hair and eyes; with basketball. Copyright 1976 by Shindana Toys, Inc. ....**$40-$50**

Estrada, Erik. Actor Estrada is best known for his role as Officer Francis "Ponch" Poncherello in the hit television series *CHiPs*, which aired from 1977 until 1983.

1. Ponch. Mego. Hong Kong. #08010/1. 1981. 3 inches. All vinyl, fully jointed, painted features; painted clothing. Copyright 1977 by Metro-Goldwyn-Mayer Film Co. ......**$10-$15**

2. Ponch. Mego. Hong Kong. #07500/2. 1981. 8 inches. All vinyl, fully jointed, painted black hair; dressed in yellow jumpsuit with gun. Copyright 1977 by Metro-Goldwyn-Mayer Film Co. ....**$20-$30**

Evans, Dale. Actress, singer and author Evans was married to leading man Roy Rogers. The couple had their own series, *The Roy Rogers Show*, on NBC from 1951 until 1957. They moved to ABC in 1962 for *The Roy Rogers and Dale Evans Show*. Besides acting on television, Evans appeared in several films.

1. Dale Evans. Duchess Doll Corp. 1948. 7 inches. Cheaply made, all plastic, fully jointed, sleep eyes, mohair wig. ....**$20-$30**

2. Dale Evans. Alexander Doll Company. U.S.A. 1951. 14 inches. All hard plastic, blue sleep eyes, mohair wig, fully jointed, "Maggie" face. ....**$600-$800**

3. Dale Evans. Zany Toys Inc. 1957. About 10 inches. Hand puppet with vinyl head, cloth body. ....**$75-$100**

4. Dale Evans. Nancy Ann Storybook Dolls, Inc. U.S.A. 1955. 8 inches. All plastic, fully jointed, sleep eyes, synthetic wig. ..**$150-$200**

5. Dale Evans, Queen of the West and her favorite horse, Buttermilk. Hartland Plastics, Inc. U.S.A. #802. 1958. 8 inches. All plastic doll. ....**$200-$250**, mint-in-box

Evans, Linda. Actress Evans started her acting career in high school. Her big break came in 1965 when she won the role of Audra Barkley in the television show *Big Valley*. The successful ABC series ran until 1969. For her role as Krystle Carrington on the television series *Dynasty* (1981-1989). Evans was the recipient of five People's Choice Awards and a Golden Globe Award for Best Actress in a Dramatic Television Series.

1. Krystle Carrington. World Doll. China. #71850. 19 inches. All vinyl, rooted blonde hair, painted features; wearing full-length white gown. Box marked: "Made exclusively by World Doll 4012 Second Avenue, Brooklyn, N.Y. 11232." Doll was sold in various outfits. ....**$75-$100**

Linda Evans as Krystle Carrington from World Doll. From the television series *Dynasty*.

5: Dale Evans, 8 inches, by Hartland Plastics. Shown without Buttermilk, her horse.

The front of the box for Krystle Carrington. *Courtesy of David Spurgeon.*

Fargas, Antonio. Actor Fargas is best known for his role as Pimp Huggy Bear in the television series *Starsky & Hutch*, which aired from September 1975 to August 1979. (See Glaser, Paul for photograph.)

Huggy Bear. Mego. Hong Kong. 1976 (Second issue). 8 inches. All vinyl, fully jointed, painted features and hair; wearing a blue jacket and pants with red and white checked shirt. Doll was sold on card with picture of car on card Copyright by Spelling Goldberg Productions. ....**$15-$20**, loose; **$40-$50**, on card

Fatone, Joey. (See N'Sync)

Fawcett, Farrah (Farrah Fawcett-Majors).
Actress Fawcett is best known for her role as Jill Munroe in the hit television series *Charlie's Angels*, which aired from September 1976 to August 1981. After the series, Fawcett began working in films, starring in such dramatic productions as *The Burning Bed* (1984) and *Jewel* (2001).

1. Farrah. Mego. Hong Kong. #77000. 1977. 12 inches. All vinyl, fully jointed, rooted blonde hair, painted green eyes with long attached eyelashes; wearing full-length dress with halter style top. Copyright by Farrah. ......**$35-$45**, loose; **$40-$50**, boxed

2. Farrah. OK Toys. Hong Kong. Circa 1970s. 11-inch doll in plastic bag wearing, red, yellow or blue bathing suit, or a white jumpsuit. ....**$30-$40**

3. Farrah as Jill. Hasbro. Hong Kong. #4863. 1977. 8 inches. All vinyl, fully jointed, rooted blonde hair, painted blue eyes. Copyright Spelling Goldberg Productions. ....**$40-$50**

4. Jill. Raynal. Belgium. 1977. 8 inches. ....**$100-$125**, boxed

5. Charlie's Angels Set. Hasbro. Hong Kong. 1977. 8 inches. Includes all three girls. ....**$175-$225**, each set

6. Farrah. Mego. Hong Kong. 1977. 12 inches. Vinyl head, rooted blonde hair, painted green eyes with long eyelashes, cheaply made plastic body; wearing one-piece white jumpsuit. ....**$50-$75**

7. Farrah. Mego. Hong Kong. #08888. 1980. 12 inches. Vinyl head, rooted blonde hair, painted green eyes with long eyelashes, cheaply made plastic body; wears a bright yellow bathing suit. Head marked: "FARRAH;" back marked: "HONG KONG." ....**$50-$75**, boxed

8. Sportgirl with her Tournament Skateboard. Circa 1970s. 11 inches. Farrah copy. Maker unknown. Manufactured for K-Mart. Cheap plastic, fully jointed for play action, rooted/washable hair, vinyl head, twist-and-turn waist; wearing blue pants and top with white boots. Package marked: "Skateboard Really Works! Manufactured in Hong Kong for Kmart Corporation Troy, Michigan 48084." Obvious copy with picture of Farrah Fawcett on packaging. Original price $1.97. ....**$20-$30**

7: Farrah, 12 inches by Mego. In original box.

8: Sportgirl, manufactured for K-Mart. *Courtesy of Suellen Manning.*

5: The front of the boxed set of Charlie's Angels. *Courtesy of Suellen Manning.*

Feldon, Barbara. Actress Feldon is best known as the beautiful Agent 99, Sue Hilton, the partner of Maxwell Smart (played by Don Adams) on the television series *Get Smart* (1965-1970).

1. Agent 99. Maker unknown. Japan. 1967. 9 inches. Cheaply made, plastic, painted features, glued-on brunette wig; wearing red plastic mini dress with gold belt and gold shoes. The doll is unmarked and the only markings on the box are "Agent 99 of Get Smart Fame 1967 Japan." The box has a picture of the character. ..**$25-$75** (Price range varies due to uncertainty of date of manufacture.)

2. Agent 99. Exclusive Toy Products, Inc. China. #19001. 1998. 6 inches. All vinyl, painted features; wearing pants, shirt and full-length tan overcoat; came with gun and display stand. Box marked: "© 1998 CBS Inc." Sold on card. ....**$15-$20**

1: Barbara Feldon as Agent 99 from *Get Smart* by an unknown maker. *Courtesy of David Spurgeon.*

2: Barbara Feldon as Agent 99 from *Get Smart* by Exclusive Toy Products, Inc., in her original box. *Courtesy of David Spurgeon.*

Field, Sally. An actress and director, Field played the role of Sister Bertrille, the Flying Nun, on the hit television series *The Flying Nun*, which aired from September 1967 to September 1970. Before that, she starred in the television series *Gidget*, which aired from September 1965 to September 1966. Field has also appeared in movies, including *Sybil* (1976). She has recently gone behind the camera as a director, directing Minnie Driver in *Beautiful* (2000).

1. Gidget. Alexander Doll Company. U.S.A. #1415. 1966. 14 inches. All vinyl, fully jointed, rooted brown hair; dressed in jumper with check. ....**$200-$250**

2. Gidget. Alexander Doll Company. U.S.A. #1421. 1966. Same as previous but wearing sailor dress and hat. ......**$200-$250**

3. Gidget. Alexander Doll Company. U.S.A. #1420. 1966. Same as previous two but wearing formal cotton outfit. ....**$200-$250**

4. Flying Nun Doll (Sister Bertrille). Hasbro. 1967. 4 inches. Vinyl, painted features, dark brown hair, bends and twists at waist; wearing white nun's habit and head covering. ....**$30-$40**, loose; **$75-$125**, boxed

5. Flying Nun Doll (Sister Bertrille). Hasbro. 1967. 11 inches. All vinyl, painted features. ....**$50-$75**, loose; **$150-$250**, boxed

6. Flying Nun Doll (Sister Bertrille). Hasbro. 1967. 18 inches. Vinyl, painted features. ......**$150-$200**, loose; **$300-$400**, boxed

5: Sally Field as the Flying Nun (Sister Bertrille), by Hasbro, from the television series *The Flying Nun*. *Courtesy of Steve Malatinsky.*

Fields, W.C. A well-known actor, comedian and screenwriter, Fields began his career in vaudeville, then moved on to plays and films. He starred in a variety of films, including *Sally of the Sawdust* (1925) and *David Copperfield* (1935).

1. W.C. Fields. Effanbee. U.S.A. 1930. 12 inches. Composition head and hands with ventriloquist dummy mechanism, mouth opens and closes, painted features; wears plaid pants, black jacket with brown trim, white shirt, red and white polka dotted tie, white top hat with black trim. ....**$300-$400**

2. W.C. Fields. Effanbee. U.S.A. 1930. 19 inches. Ventriloquist doll with composition head and hands, ventriloquist dummy mechanism, mouth opens and closes, painted features; wears plaid pants, black jacket with brown trim, white shirt, red and white polka dotted tie, white top hat with black trim. ....**$600-$700**

3. W.C. Fields. Knickerbocker. Taiwan. 1972. 16 inches. All stuffed cloth, talking doll with printed features and clothing. Tag reads: "DOLLS OF DISTINCTION//©KNICKERBOCKER//MADE IN TAIWAN." ......**$30-$50**

4. W.C. Fields. Peggy Nisbet. England. #P759. 1970s. 7 inch. All hard plastic, jointed at arms, painted features and hair; dressed as the character Micawber from the movie *David Copperfield.* Copyright 1935 by MGM. ....**$100-$150**

5. W.C. Fields. Effanbee Doll Company. China. 1980. 15 inches. Vinyl, fully jointed, red hair, painted blue eyes. Head marked: "W.C.FIELDS// EFFANBEE//19©80;" back marked: "W.C. FIELDS//EFFANBEE//©1979// W.C. FIELDS PROD.INC." The Effanbee Doll Co. produced a variety of limited-edition dolls with numbered certificates. Many of the dolls could only be purchased through Effanbee's Limited Edition Doll Club or the secondary market. Part of the Legend Series. ....**$250-$300**

3: Knickerbocker's 16-inch cloth version of W.C. Fields. *Author's collection.*

6. W.C. Fields. Juro. China. 1980. 30 inches. Ventriloquist doll by Juro, a division of Goldberger Doll Mfg. Co. Inc. Vinyl head and hands, painted red/blonde hair, painted blue eyes, painted teeth, stuffed cloth body. Head marked: "W.C. FIELDS©1980//W.C. FIELDS PRODUCTIONS, INC.//EEGEE CO." ....**$100-$150**

Finney, Albert. Actor Finney played the part of Daddy Warbucks in the 1982 film *Annie,* based on the comic strip "Little Orphan Annie." He started his career on the stage, appearing in many Shakespearean roles.

Daddy Warbucks. Knickerbocker Toy Co. Inc. U.S.A. #3869. 1982. 7 inches. All vinyl, fully jointed, bald head, painted features; wearing black suit with buttons and black bow tie. Copyright by Columbia Pictures Industries, Inc. ....**$35-$50**

Fisher, Carrie. Actress and screenwriter Fisher is best known for her role as Princess Leia in the movie *Star Wars* (1977). Fisher also starred in the movie *Shampoo* (1975) with Warren Beatty. She is the daughter of Debbie Reynolds and Eddie Fisher.

1. Princess Leia Organa. Kenner. Hong Kong. #38190. 1978. 3 inches. All vinyl, fully jointed, painted features; with different outfits, including Bespin gown and Hoth outfit. ....**$20-$25**

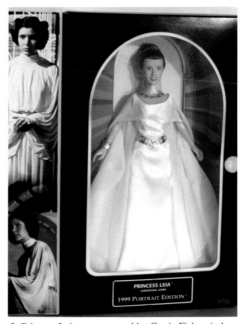

3: Princess Leia, as portrayed by Carrie Fisher, in her ceremonial gown, by Hasbro, Inc. *Courtesy of David Spurgeon.*

2. Princess Leia Organa. Kenner. Hong Kong. #38070. 1978. 11 inches. All vinyl, fully jointed, rooted brown hair, painted brown eyes; wearing long white dress (Bespin gown) from *Star Wars* film. Head marked: "© G.M.F.G.I. 1978." Copyright 1977 by Twentieth Century Fox Film Corp. and copyright 1978 by General Mills Fun Group. ....**$150-$200**

3. Princess Leia. Hasbro, Inc. China. #61772. 1999. 11 inches. All vinyl, jointed, rooted dark braided hair, painted features; dressed in ceremonial gown. Box marked: "© Lucasfilm Ltd. TM © 1998 Hasbro Inc." A "1999 Portrait Edition." ....**$30-$40**

Flintstone, Pebbles. Pebbles is the fictional daughter of Fred Flintstone from the television hit cartoon series *The Flintstones.* Her neighbor, and later her boyfriend, was Bamm-Bamm Rubble, son of Fred's neighbor, Barney.

Pebbles and Bamm-Bamm. Ideal Toy Corp. U.S.A. 1963. Pebbles came in two sizes: 8 inches. **$75-$100**; 12 inches, **$100-$150**. Bamm-Bamm came in two sizes: 12 inches, **$75-$100**; 16 inches, **$100-$150** (If found with original boxes, prices nearly double.)

Pebbles Flintstone and Bamm-Bamm Rubble, cartoon characters, shown with Dino, Pebbles' pet dinosaur. *Author's collection.*

Original 1963 box covers for Pebbles Flintstone (left) and Bamm-Bamm Rubble (right).

Ford, Harrison. This actor was the "other" Harrison Ford, who made a name for himself in silent films from 1916 through the 1920s. A ladies' man on screen, Ford appeared in *The Primitive Lover* (1916), *Foolish Wives* (1919) and *The Average Woman* (1924), among others. Ford's last film was *Love in High Gear* (1932).

Harrison Ford. Maker unknown. 14 inches. Composition and cloth, mohair wig, beautifully hand-painted facial features; wearing black suit with white shirt and vest, black bow tie. Extremely rare. ....**$750-$1,000**

Harrison Ford, an actor from the silent screen era, by an unknown maker, shown with a photograph of the actor. *Courtesy of Billie Nelson Tyrrell.*

Ford, Harrison. Contemporary actor Ford has been a favorite movie-screen personality since the 1980s. He has appeared in a variety of films, including *Star Wars* (1977) and *The Empire Strikes Back* (1977) (as the character Han Solo) as well as *Raiders of the Lost Ark* (1981), *Blade Runner* (1982) and *Witness* (1985).

1. Han Solo. Kenner. Hong Kong. #38260. 1978. 3 inches. All vinyl, fully jointed with painted features and clothing. ....**$75-$100**

2: Han Solo from *Star Wars*, as portrayed by Harrison Ford. *Courtesy of Sunnie Newell.*

2. Han Solo. Kenner. Hong Kong. #39170. 1979. 12 inches. All vinyl, fully jointed, painted red hair, brown eyes. Head marked: "© G.M.F.G.I. 1979;" back marked: "© G.M.F.G.I. 1978 KENNER PROD.//CINCINNATI, OHIO 45212//MADE IN HONG KONG. Copyright 1977 by Twentieth Century Fox Film Corporation." ....**$200-$300** (See photo on page 59.)

3. Han Solo. Kenner. Hong Kong. #39790. 1980. 3 inches. All vinyl, painted features; wearing white shirt and brown dark pants and vest, came with guns. Copyright 1977 by Twentieth Century Fox Film Corporation. ......**$150-$200**, loose; **$300-$400**, mint-in-box

4. Indiana Jones. Kenner. Hong Kong. #46000. 1981. 12 inches. All vinyl, fully jointed, painted features; wearing brown pants, jacket, boots, belt and white shirt, came with whip and pistol. Marked: "L.F.L. 1981 KENNER PROD. CINCINNATI, OH 45202// MADE IN HONG KONG." Copyright by Lucasfilms Ltd. ....**$75-$100**, mint-in-box

5. Indiana Jones. Kenner. Hong Kong. #46010. 1982. 4 inches. All vinyl, fully jointed, painted features. Copyright by Lucasfilms Ltd. ....**$20-$30**

Forrest, Steve. Actor Forrest played a wide variety of supporting parts. He is best known as Lt. Dan "Hondo" Harrelson on the television series *S.W.A.T.*, which aired on ABC from February 1975 to July 1976. (For group photograph, see Perry, Rod.)

1: Hondo from the television series *S.W.A.T.*, as portrayed by Steve Forrest, by L.J.N. Toys Ltd. *Courtesy of Suellen Manning.*

1. Hondo from *S.W.A.T.* L.J.N. Toys Ltd. Hong Kong. #6600. 1975. 7 inches. All vinyl, fully jointed, painted hair and features; dressed in *S.W.A.T.* gear. Copyright 1975 by Spelling Goldberg Productions. ....**$15-$30**

2. Hondo from *S.W.A.T.* L.J.N. Toys Ltd. Hong Kong. #6850. 1976. 7 inches. All vinyl, fully jointed, painted hair and features. Copyright 1975 by Spelling Goldberg Productions. ....**$15-$30**

Foxx, Redd. Actor and comedian Foxx is best known for his role as Fred Sanford on the television series *Sanford and Son*, which aired on NBC from January 1972 until September 1977.

Redd Foxx. Shindana. 1976. 16 inches. Two-sided doll with printed features and clothing. Marked on tag: "© 1976//REDD FOXX ENTERPRISES//SHINDANA TOYS, INC." ....**$25-$30**

Francis, Anne. Actress Francis is best known for her role as private detective Honey West, from the television show by the same name, which aired on ABC from September 1965 until September 1966. Francis also appeared in films and played the role of Terri Dowling on the television series *My Three Sons* on CBS from 1971 until 1972. (See Vaughn, Robert for additional photograph.)

1. Honey West. Gilbert. Hong Kong & Japan. #16114. 1965. 11¾ inches. Vinyl head and arms, plastic legs and torso, rooted blonde hair, painted eyes, painted beauty mark near mouth; dressed several ways including in a black trench coat, in black tights and black coat with boots and in a one-piece black jumpsuit. Sold with unmarked plastic leopard. Head marked: "K73." Copyright by Four Star Television and A.C. Gilbert Co. ....**$100-$150**

2: Anne Francis as Honey West by Exclusive Toy Products, Inc. *Author's collection.*

2. Honey West. Exclusive Toy Products, Inc. China. #28002. 1997. 6 inches. All vinyl. Box marked: "© 1962 Danjaq, LLC & United Artists Corp. © 1988 Danjaq, LLC & United Artists Corp. © 1997 Danjaq, LLC & United Artists Corp. Dr. No. © 1962. Danjaq, LLC & United Artists Corp." ....**$20-$30**

Franklin, Benjamin. A statesman, scientist and printer, Franklin helped to establish the University of Pennsylvania and is best known for his role in drafting the Declaration of Independence.

1. Benjamin Franklin. Peggy Nisbet. England. #P729. Circa 1970s. 8 inches. Plastic; dressed in short pants with button-down coat. ....**$50-$75**
2. Benjamin Franklin. S.S. Kresge Company. 1976. 7 inches. Vinyl head, jointed plastic body, swivel waist, painted hair and features; wearing blue and yellow outfit with white ruffled shirt. Marked on back: "MADE IN//HONG KONG." Part of a series called the Heroes of the American Revolution. Original price was $1.50. ....**$15-$25**
3. Benjamin Franklin. Hallmark. Taiwan. #250DT900-3. 1979. 7 inches. All cloth with printed features and clothing, came with box shaped like brick building. ....**$10-$20**

2 A: Benjamin Franklin from the Heroes of the American Revolution series by the S.S. Kresge Company. *Courtesy of Suellen Manning.*

2 B: The back of the box for Benjamin Franklin shows the rest of the Heroes of the American Revolution series, which included, in addition to Franklin, Daniel Boone, John Paul Jones, Paul Revere, Thomas Jefferson, the Marquis de Lafayette, George Washington, Patrick Henry and Nathan Hale. *Courtesy of Suellen Manning.*

Freeman, Morgan. Actor Freeman has performed on stage and in television and films. He was nominated for an Academy Award for his role in the 1987 film *Street Smart*, and again in 1989, for the film *Driving Miss Daisy*. His third nomination, in 1994, was for his role in *The Shawshank Redemption*. Freeman also had a starring role in the film *Robin Hood-Prince of Thieves* (1991).

Azeem—Prince of Thieves. Kenner. Hong Kong. 1991. 4 inches. All plastic, poseable, painted hair and features; painted clothing with fabric and vinyl clothing pieces. Marked: "©MCP&WBI 91." Sold on card with picture of star. Copyright by Warner Brothers. ....**$15-$20**

Kenner's Azeem-Prince of Thieves, as portrayed by Morgan Freeman, in the movie *Robin Hood-Prince of Thieves*. In original box.

Furrier, Vincent Damon. (See Cooper, Alice.)

G

Gabor, Eva. Hungarian actress Gabor is best known for her role as Lisa Douglas on the hit television series *Green Acres*, which aired from September 1965 to September 1971.

    1. *Green Acres* Paper Dolls Booklet. Whitman. 1967. Shows Eddie Albert with co-star Eva Gabor on cover. ....**$50-$60**, uncut

    2. *Green Acres* Paper Dolls. Whitman. 1968. Shows Eddie Albert with co-star Eva Gabor on cover. ....**$40-$50**, uncut

Gamonet, Roberto. Actor Gamonet is best known for his role as Pufnstuf in the television series *H.R. Pufnstuf*, which aired from September 1969 to September 1971. He wore the suit of the character H.R. Pufnstuf. The star of the show was Jack Wild, who played the part of Jimmy.

    1. Pufnstuf. My-Toy. China. 1970. 22 inches. Stuffed doll with character face. ......**$350-$600**, loose; **$650** and up, boxed

    2. Pufnstuf. Krofft. China. Circa 1990s. 6 inches. All vinyl, painted and molded features, jointed at the arms, legs and neck. Sold on card with plastic box that looks like a television set. Part of the Superstars Series. ....**$20-$25**

2: Roberto Gamonet as Pufnstuf, from the television series *H.R. Pufnstuf*, by Krofft.

Garber, Matthew. Actor Garber is best known for his role as Michael in the 1964 Disney hit *Mary Poppins*. (See Andrews, Julie for photograph.) Jane was played by Karen Dotrice.

    Michael. Horsman. U.S.A. 1964. 8¼ inches. All vinyl, fully jointed, rooted blonde hair, painted blue eyes. Marked on head: "©11//HORSMAN DOLLS INC.// 6682." ....**$20-$30**

Garland, Judy. Actress and singer Garland is best remembered for her role as Dorothy in the 1939 movie *The Wizard of Oz*. She appeared in several other films, including *Meet Me in St. Louis* (1944), and was once MGM's top-grossing star. Garland's daughter is singer Liza Minnelli.

    1. Judy Garland as Dorothy. Ideal Toy Corp. U.S.A. 1939 to 1940. 13 inches, 15 inches and 18 inches. Composition, fully jointed, auburn hair, dark brown or black human hair wig in braids, brown glass eyes, open mouth with tongue and six teeth; dressed in blue and white-checked "Dorothy" jumper/dress outfit, also sold in red and white checked outfit. Marked on head (15-inch): "15//IDEAL DOLL//Made in U.S.A.;" marked on body: "U.S.A. 16." Sculpted by Bernard Lipfert. Original price was $3.00 to $5.00. ....13 inches, **$1,000-$1,200**; 15 inches, $1,200-$1,800; 18 inches, **$1,500-$2,200**

    2. Judy Garland as Teenager. Ideal Toy Corp. U.S.A. 1940 to 1942. 15 inches and 21 inches. Composition, brown or auburn human hair wig, green or brown glass sleep eyes, open mouth with four teeth; dressed in pink dress with red and blue flowers from the movie *Strike Up the Band* (1940), also sold in outfit from

1: Ideal's 15-inch Judy Garland as Dorothy from *The Wizard of Oz* (shown with the Cowardly Lion) sold for $2,800 at a McMasters doll auction in 1996. *Courtesy of McMasters Doll Auctions.*

2: A rare Ideal 21-inch Judy Garland with lighter hair was used for only one year. All original, she is wearing a long white dress with stripes of colored designs, a straw hat with a large ribbon bow and is marked "Miss Liberty." $1,000 up. *Courtesy of Patricia Wood.*

3B: The boxed set of characters from the film *The Wizard of Oz* by Mego.

the 1941 movie *Babes on Broadway*. Marked on head: "MADE IN U.S.A.;" marked on body: "IDEAL DOLL//21 [21 is backwards];" tag on dress marked: "Judy Garland//A Metro Goldwyn Mayer//STAR//in//'Little Nellie/ Kelly;'" original pin on dress reads: "JUDY GARLAND//A METRO GOLDWYN MAYER STAR." Designed by Bernard Lipfert. Body used was from the Deanna Durbin mold. ....15 inches, **$400-$600**; 21 inches, **$600-$700**

3. Dorothy. Mego. Hong Kong. 1974. 8 inches. All vinyl, jointed, painted features, braids in hair; wearing outfit from *The Wizard of Oz.* ....**$30-$50**, for each figure in the set

3A: Mego's eight-inch characters from the film *The Wizard of Oz.*

4. Judy Garland as Dorothy. Effanbee Doll Company. China. 1984. 16 inches. Vinyl, painted features; wearing traditional Dorothy outfit. The Effanbee Doll Co. produced a variety of limited-edition dolls with numbered certificates. Many of the dolls could only be purchased through Effanbee's Limited Edition Doll Club or on the secondary market. Part of the Legend Series. ....**$100-$125**

5. Judy Garland as Dorothy. Ideal Toy Corp. 1984 to 1985. 9 inches. Vinyl, six-piece poseable body; wearing Dorothy outfit from movie. Marked on head: "CBS INC//H4-22;" marked on back: "LOEW'S REN.//1966// MGM//MFG BY CBS INC//B107." ....**$30-$50**

Garner, James. Actor Garner began his career on stage and then moved on to television and movies. He is known for many roles, including Bret Maverick from the ABC television series *Maverick*, which aired from 1957 until 1960 and as Jim Rockford on the NBC series *The Rockford Files*, which aired from 1974 until 1980. Recently, Garner starred in *Space Cowboys*, a 2000 movie co-starring Clint Eastwood.

James Garner as Maverick. Hartland Plastics, Inc. U.S.A. #762. 1958. 8 inches. All plastic. .... **$50-$100**, mint-in-box

Garth, Jenny. Actress Garth played the role of Kelly Taylor on the hit Fox television series *Beverly Hills 90210*.

1. Kelly. Mattel, Inc. China. 1991. 11 inches. All vinyl, jointed, painted features; wearing a black mini dress with burgundy trim, sold with yellow one-piece bathing suit. ....**$15-$20**

Jenny Garth as Kelly Taylor from the television series *Beverly Hills 90210*. From Mattel, Inc.

Geer, Will. Actor Geer is best known for his role as Zeb "Grandpa" Walton on the CBS television series *The Waltons*, which aired from September 1972 to August 1981.

Grandpa. Mego. Hong Kong. 1974. 8 inches. Vinyl, jointed, painted gray hair, painted gray eyes; wearing blue jean overalls with blue and white plaid shirt. Head marked: "© 1974 LORI-MAR//PROD.INC." Sold as a pair with Grandma and also sold singly. ....**$15-$20**, loose; **$25-$30**, boxed singly; **$40-$50**, boxed pair (See Corby, Ellen for photograph.)

Gerard, Gil. Actor Gerard is best known for his role as Buck Rogers in the NBC television series *Buck Rogers in the 25th Century*, which aired from 1979 to 1981. He also starred in several films in the 1980s.

1. Buck Rogers. Mego. Hong Kong. #85000/1. 1979. 3 inches. All vinyl, fully jointed, painted features; painted clothing. Copyright by Robert C. Dille. ....**$15-$25**

2. Buck Rogers. Mego. Hong Kong. #85001/1. 1979. 12 inches. All vinyl, fully jointed, painted black hair, painted blue eyes; wearing white pants with long-sleeved white jacket, black belt with gun. Head marked: "© 1978 ROBERT//C.DILLE;" back marked: "© 1979 MEGO CORP.//MADE IN HONG KONG." ....**$40-$50**

Gibb, Andy. Inspired by the success of his famous singing brothers' (The Bee Gees) soundtrack for the film *Saturday Night Fever*, Andy Gibb began his own solo singing career. Following the disco style of his brothers, his first three singles—"I Just Want To Be Your Everything," (Love Is) Thicker Than Water" and "Shadow Dancing"—all hit number one. Three more consecutive top-ten hits followed.

Andy Gibb. Ideal. Hong Kong. #1470-4. 1979. 7 inches. Andy Gibb doll with Brandi. Disco Dancin' with the Stars. Vinyl, rooted blonde hair, painted eyes, arms swing and body sways when put on dancing stand, with two dancing stands and light show with strobe lighting; wearing a white jumpsuit with red vest. Marked on back: "ANDY GIBB//IDEAL TOY CORP.//HONG KONG;" marked on head: "S.G.L. IDEAL." ....**$50-$75**

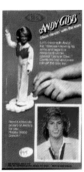

Ideal's seven-inch Andy Gibb. Front and back of box shown.

Gibbs, Marla. Actress Gibbs is best known for her role as the sassy maid Florence on the CBS television series *The Jeffersons*, which began in 1975. In 1980, Gibbs starred in her own show, a less-successful spinoff of *The Jeffersons*, called *Checking In*.

Marla Gibbs by Shindana, in her original box. *Courtesy of Suellen Manning.*

Marla Gibbs. Shindana. Hong Kong. #1048. 1978. 15 inches. All vinyl, fully jointed, rooted black hair, painted brown eyes; wearing multi-colored, patchwork-styled dress with white apron, packaged with an extra outfit of a long red gown with gold trim. Box marked: "Copyright by Marla Gibbs Enterprises, Inc. Los Angeles, CA 90001" and "Shindana Toys, Inc." ....**$35-$50**

Gilbert, John. The son of an actress, Gilbert made his first stage appearance as an infant and played an extra in films during his childhood. The film *The Merry Widow* brought him fame in 1925 and by 1928 he was the highest-paid actor in Hollywood. Gilbert is best known for his role in *The Big Parade*, probably the most successful film of the silent era. He made nearly 100 films before his death in 1936.

John Gilbert. Maker unknown. 1928. 20 inches. All wax, painted hair and features; wearing outfit from the film *The Merry Widow*. ..**$750-$1,000**

John Gilbert, an actor from the silent screen era, by an unknown maker, shown with Mae Murray. *Courtesy of Billie Nelson Tyrrell.* (See also Murray, Mae.)

Gilbert, Melissa. Actress Gilbert is best known for her role as Laura Ingalls on the television series *Little House on the Prairie*, which aired from September 1974 to September 1982. Since the series ended, Gilbert has appeared in many films including *Seduction in a Small Town* (1997) and *The Soul Collector* (1999).

Laura. Knickerbocker. Taiwan. 1978. 12 inches. Vinyl head and lower arms, stuffed cloth body, rooted blonde hair in braids, painted green eyes; dressed in period clothes with tag marked: "Little House on the Prairie." Head marked: "©ED FRIENDLY PRODS.INC.//LIC JLM// MADE IN TAIWAN T-1." Box shows the cast of the series. ....**$50-$75**

Gisondi, Toni Ann. Actress Gisondi played the part of Molly in the 1982 film version of *Annie* based on the comic-strip character "Little Orphan Annie."

Molly. Knickerbocker Toy Co. #3868. 1982. 6 inches. All vinyl, fully jointed, rooted brown hair, painted features; wearing knee-length dress with printed collar and sleeves. Copyright by Columbia Pictures Industries, Inc. ....**$25-$35** (See Burnett, Carol for photograph.)

Glaser, Paul Michael. Actor and director Glaser is best known for his role as Detective Dave Starsky on the television series *Starsky & Hutch*, which aired from September 1975 to August 1979. After his wife Elizabeth died from AIDS transmitted through a blood transfusion, Glaser founded the Elizabeth Glaser Pediatric Aids Foundation, which has raised millions of dollars for AIDS research.

1. Starsky. Mego. Hong Kong. 1975. 8 inches. All vinyl, fully jointed, painted black hair, painted features; wearing blue jeans with blue turtleneck. Doll is on card with picture of car on it. First issue. Card shows two photographs on back. ....**$15-$20**, loose; **$40-$50**, on card (See photo on page 66.)

2. Starsky. Mego. Hong Kong. #62800/1. 1976. 8 inches. All vinyl, fully jointed, painted black hair, painted features; wearing blue jeans and black sweater. Doll is on card with picture of car on card. Five photographs on back of card. ....**$15-$20**, loose; **$30-$40**, on card.

3. Chopper. Mego. Hong Kong. 1976. 8 inches. All vinyl, fully jointed, painted black hair, painted features; wearing red and white sweater and blue jeans. On card with picture of car on card. Five photos on back of card. ....**$20-$30**

4. Starsky. Palitoy. United Kingdom. 1977. 8 inches. All vinyl, jointed, painted hair and features. Looks like Mego-type dolls. Sold on card. Card has illustrations. ....**$20-$30**, loose; **$75-$100**, on card

5. Starsky and Hutch. Palitoy. United Kingdom. 1977. 8 inches. All vinyl, jointed with painted hair

and features. Sold in pack with both dolls. Looks like Mego-type dolls. ....**$150-$200**, boxed

Gleason, Jackie. Born in Brooklyn, New York, actor Gleason is known as the man who defined television in the 1950s with his unique brand of humor in the series *The Honeymooners.* After the series ended, Gleason returned to films, playing in such movies as *The Hustler* (1961) and *Smokey and the Bandit* (1977). He was nominated for an Oscar for his performance as the billiard king Minnesota Fats in the film *The Hustler.*

Jackie Gleason. Unmarked. Circa 1950s. 18 inches. Cloth body, celluloid face. ....**$150-$250**, mint

Unmarked Jackie Gleason shown with a game. Game's value is $25-50. He is missing his hat and his jacket appears to have been cut. *Courtesy of Steve Malastinsky.*

Goddard, Mark. Actor Goddard is best known for his role as Major Don West on the television series *Lost in Space,* which aired on CBS from 1965 until 1968.

Major Don West. Trendmasters, Inc. China. #09503. 1998. 11 inches. All vinyl, fully jointed, painted hair and features; wearing silver space jumpsuit with silver boots, with laser assault weapon. Box marked: "© Trendmasters, Inc." ....**$20-$30**

Mark Goddard as Major Don West from the television series *Lost in Space,* by Trendmasters, Inc. *Author's collection.*

Barry Goldwater by Remco from 1964. *Courtesy of David Spurgeon.*

Goldwater, Barry M. Politician Goldwater was the Republican nominee for President in 1964, but was defeated by Lyndon Johnson. He served as Senator from the state of Arizona.

Barry Goldwater. Remco. Hong Kong. #1816. 1964. 5 inches. Painted features and clothing; wearing white plastic hat and large pin that says "Barry." Box marked: "© 1964 Remco Industries Inc. Harrison, NJ. Senator Barry M. Goldwater. REMCO;" also: "Sticks to Dashboard." ....**$50-$75**

Goodman, John. Actor Goodman is best known for his role as Roseanne's husband on the hit television series *Roseanne*, which aired from 1988 to 1997. After *Roseanne* was canceled, Goodman moved on to film work, starring as Fred Flintstone in the 1994 movie *The Flintstones*.

1. Fred Flintstone. Mattel, Inc. China. #11667. 1993. 8 inches. Vinyl head, painted hair and features, cloth body; wearing authentic Fred Flintstone outfit of orange oversized shirt with black marks and blue tie. Box marked: "© 1993 Mattel, Inc." ....**$10-$15**

2. Fred Flintstone-Yabba-Dadda Doo Fred. Mattel, Inc. China. 1994. 8 inches. All vinyl, painted features and clothing, with green bird. Push button to hear two different "Fred" phrases. ....**$10-$15**

2: Fred Flintstone, portrayed by John Goodman, by Mattel, from 1994. *Author's collection.*

1: Fred Flintstone, portrayed by John Goodman, by Mattel, from 1993. *Author's collection.*

Gordeeva, Ekaterina ("Katia"). Gordeeva is a Russian ice skater who competed in the Winter Olympics. Her titles include two-time Olympic Champion and four-time World Champion in pairs figure skating with her late husband, Sergei Grinkov. She also performs for Stars on Ice, a traveling ice-skating show that visits more than sixty cities across the United States.

Katia. Playmates. China. Asst. #52500. Stock #52509. 1998. 11 inches. All vinyl, jointed, rooted brown hair, painted blue eyes, painted features with smiling mouth and teeth; wearing baby blue top with short ice-skating skirt, white sparkle tone hose and white ice skates, with stand and Stars on Ice medal. Box marked: "© 1998 Playmates Toys Inc. STARS ON ICE is a trademark of IMG." ....**$20-$30**

Ekaterina "Katia" Gordeeva from the Stars on Ice series by Playmates. *Author's collection.*

Goya, Chantal. Goya was a top French singing star in the late 1970s and early 1980s.

1. Chantal Goya. Mattel, Inc. Taiwan. #8935-63. 1980. 11 inches. All vinyl, jointed, on Barbie body with bent arm holding a microphone; wearing flowered print dress with lace collar, white socks and red tie-on shoes, later editions are dressed in different outfits, including a long white gown with pink ribbon. Marked on back of head: "© C. GOYA 1979 TAIWAN;" marked on rear: "© MATTEL INC//1966//TAIWAN." Copyright by C. Goya and Mattel, Inc. Distributed in France. ....**$75-$100**

2. Chantel Goya fashions. #8938; 1980; blue floral print jumpsuit with orange belt and shoes. #8937; 1980; two-piece yellow floral print gown with shoes. Others were also available. Copyright by C. Goya and Mattel, Inc. ....**$40-$50**, each for outfits in packages

Grandy, Fred. Actor and politician Grandy is best known as an actor for his role as Burl "Gopher" Smith in the hit television series *The Love Boat*, which aired from September 1977 to September 1986. Grandy left the world of acting to pursue a career in politics.

Gopher. Mego. Hong Kong. #23005/5. 1981. 3 inches. Vinyl, fully jointed, with painted hair and features; painted clothing, on card. Copyright by Aaron Spelling Productions, Inc. Shows picture of cast on card. ....**$15-$25**

Gray, Erin. Actress Gray played the role of Wilma Deering in the NBC television series *Buck Rogers in the 25th Century*. The show aired from 1979 to 1981.

Wilma Deering. Mego. Hong Kong. #85000/3. 1979. 3 inches. All vinyl, fully jointed, painted features; painted clothing. Copyright Robert C. Dille. ....**$10-$20**

Greenbusch, Lindsay and Sidney. The Greenbusch sisters are identical twins who played Carrie on the television series *Little House on the Prairie*, which aired from September 1974 to September 1982.

1. Carrie. Knickerbocker. Taiwan. 1978. 12 inches. Vinyl head and lower arms, stuffed cloth body, rooted brown hair, painted blue eyes; wearing period clothes marked: "Little House on the Prairie." Marked on head: "© 1978 ED FRIENDLY PRODS. INC//LIC JLM//MADE IN TAIWAN T-2." Box shows photograph of the cast from the series. .... **$50-$75**

Greene, Lorne. Actor Greene is best known for his role as Ben Cartwright on the NBC television series *Bonanza*, which aired from September 1959 until January 1973. The show was one of NBC's longest-running series. From 1978 until 1979, Greene played the role of Commander Adama on the television series *Battlestar Galactica*.

1. Ben Cartwright. American Character. U.S.A. 1965. 8 inches. All plastic, fully jointed action figure; molded and painted clothing and features. ....**$40-$50**

2. Commander Adama. Mattel, Inc. Hong Kong. #2868. 1978. 4 inches. All vinyl, fully jointed, painted features and hair; painted clothing, came with cloth cape on card. Copyright by Universal City Studios, Inc. Package shows picture of Lorne Greene and the spaceship from the show. ....**$25-$35**

Gretzky, Wayne. Hockey player Gretzky joined the World Hockey Association with the Indianapolis Racers at the age of seventeen. After eight years, his contract was sold to the Edmonton Oilers. Gretzky also played for the L.A. Kings, the St. Louis Blues and the New York Rangers. He received ten Art Ross trophies as scoring champion, two Conn Smythe trophies for playoff MVP and four Lady Byng trophies for most gentlemanly player. In his career, Gretzky set sixty-one single-game, one-season and career-scoring records.

1. Wayne Gretzky. Mattel. China. 1982. 11 inches. All vinyl, molded hair, painted features, painted blue eyes, yellow-blonde hair; wearing hockey outfit from Edmonton Oiler. ....**$40-$50**

2. Wayne Gretzky. Hasbro. China. #26101. 1999. All vinyl, fully jointed, poseable, painted yellow hair, painted blue eyes and features; wearing Edmonton Oilers uniform with hockey stick and helmet. Box marked: "© By Wayne Gretzky. Official Licensed Product of the NHL. © 1999 NHL. © NHLPA." Part of the Starting Line-Up series. ....**$20-$30**

Guinness, Sir Alec. Actor Guinness worked in films and on stage and won an Academy Award for his role in the film *The Bridge on the River Kwai* (1957). He played the part of Obi-Wan Kenobi in *Star Wars* (1997) and *The Empire Strikes Back* (1997).

1. Ben (Obi-Wan) Kenobi. Hong Kong. #38250, 1978. 3 inches. All vinyl, fully jointed, painted features. ....**$25-$50**

2. Ben (Obi-Wan) Kenobi. Kenner. Hong Kong. #39340. 1980. 12 inches. All vinyl, fully jointed, painted hair and features; wearing white and brown robes. ....**$50-$75**

H

Deidre Hall as Marlena Evans. Mattel, Inc. China. Circa 1990s. 11 inches. All vinyl, jointed, painted features, shoulder-length blonde hair; wearing long white wedding dress with bouquet of white flowers. ....**$40-$50**

Deidre Hall as Marlena Evans, by Mattel, from the television series *Days of Our Lives. Author's collection.*

Haggerty, Dan. Actor Haggerty is best known for his role as James "Grizzly" Adams on the television show *The Life and Times of Grizzly Adams*, which aired from February 1977 to July 1978.

1. Grizzly Adams. Mattel, Inc. Hong Kong. #2377. 1978. 10 inches. Vinyl, jointed; wearing a white shirt with brown pants and suspenders. Marked on side of neck: "© SCHICK SUNN 1978 HONG KONG;" marked on back: "© 1971 MATTEL, INC.//U.S. & FOREIGN PATENTED//HONG KONG." ....**$20-$25**, loose; **$40-$50**, boxed

2. Grizzly Adams and Ben. Mattel, Inc. Hong Kong. #2378. 1978. Ben, the bear, was Grizzly Adams' sidekick in the show. Came as packaged set. ....Both: **$40-$50**, loose; **$80-$100**, boxed

Hale, Alan, Jr. Actor Hale is best known for his role as Jonas "Skipper" Grumby on the hit television series *Gilligan's Island*, which aired from September 1964 to September 1967. He also starred in several films during his career.

Skipper. Playskool. 1977. 3 inches. Soft rubber, painted features; from the cartoon series. Companion dolls were Gilligan and Mary Ann. ....**$10-$15**, each

Haley, Jack. Actor Haley performed in vaudeville, on stage and in films. His most famous role was as the Tin Man in the 1939 classic, *The Wizard of Oz.*

1. Tin Woodsman. Mego. Hong Kong. #51500/2. 1974. 8 inches. All vinyl, fully jointed, painted features. Head marked: "©1974 MGM//INC." ....**$35-$50** (See Garland, Judy for photo.)

2. Tin Woodsman. Mego. Hong Kong. #59037. 1974. 17 inches. Vinyl head with cloth body, painted features. Sold in window box. Copyright 1974 by MGM, Inc. ......**$125-$175**

Hall, Deidre. Actress Hall has starred in a variety of films and on television. She is best known for her role as Marlena Evans in the long-running television soap-opera *Days of Our Lives.*

The back of the box for Diedre Hall as Marlena Evans. *Author's collection.*

Halliwell, Geraldine. (See Spice Girls)

Hamill, Dorothy. Hamill won the Olympic Gold Medal in Women's Figure Skating in the 1976 Olympics. After the Olympics, Hamill continued to perform for many years. She headlined for the Ice Capades, a traveling ice-skating show.

Dorothy Hamill by Ideal, circa 1977.

Dorothy Hamill. Ideal. Hong Kong. #1290-6. 1977. 11 inches. Vinyl head, plastic poseable body, rooted brown hair, on ice rink with skates; six outfits sold separately and shown on box. Marked on body: "1975 IDEAL//US//PAT. NO. 3903640//HOLLIS, NY 11423// HONG KONG P;" marked on head: "1977 DH/IDEAL" ....**$35-$50** (See photo on page 69.)

Hamill, Mark.
Actor Hamill has appeared on television and in films. He is best known for his role as Luke Skywalker in the films *Star Wars* (1977) and *The Empire Strikes Back* (1982).

1. Luke Skywalker. Kenner. Taiwan. #38180. 1978. 3 inches. All vinyl, painted and molded hair, painted features. Copyright 1977 by Twentieth Century Fox Film Corporation. ....**$25-$40**

2. Luke Skywalker. Kenner. Hong Kong. #38080. 1978. 12 inches. All vinyl, fully jointed, painted and molded blonde hair, painted blue eyes. Head marked: "© G.M.F.G.I. 1978;" back marked: "© G.M.F.G.I. 1978 KENNER PROD.//CINCINNATI,OHIO 45202//MADE IN HONG KONG." Copyright 1977 by Twentieth Century Fox Film Corporation. ....**$100-$150**

3. Luke Skywalker. Kenner. Hong Kong. #39780. 1979. 3 inches. All vinyl, painted and molded hair, painted features; dressed in Bespin Fatigues. Copyright 1977 by Twentieth Century Fox Film Corporation. Copyright 1980 by Lucasfilm Ltd. ....**$10-$15**

4. Luke Skywalker. Kenner. Hong Kong. #39060. 1980. 3-7/8 inches. All vinyl, painted and molded hair, painted features; dressed in X-Wing Pilot outfit. Copyright 1977 by Twentieth Century Fox Film Corporation. Copyright 1980 by Lucasfilm Ltd. ....**$15-$20**

Hamilton, Bernie.
Actor Hamilton is best known for his role as Captain Harold Dobey in the television series *Starsky & Hutch*, which aired from September 1975 to August 1979.

Dobey. Mego. Hong Kong. #62800/4. 1976. 7 inches. Wearing black jacket, pants, shirt and white buttons. Doll is on card with picture of car on card. ......**$15-$20**, loose; **$40-$50**, on card

Hamilton, Margaret.
Actress Hamilton's most famous role was as the Wicked Witch in the 1939 classic *The Wizard of Oz*.

1. The Wicked Witch of the West. Mego. Hong Kong. #51500/6. 1974. 7 inches. All vinyl, fully jointed, rooted black hair, green painted face and features. Copyright 1974 by Metro-Goldwyn-Mayer, Inc. ....**$45-$65** (See Garland, Judy for photo.)

2. The Wicked Witch of the West. Mattel, Inc. China. 1995. 11 inches. All vinyl, painted green face; wearing black costume from the film. ....**$40-$50**

Hamlin, Harry.
Actor Hamlin has appeared both in films and on television, including the film *The Clash of the Titans* (1981), in which he played the role of Perseus, the hero son of Zeus and Danae. From 1986 until 1992, he portrayed attorney Michael Kuzak on the NBC series *L.A. Law*.

1. Perseus. Mattel, Inc. Philippines. #3268. 1981. 4 inches. All vinyl, fully jointed, painted brown hair, painted features; painted clothing. Copyright 1980 by Metro-Goldwyn-Mayer Film Co. ....**$15-$20**

2. Perseus. Mattel, Inc. Philippines. 1981. 4 inches. All vinyl, fully jointed. Same as previous doll except packaged with Pegasus, the winged horse. Copyright 1980 by Metro-Goldwyn-Mayer Film Co. ....**$20-$30**

Hammer, M.C. (Stanley Kirk Burrell)
Singer and actor Hammer is an all-around entertainer, often surrounded by his "posse" of dancers on stage. The posse sported Hammer's trademark baggy-style pants. Hammer has appeared in several films, including *Private Parts* (1997).

M.C. Hammer. Mattel, Inc. Malaysia. #1089. 1991. 12 inches. All vinyl, jointed, painted features; wearing gold jumpsuit. Box marked: "© 1991 Bustin' Productions, Inc." ....**$15-$20**

M.C. Hammer by Mattel in his trademark clothes.

The back of M.C. Hammer's box.

Hammond, Nicholas. Actor Hammond is best known for his role as Friedrich in the 1965 classic *The Sound of Music*. Hammond also played a dual role of Spider Man and Peter Parker for the television series *The Amazing Spiderman*.

1. Friedrich from *The Sound of Music*. Alexander Doll Company. U.S.A. #1001. 1965. 8 inches. All hard plastic, fully jointed, blonde wig; wearing costume from the movie, with hat. Part of set. ....**$200-$250**

2. Friedrich from The Sound of Music. Alexander Doll Company. U.S.A. #1007. 1965 to 1966. 11 inches. Plastic and vinyl, rooted blonde hair, sleep eyes with eyelashes; wearing costume from the movie, with hat. Head marked: "ALEXANDER//19©65." Part of set. **$200-$250**

3. Friedrich from The Sound of Music. Alexander Doll Company. U.S.A. #0807. 1971. 8 inches. Plastic and vinyl, rooted blonde hair, blue sleep eyes; wearing costume from the movie, with hat. Marked on back "ALEX." Part of set. ....**$150-$200**

Hardy, Oliver. Part of a famous comedy duo with Stan Laurel, actor Hardy appeared in many films with his partner. He was considered the "big one" of the two. His film career began in the early 1900s. (See also Laurel, Stan.)

1. Laurel & Hardy. Lenci. Italy. Circa 1930s. 10 inches. All felt, hand-finished faces; each figure wearing eighteenth-century costumes including tri-cornered hats. ......**$2,000-$3,000**, pair.

2. Oliver Hardy. Dakin. 1974. 5 inches. All vinyl with wind-up dancing/skating mechanism. **$45**

3. Laurel & Hardy. Exclusive Toy, Inc. 1997. 9 inches. All vinyl, painted features; wearing traditional Laurel and Hardy outfits. Sold separately in window boxes. Limited edition. ....**$20-$25**, each

4: Laurel & Hardy Bean Bag Collectibles. *Courtesy of David Cox.*

4. Laurel & Hardy Bean Bag Dolls. Highlight Starz Sun Times Enterprises, Inc. China. 1999. 10 inches. All cloth with beans inside; sewn-on hats with stitched features. Box marked: "Highlight Starz Laurel & Hardy Bean Bag Collectibles." ....**$25-$35**, pair

5. Laurel & Hardy. Comedy Classic Headliners. Equity Marketing Inc. China. 2000. 6 inches. Very realistic looking, molded vinyl, molded and painted features; both wearing molded black hats and molded black suits; Laurel is wearing a black-and-white spotted bow tie and Hardy is wearing a black and white-spotted tie. Each stands on base with his name engraved on it. Limited edition of 20,000. ....**$10-$15**, each

5: Laurel & Hardy Comedy Classic Headliners by Equity Marketing, Inc. *Courtesy of David Cox.*

3: Stan Laurel and Oliver Hardy — Laurel & Hardy — by Exclusive Toy Inc. *Courtesy of David Cox.*

Harrison, George. (See Beatles, The)

Harrison, Rex. Actor Harrison played many roles on stage and in film, including that of Doctor Doolittle in the popular 1967 musical motion picture of the same name, and Henry Higgins in *My Fair Lady* with Audrey Hepburn. One of his last films was *Heartbreak House* in 1986.

1. Doctor Doolittle. Mattel, Inc. Japan. #3575. 1968. 6 inches. Vinyl; wearing black coat jacket, tie and top hat, with parrot named Polynesia who has moving eyes. Marked: "©MATTEL, INC//JAPAN." ....**$75-$100**, boxed

2. Doctor Doolittle. Mattel, Inc. Japan. #3579. 1968. 6 inches. Wearing black jacket with top hat. Parrot is sewn to his coat. With two-headed Pushmi-Pullyu. Marked on animal's tag: "Quality originals by Mattel ®//PUSHMI-PULLYU." ....**$75-$100**

3. Doctor Doolittle Talking Hand Puppet. Mattel, Inc. Hong Kong. #3565. 1968. 24 inches. Talking puppet with cloth print body showing coat jacket, vest, collar, top hat and Polynesia the parrot. Pull string at lower left side allows puppet to speak. Rex Harrison's voice was used. ....**$150-$200**

4. Doctor Doolittle Presents the Talking Pushmi-Pullyu. Mattel, Inc. #5225. 1968. Features the Pushmi-Pullyu with pull-string talking feature in a 9-inch by 13-inch box. ....**$125-$150**

5. Pushmi-Pullyu. Mattel, Inc. #3578. 1968. Advertised as "Marvelous Movie Pet." Animal only. ....**$50-$75**

6. Doctor Doolittle Cottage. Mattel, Inc. #5125. 1968. Vinyl home for Doctor Doolittle. With hang tag and carry handle, plastic animals and Doctor Doolittle stand. ....**$100-$150**

7. Doctor Doolittle Talking Doll. Mattel, Inc. #5349. 1968. 24 inches. Soft body with vinyl head; wearing his trademark clothing. Marked on tag: "Quality Originals BY//MATTEL ®//DOCTOR DOOLITTLE// MCMLXVII Twentieth Century-Fox//Film Corporation// and Apjac//Productions. Inc.//All Rights Reserved// ©Mattel, Inc." The doll says ten different phrases. Great likeness to Rex Harrison. ..**$150-$200**

1: Rex Harrison as Dr. Doolittle, by Mattel. *Courtesy of McMasters Doll Auctions.*

Hart, Melissa Joan. Actress Hart has appeared in several films, including *Can't Hardly Wait* (1998) and *Drive Me Crazy* (1999). She starred in the title role on the Nickelodeon series *Clarissa Explains It All* (1991 to 1994). Hart currently stars in the Warner Brothers television series *Sabrina, The Teenage Witch.* Having made her first national television commercial at age four, Hart is now a veteran of television, film and theater.

Sabrina The Teenage Witch. Kenner. China. 1997. 11 inches. All vinyl, jointed, rooted blonde hair, painted features; wearing short pink dress with silver glitter overlay, pink boots; came with black cat and magic card. Box marked: "© 1997 Viacom Productions, Inc." ....**$15-$25**

Kenner's Sabrina The Teenage Witch portrayed by Melissa Joan Hart. *Author's collection.*

Hartline, Mary. Hartline was the hostess for the television show *Super Circus*, which premiered in Chicago in 1949. The show moved, a few years later, to New York and added personality Jerry Cologna. Hartline and Cologna were a winning combination for *Super Circus*, making the show a favorite of the time. Hartline's popularity earned her a contract with Canada Dry Ginger Ale as the company's official spokesperson.

The Mary Hartline dolls were marked differently depending on their size. For example, the 16-inch doll is marked "IDEAL DOLL 16" or "P-91" on the back and "P-91/IDEAL DOLL/MADE IN U.S.A." on the head. The 22-inch doll is marked "IDEAL DOLL/P-94" on the back and "IDEAL DOLL" on the head.

1. Mary Hartline. Ideal Toy Corp. U.S.A. #1250. 1952. 7 inches. Hard plastic, jointed neck and arms, blonde nylon wig, blue or yellow sleep eyes, painted eyelashes; molded white boots. Marked on back: "IDEAL." ......**$65-$85**

2. Mary Hartline. Ideal Toy Corp. U.S.A. 1952. 16 inches. Hard plastic head, blue sleep eyes with real eyelashes and eye shadow, closed mouth, original wig, five-piece hard plastic body; dressed in original marked dress, original panties and majorette boots. A baton and Rayve Toy Wave Kit also included. Marked on back of head: "P-91//IDEAL DOLL//MADE IN U.S.A.;" marked on body: "IDEAL DOLL, P-91." ....$300-$400, mint-in-box

3. Mary Hartline. Ideal Toy Corp. U.S.A. 1952. 16 inches. Blonde hair with extra thick bangs to side, eye shadow above blue sleep eyes; dressed in harder-to-find blue musical dress with attached slip and matching panties, white leatherette majorette boots with gold tassels; also has red wood baton. ....$400-$500

4. Mary Hartline. Ideal Toy Corp. U.S.A. 1952. 14 inches. ....$350-$400

5. Mary Hartline. Ideal Toy Corp. U.S.A. 1952. 16 inches. Original outfit. ......$400-$500

6. Mary Hartline Paper Dolls. Whitman Publishing Co. U.S.A. 1953. Came with two dolls and a variety of clothing. Box marked: "Copyright,

1953 by WHITMAN PUBLISHING CO. Racine, Wisconsin, Printed in U.S.A." ....$20-$30

7. Mary Hartline Plastic Figure. Louis Marx. U.S.A. Circa. 1950s. 1 inches. Made of off-white molded plastic. Came with various figures including Cliffy and Scampy. ....$10 each

3: A hard-to-find Ideal Mary Hartline in her blue musical dress.

5: Mary Hartline by Ideal, 16-inches.

Hayes, Billie.
Actor Hayes is best known for her role as Witchiepoo in the television series *H.R. Pufnstuf*, which aired from September 1969 to September 1971. The star of the show was Jack Wild, who played the part of Jimmy.

1. Witchiepoo. My-toy. 1970. 19 inches. Stuffed with green face and hands, open mouth; wearing witch clothes. ....$250-$350, loose; $600-$800, boxed

2. Witchiepoo Hand Puppet. Remco. Hong Kong. 1971. 11 inches. Lifelike head, cloth puppet body, string hair. ....$100-$125, loose; $200-$300, boxed

Hegyes, Robert.
Actor Hegyes is well known for his role as Juan Epstein on the television series *Welcome Back Kotter*, which aired on ABC from 1975 until 1979.

Epstein. Mattel, Inc. Taiwan. #9774. 1976. 9 inches. All vinyl, fully jointed, painted features and hair; dressed in jean pants and vest with blue shirt. Marked on back of head: "©WOLPER// KOMACK;" marked on back: "©1973//MATTEL INC//TAIWAN." On card with an accessory piece, like each doll in this series. Copyright by the Wolper Organization, Inc. and Komack Company, Inc. ....$15-$20, loose; $40-$50, on card

1-2: Three sizes of Ideal Mary Hartline dolls: 16 inches, 7 inches (in front) and 22 inches. *Courtesy of Sue Munsell.*

7: Louis Marx's one-inch Mary Hartline doll, shown with Cliffy and Scampy.

Henie, Sonja. Born in Olso, Norway, Henie won the World Championships in ice skating ten consecutive times. She also won the Gold Medal in the Olympics for figure skating in 1928, 1932 and 1936. Henie went on to star in twelve films, including *One in a Million* (1939). The Alexander Doll Company was the only company licensed to produce Sonja Henie dolls, although other companies did produce look-alike versions.

1. Sonja Henie. Alexander Doll Company. U.S.A. 1939. 7 inches. All composition, jointed legs and arms, mohair wig, painted blue eyes; wears white dress. Marked on back: "MME// ALEXANDER." ....**$350-$450**

2. Sonja Henie. Alexander Doll Company. U.S.A. 1939. 13 inches. All composition, jointed legs and arms, blonde human hair wig, blue sleep eyes with eyelashes and eye shadow, open mouth with teeth. Back marked: "WENDY ANN//MME.ALEXANDER//NEW YORK." ....**$600-$700**

3. Sonja Henie. Alexander Doll Company. U.S.A. 1939. 14 inches. All original doll shown with advertisement for Drene hair care products. ....**$600-$700**

4. Sonja Henie. Alexander Doll Company. U.S.A. 1939. 14 inches. All original in pink skating outfit. ....**$600-$700**

5. Sonja Henie. Alexander Doll Company. U.S.A. 1939. 14 inches. All composition, jointed legs and arms, blonde human hair wig, blue sleep eyes with eyelashes and eye shadow; dressed in skating outfit. Head marked: "MADAME ALEXANDER//SONJA//HENIE." ..**$600-$700**

Publicity photo showing (from left) Frances Scully, Irene Rich, Tom Breneman and Sonja Henie. Copyright by Kellogg Co. 1945.

8: A 21-inch Sonja Henie in a black skating costume. *Courtesy of Patricia Wood.*

4: An all-original 14-inch Sonja Henie in her pink skating outfit. *Author's collection.*

6. Sonja Henie. Alexander Doll Company. U.S.A. 1939. 17 to 18 inches. All composition, jointed legs and arms, blonde human hair wig, blue sleep eyes with eyelashes and eye shadow; dressed in skating outfit. Head marked: "MADAME ALEXANDER//SONJA//HENIE." ....**$800-$900**

7. Sonja Henie. Alexander Doll Company. U.S.A. 1939 to 1941. An all-original doll with trunk and extra clothing. ....**$1,000** up

8. Sonja Henie. Alexander Doll Company. U.S.A. 1940. 21 inches. All composition, jointed legs and arms, blonde human hair or mohair wig, blue sleep eyes with eyelashes and eye shadow; dressed in black skating outfit. Head marked: "MADAME ALEXANDER// SONJA// HENIE." ....**$1,000-$1,200**

This 17-inch Sonja Henie sold for $625 at auction in 2000. *Courtesy of McMasters Doll Auctions.*

A Sonja Henie wearing blue ski pants with a red jacket, accessorized with skis and ski poles. *Courtesy of McMasters Doll Auctions.*

9. Sonja Henie. Arranbee Doll Company. U.S.A. Circa 1940s. 20 inches. All original, all composition, sleep eyes, mohair wig. An unauthorized doll made to look like Sonja Henie. ....**$400-$500**

10. Sonja Henie. Alexander Doll Company. U.S.A. 1951. 14 inches. Vinyl head, plastic body, blonde wig, blue sleep eyes with eyelashes; dressed in skating outfit. Head marked: "ALEXANDER 1951." "Madeline" face, made for only one year. ....**$500-$600**

Henry, Patrick. A politician, revolutionary patriot and statesman who was known as the "Voice of the Revolution," Henry was Virginia's first governor after the Commonwealth declared independence from Great Britain. He is known for his Stamp Act Speech of 1765 and his famous Liberty or Death speech of 1775.

Patrick Henry. S.S. Kresge Company. Hong Kong. #48-245941976. 7 inches. Vinyl head, painted features and hair, fully jointed plastic body; wearing blue suit with white shirt in revolutionary era style. Marked on back: "MADE IN//HONG KONG." Part of a series called the Heroes of the American Revolution. The dolls in this series were distributed by Montgomery Ward & Co. Inc. ....**$15-$25**

7: An all-original Sonja Henie with a trunk and extra clothing. *Courtesy of Sharron's Dolls.*

Patrick Henry from the Heroes of the American Revolution series by the S.S. Kresge Company. *Courtesy of Suellen Manning.* For a view of the back of the box, see Franklin, Benjamin.

Hensley, Pamela. Actress Hensley played the role of Ardella in the NBC television series *Buck Rogers in the 25th Century*, which aired from 1979 to 1981.

Ardella. Mego. Hong Kong. #85000/7. 1979. 3 inches. All vinyl, fully jointed, painted features; painted clothing; molded hat. Copyright by Robert C. Dille. ....**$5-$10**

Two award-winning Sonja Henie dolls. *Courtesy of Patricia Wood.*

Henville, Alexandria Lee (Baby Sandy).

Henville was a child star for Universal Studios. Baby Sandy was featured in several films in the late 1930s and early 1940s, including *East Side of Heaven, Unexpected Father* and *Little Accident (all 1939)*.

1. Baby Sandy. Ralph Freundlich, Inc. U.S.A. 1939 to 1942. Dolls were made in a variety of sizes. All composition, fully jointed with molded hair, blue sleep tin eyes. The 8-inch version hads blonde molded hair and painted blue eyes. Heads are marked: "BABY SANDY." The doll was advertised as "A Doll plus A Personality." Licensed by Mitchell J. Hamilburg for Universal Pictures. ....8 inches, **$200-$250**; 11 inches, **$250-$300**; 14-15 inches, **$300-$400**; 16-17 inches (also with blonde mohair wig), **$400-$500**; 20 inches, **$600-$700**

2. Baby Sandy. Ralph Freundlich, Inc. U.S.A. 1939 to 1942. 15 inches. All composition, fully jointed, molded hair; re-dressed in blue jumper with white blouse. ....**$200-$300**

3. Baby Sandy. Ralph Freundlich, Inc. U.S.A. 1939 to 1942. 17 inches. All composition, fully jointed, molded hair; re-dressed red and white dress. ....**$300-$400**

2: Baby Sandy by Ralph Freundlich, Inc., 15 inches. *Courtesy of Sunnie Newell.*

3: Baby Sandy by Ralph Freundlich, Inc., 17 inches. *Courtesy of Lynnae Ramsey.*

Hiawatha.

American Indian Hiawatha was a leader among the Iroquois people in the late 1500s and the subject of a classic poem by author Henry Wadsworth Longfellow.

1. Hiawatha. Alexander Doll Company. U.S.A. Circa 1930s. 7 inches. All composition, jointed; dressed in Indian outfit. .... **$350-$400**

2. Hiawatha. Alexander Doll Company. U.S.A. Circa 1930s 18 inches. All cloth; dressed in Indian outfit. ....**$600-$700**

3. Hiawatha. Alexander Doll Company. U.S.A. #720. 1967 to 1969. 8 inches. All plastic, fully jointed, black synthetic wig, brown sleep eyes and molded eyelashes; dressed in Indian outfit. Part of the American Series. ....**$300-$350**

Hilton-Jacobs, Lawrence.

Actor Hilton-Jacobs is well known for his role as Frederick "Boom Boom" Washington on the television series *Welcome Back, Kotter*, which aired from 1975 until 1979.

Washington. Mattel, Inc. Taiwan. #9773. 1976. 9 inches. All vinyl, fully jointed; dressed in blue jeans, yellow jacket and T-shirt. Marked on back of head: "©WOLPER/KOMACK;" marked on back: "©1973/MATTEL INC/TAIWAN." On card with an accessory piece as is each doll in this series. ....**$15-$20**, loose; **$40-$50**, on card

Holder, Geoffrey.

Actor Holder played the part of Punjab in the 1982 film version of *Annie* based on the comic strip character Little Orphan Annie. Also a stage actor, Holder received two Tony Awards for his role in the Broadway show *The Wiz*.

Punjab. Knickerbocker Toy Co., Inc. U.S.A. #3866. 1982. 7 inches. All vinyl, fully jointed, painted features; wearing white gown and turban. Copyright by Columbia Pictures Industries, Inc. ....**$15-$30**

Holtz, Lou.

Football coach and author Holtz is a motivational coach who revitalized the Notre Dame football program by leading the team to nine bowl games and a National Championship. During his twenty-seven years as a head football coach, Holtz garnered a 216-95-7 career record. He also coached the Arkansas Razorbacks Football team and is now coaching at the University of South Carolina. Holtz is the author of *Winning Every Day*.

Coach Lou Holtz. Maker unknown. Hong Kong. 1978. 11 inches. All vinyl, painted features, molded and painted yellow hair; wearing red and white plaid pants, a red sweater with white collar, white shoes and light red sunglasses. ....**$15-$20**

Coach Lou Holtz by an unknown maker. *Author's collection.*

Howard, Ron. A multi-talented actor, director and producer, Howard played the role of Opie on the CBS television series *The Andy Griffith Show*, which aired from 1960 until 1968. He then starred as Richie Cunningham on the hit television series *Happy Days*, which aired from January 1974 to July 1984. He has directed several major film hits including *Cocoon* (1985) and *How the Grinch Stole Christmas* (2000).

Richie. Mego. Hong Kong. #63001/1. 1976. 8 inches. All vinyl, fully jointed, painted hair and features; dressed in pants and striped shirt with long sweater, shoes. Head marked: "© MEGO PARAMOUNT//PICTURES CORP.;" back marked: "© MEGO CORP. 1974//REG US PAT OFF//PAT PENDING//HONG KONG." Sold on card. **$50-$60**

Mego's Richie from the *Happy Days* television series, shown with Potsie, portrayed by Anson Williams. *Courtesy of McMasters Doll Auctions.*

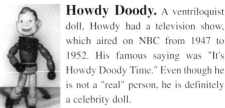

Howdy Doody. A ventriloquist doll, Howdy had a television show, which aired on NBC from 1947 to 1952. His famous saying was "It's Howdy Doody Time." Even though he is not a "real" person, he is definitely a celebrity doll.

1. Howdy Doody. Effanbee Doll Company (Noma Electric) U.S.A. Designed by Joseph Kallus. Circa 1947. 13 inches. All composition, jointed, red upper body with blue scarf. ....**$350-$500**

2. Howdy Doody. Ideal Toy Corp. U.S.A. 1950-1952. Several sizes. Hard plastic ventriloquist head with pull string for mouth, stuffed cloth body and limbs with vinyl hands. Marked on head: "IDEAL." ....18 inches, **$200-$250**; 20 inches, **$250-$300**; 24 inches, **$300-$350**

3. Howdy Doody. Ideal Toy Corp. U.S.A. 1953 to 1955. Several sizes. This ventriloquist doll has a hard plastic head and cloth body with the clothing sewn to the body. ....20 inches, **$200-$250**; 25 inches, **$250-$300**

4. Howdy Doody. No markings as to company origin. Circa 1950s. 16 inches. Composition head, cloth body, painted features with large freckles, open mouth with teeth; wearing red pants, red and white checked shirt with blue scarf that reads "Howdy Doody." ....**$350-$450**

5. Howdy Doody. Kohner. U.S.A. #180. Circa 1950s. 4 inches. Plastic base and head, wood jointed body; wearing a green felt scarf around neck. Marked on base: "NBC ©Bob Smith" with patent number. A push-up toy. ....**$50-$75** (See photo on page 78.)

4: Howdy Doody with a composition head by an unknown maker.

4. Truly Scrumptious. Mattel, Inc. Japan. 1968. #1108. 11 inches. Similar to other dolls except this one has straight legs and a no-twist body; wears a pink gown with feathered hat. Marked: "Midge// © 1963//Barbie ®//© 1958//By//MATTEL INC.// PATENTED." ....**$400-$500**

2: Talking Truly Scrumptious from *Chitty Chitty Bang Bang* lavender gown with black dotted net overlay. By Mattel. *Courtesy of McMasters Doll Auctions.*

Howes, Sally Ann. Actress Howes is best known for her role as Truly Scrumptious in the 1968 motion picture *Chitty Chitty Bang Bang*, which starred Dick Van Dyke.

1. Chitty Chitty Bang Bang Miraculous Movie Car. Mattel, Inc. Japan. 1969. #6150. Contains molded passengers in car depicting Mr. Potts, Truly Scrumptious and the two children. Car rolls and has an inflatable raft for floating on water. ....**$175-$200**

2. Truly Scrumptious Talking Doll. Mattel, Inc. Japan. #1107. 1969. 11 inches. Rooted eyelashes, bendable legs; wears lavender gown with black dotted net overlay. Pull string to hear several phrases including "Do you invent things?," "What a nice friend" and "Let's go for a drive." Marked on neck: "©1965 MATTEL, INC//JAPAN;" marked on rear: "© 1967//MATTEL, INC.//U.S. & FOREIGN//PATS.PEND// MEXICO;" dress is labeled: "Truly Scrumptious ®//©1968 GLIDROSE PRODUCTIONS, LTD.//AND WARFIELD PRODUCTIONS, LTD.//MADE IN JAPAN// © 1968 MATTEL, INC." Barbie's body and Francie's head were used on this doll. ....**$350-$400**

3. Chitty Chitty Bang Bang Liddle Kiddles. Mattel, Inc. Japan. #3597. 1969. Adults are 2 inches tall, children are 1 inch tall. Tiny doll versions of Mr. Potts and Truly Scrumptious with the two children. ....**$300-$350**, set, mint-in-package

4A: Mattel's Truly Scrumptious from *Chitty Chitty Bang Bang* wears a pink gown. *Courtesy of McMasters Doll Auctions.*

4B: Close-up of Truly Scrumptious in her pink gown, with her pink and green bonnet. *Courtesy of McMasters Doll Auctions.*

(See Van Dyke, Dick for photo.)

J

Jackson, Alan. Singer Jackson is one of country music's best-loved singers. In the 1990s he sold more than thirty million records.

Alan Jackson. Exclusive Toy, Inc. Signature Superstars. China. #18076. 1998. 9 inches. All vinyl, panted features. Box marked: "© 1998 Alan Jackson. Manufactured by Exclusive Toy, Inc. Metuchen, NJ. 08840." ....**$20-$30**

Jackson, Kate. Actress Jackson is best known for her role as Sabrina Duncan in the hit television series *Charlie's Angels*, which aired from September 1976 to August 1981. (See also Fawcett, Farrah and Ladd, Cheryl.)

1. Sabrina. Hasbro. Hong Kong. #4861. 1977. 8 inches. All vinyl, fully jointed, rooted brown hair, painted brown eyes; wearing one-piece jumpsuit. Copyright Spelling-Goldberg Productions. ....**$25-$40**

2. Charlie's Angels Set. Hasbro. Hong Kong. 1977. 8 inches. Includes all three girls. ....**$175-$225**, each set

3. Sabrina. Raynal. Belgium. 1977. 8 inches. ....**$100-$125**, boxed

4. Kate Jackson. Mattel, Inc. Korea. #2495. 1978. 11 inches. All vinyl, fully jointed, rooted brown hair, painted brown eyes; wearing sexy dress with high neck. Marked on back of head: "© MATTEL INC 1978;" marked on rear: "© MATTEL INC//1966//KOREA;" box marked: "She's a beauty with brains—so watch out! Copyright by C & D Enterprises." ......**$40-$50**

Jackson, Michael. Singer and entertainer Jackson is one of the top singers of all time. He began his career singing with his brothers in the group The Jackson Five. When he went solo, he sold millions of records. During his world tour "Dangerous," he played to sold-out audiences. Jackson has won just about every music award imaginable.

Michael Jackson. Christmas Corp. China. Circa 1990s. 6 inches. Spoof doll, wearing red top with gold trim, black pants and shoes. Box marked: "© Celebrity Spoof Licensing Corp." ....**$20-$25**

Michael Jackson, by Christmas Corp., copyright by Celebrity Spoof Licensing Corp.

James Bond. (See Connery, Sean and Moore, Roger)

Jefferson, Thomas. The third president of the United States, Jefferson was one of the authors of the Declaration of Independence.

Thomas Jefferson. S.S. Kresge Company. Hong Kong. #48-245941976. 7 inches. Vinyl head, painted features and hair, fully jointed plastic body; wearing blue suit with white shirt in revolutionary era style. Marked on back: "MADE IN//HONG KONG." Part of a series called the Heroes of the American Revolution. The dolls in this series were distributed by Montgomery Ward & Co. Inc. ....**$15-$25**

Thomas Jefferson from the Heroes of the American Revolution series by the S.S. Kresge Company. For a view of the back of the box, see Franklin, Benjamin. *Courtesy of Suellen Manning.*

John, Sir Elton. A musician, singer, producer and composer who has been producing hits for over two decades. John has won an array of awards. One of his best-selling songs was composed following the death in 1997 of his friend, Princess Diana. It was a remake of his hit "Candle in the Wind," originally written about actress Marilyn Monroe.

Elton John. Yaboom. China. 2000. 12 inches. All vinyl, painted and molded features; dressed

Elton John by Yaboom. *Author's collection.*

The back of the box for the two-doll pack containing the Yellow and Pink Power Rangers. *Courtesy of David Spurgeon.*

in different outfits, including an all-black outfit and a red suit with white designs. Sold in a boxed package with microphone, shoes and stand. Push button to hear him sing "Crocodile Rock." ....$50-$75

Johnson, Amy Jo. Actress Johnson played the role of Kimberly, the Pink Power Ranger in the movie and television series *Mighty Morphin Power Rangers*, which aired from 1993 to 1996.

Kimberly. Bandai. China. #2222. 1994. 9 inches. Power Rangers for Girls. Wearing pink dress with flower skirt, boxed with Power Ranger outfit and helmet. Box marked: "© 1994 Bandai America, Inc." Sold as two-doll pack with yellow Power Ranger and also sold separately. ....$15-$20, individually; $25-$35, set

Kimberly, the Pink Power Ranger, shown on the right with Trini, the Yellow Power Ranger, in the two-doll pack. *Courtesy of David Spurgeon.*

Johnson, Julanne. Actress Johnson was a film star in the early 1920s. She starred with Douglas Fairbanks, Sr. in the movie *Thief of Bagdad* (1924).

Julanne Johnson. Maker unknown. Circa 1920s. Molded cloth, painted features; wearing costume from the Thief of Bagdad. ....$500-$700

Julanne Johnson by an unknown maker. *Courtesy of Billie Nelson Tyrrell.*

Johnson, Lyndon B. Thirty-sixth president of the United States, Johnson was sworn into office after the assassination of President John F. Kennedy in 1963. In 1964, he won the presidential election and stayed in office, beating out Barry Goldwater.

President Lyndon Johnson. Remco. Hong Kong. #1815. 1964. 5 inches. All vinyl, painted features; with molded hat, molded painted clothing. Box marked: "© 1964 Remco Industries Inc. Harrison, NJ;" also marked: "President Lyndon B. Johnson, LJB HIMSELF By REMCO." ....**$75-$100**

President Lyndon B. Johnson by Remco. *Courtesy of David Spurgeon.*

Jones, Anissa. Actress Jones is best known for her role as Buffy in the hit television series *Family Affair*, which aired from 1966 to 1971. Jones was frequently seen in the show holding her doll, Mrs. Beasley.

1. Buffy and Mrs. Beasley. Mattel, Inc. Japan. 1967. 6 inches. All vinyl Buffy with cloth Mrs. Beasley. ....**$175-$225**

2. Buffy and Mrs. Beasley. Mattel, Inc. Japan. #3577. 1967. Talking 10-inch Buffy with 4-inch Mrs. Beasley. Buffy wears white dress with red polka dots and short red skirt; Mrs. Beasley wears blue-and-white polka-dotted outfit and has glasses. Buffy is marked on neck: "©MATTEL INC. JAPAN;" marked on back: "© 1965//MATTEL, INC//JAPAN//23." Mrs. Beasley's cloth tag is marked: "Mrs. Beasley ®//© 1967 FAMILY// AFFAIR CO.// © 1967 MATTEL// INC. JAPAN." ....**$250-$300**, boxed (See photo on page 82.)

3. Mrs. Beasley Rag Doll. Mattel, Inc. 1968. 10 inches. Dressed in a red dress with white dots or blue dress with white dots. ....**$20-$30**, each

4. Buffy and Mrs. Beasley Talking Dolls. Mattel, Inc. Japan. 1968. #3107. Features 10-inch Buffy with large Mrs. Beasley doll. When you pull the string at the back of the neck, Buffy says eight different phrases including "I'm always asking questions" and "Count my Freckles, Ha! Ha!" Marked on neck: "©MATTEL INC.//HONG KONG;" marked on back: "© 1967 MATTEL INC.//US & FOR.//PATS. PEND/MEXICO." ....**$300-$350**, mint-in-box

5. Mrs. Beasley Talking Doll. Mattel, Inc. 1969 until 1973. 22 inches. Hard to find in original box. Some of her phrases include "Would you like to try on my glasses?" and "Long ago I was a little girl just like you." ....**$150-$200**, loose, with glasses; **$400-$500**, boxed

6. Jody and Buffy Paper Dolls. Whitman. U.S.A. 1970 and 1974. Buffy and Jody (1970), Family Affair (1970) and Mrs. Beasley (1974). ....**$20-$25**, each, cut; **$40-$50**, uncut

7. Mrs. Beasley Rag Doll. Mattel, Inc. China. 1973. 14 inches. All cloth; wearing blue outfit with white dots. ..**$50-$75**, boxed

6: Buffy and Jody Paper Dolls by Whitman. *Courtesy of McMasters Doll Auctions.*

1: Mattel's Buffy and Mrs. Beasley. *Courtesy of McMasters Doll Auctions.*

2: Mattel's 10-inch Talking Buffy, shown without Mrs. Beasley.

Joyner, Florence Griffith (Flo Jo).

Joyner was a United States Olympic track star who was once dubbed the world's fastest woman. Joyner won three gold medals in track in the 1988 Olympics in Seoul, South Korea. She died in her sleep at the age of thirty-eight in 1998.

Flo Jo. LJN Toys Ltd. China. #2501. 1989. 11 inches. Wearing pink unitard with blue panties designed by Flo Jo; with accessories and tan bag. Box marked: "© 1989 LJN Toys Ltd." ....**$15-$20**

Flo Jo (Florence Griffith Joyner) by LJN Toys Ltd. Dressed in her signature one-legged unitard. *Courtesy of David Spurgeon.*

Jones, Davy. (See Monkees, The)

Joplin, Janis. Rock singer Joplin, with her unique brand of expression, became a household name in the 1960s. When she died of a drug overdose at age twenty-seven, her death symbolized the end of a turbulent and reckless decade.

Janis Joplin. McFarlane Toys. China. 2000. 6 inches. All vinyl, painted and molded features; with elaborate stand with Janis at the microphone. ....**$20-$30**

McFarlane Toys' Janis Joplin, six inches. On original card.

The back of Flo Jo's box. *Courtesy of David Spurgeon.*

Julia. (See Carroll, Diahann)

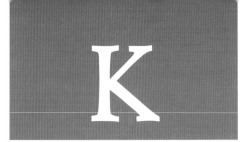

K

Kaplan, Gabe. Actor Kaplan is best known for his role as the teacher Gabe Kotter on the ABC television series *Welcome Back Kotter*, which aired from 1975 until 1979.

1. Kotter. Mattel, Inc. Taiwan. #9770. 1976. 9 inches. All vinyl, fully jointed; dressed in brown pants, white shirt, green tie and brown-tone jacket. Marked on head: "©WOLPER/KOMACK;" marked on back: "©1973/MATTEL INC/TAIWAN." Copyright by Wolper Organization, Inc. and the Komack Company, Inc. On card with an accessory piece, like each doll in this series. ......**$15-$20**, loose; **$40-$50**, on card

2. Mr. Kotter Paper Dolls. Toy Factory. 1976. Shows illustration of Mr. Kotter waving on cover. ....**$10-$15**, cut; **$25-$30**, uncut

Karath, Kym. Child actress Karath starred as Gretl in the 1965 movie *The Sound of Music*.

1. Gretl. Alexander Doll Co. U.S.A. #1000. 1965. 8 inches. All hard plastic, dark-colored wig. Part of set. ....**$200-$250**

2. Gretl. Alexander Doll Co. U.S.A. #1001. 1965 to 1970. 12 inches. Vinyl head, rooted blonde hair, blue sleep eyes, vinyl and plastic body; wearing flowered dress. Marked on head: "ALEXANDER//19©64." Part of set. ....**$250-$300**

3. Gretl. Alexander Doll Co. U.S.A. 1966. 12 inches. Vinyl head, rooted blonde hair, vinyl and plastic body; dressed in sailor outfit. Part of set. ....**$250-$300**

4. Gretl. Alexander Doll Co. U.S.A. #0801. 1971 to 1973. 8 inches. All hard plastic, fully jointed with bent knees. Head marked: "ALEXANDER//19©64." Part of set. ....**$200-$250**

Kaye, Danny. Actor Kaye performed in vaudeville before moving into films and then later television with *The Danny Kaye Show*, which aired from 1963 until 1967.

1. Danney Kaye Nodder. Unmarked. Circa 1950s. Made of plastic-type material, all painted. First name on base is misspelled "Danney" and the bottom says "Danney Kaye." ..**$30-$40**

2. Danny Kaye in *Hans Christian Andersen*. Peggy Nisbet. England. #P763. 1970s. 8 inches. All plastic. ....**$50-$75**

1: Unmarked Danny Kaye nodder, circa 1950s.

Keeshan, Robert (Captain Kangaroo).
A television personality, Keeshan played Clarabelle the Clown on the television show *The Howdy Doody Show*, which aired on NBC from 1947 to 1952. Beginning in 1955, Keeshan starred as Captain Kangaroo on his own television show of the same name, which aired for nearly three decades.

1. Clarabelle. Alexander Doll Company. U.S.A. 1951 to 1953. Various sizes. Stuffed cloth body with applied features, fully jointed; wearing Clarabelle costume. ....19 inches, **$300-$400**; 29 inches, **$500-$600**; 49 inches, **$700-$800**

2. Clarabelle. Pelham Puppets. England. 1953. 15 inches. Composition head, painted features, moving mouth, composition hands and feet with wooden section for torso. Unmarked. Copyright by Bob Smith. ....**$200-$300**

3. Clarabelle. Ideal Toy Corp. 1954. 16 and 20 inches. Mask face with cloth body, later version made with vinyl face; dressed in satin Clarabelle outfit with noise box and horn. ....16 inches, **$50-$75**; 20 inches, **$75-$100**

4. Captain Kangaroo. Baby Barry Toy. Circa 1950s. 21 inches. Vinyl head and hands, stuffed cloth body, painted gray hair and mustache, blue inset eyes, black vinyl feet. Marked on neck: "©//B.B.;" marked on clothing: "EXCLUSIVE LICENSEE//BABY BARRY//TOY N.Y.C.;" other side of tag marked: "CAPTAIN//KANGAROO." ....**$100-$125**

5. Captain Kangaroo. Mattel, Inc. #5334. 1967. 20 inches. All-cloth doll with printed features and clothing, with attached extra clothing. Tag on clothing marked: "©ROBERT KEESHAN//ASSOCIATES, INC.//ALL RIGHTS RESERVED//© MATTEL, INC." ....**$30-$50**

Keith, Richard. Child actor Keith played the role of Little Ricky (Ricky Jr.) on the television series *I Love Lucy* from 1956 until 1957. (See also Ball, Lucille.)

1. Little Ricky (Ricky Jr.). Zany Toys, Inc. 1953. 8 inches. Vinyl head, hands and feet attached to a blanket with pajamas, painted brown hair, painted blue eyes. Tag on blanket reads: "I AM//RICKY, JR//©LUCILLE BALL//AND DESI ARNAZ." Used as a puppet. ......**$75-$100**

2. Little Ricky (Ricky Jr.). American Character. U.S.A. 1953. 21 inches. Vinyl head, jointed vinyl body, molded and painted hair, blue sleep eyes with eyelashes, open mouth; wearing shirt that reads: "Ricky Jr." Head marked: "AMER. CHAR. DOL." Original price was $15.98. ....**$250-$300**

3. Little Ricky (Ricky Jr.) American Character U.S.A. 1955. 14 inches. Vinyl head, jointed vinyl body, molded and painted hair, blue sleep eyes with eyelashes, open mouth; wearing red-and-white plaid shirt with tan one-piece long jumper that reads "Ricky Jr." The catalog price was $10.98. ....**$150-$200**

2: American Character's 21-inch Little Ricky.

3: American Character's 14-inch Ricky Jr. is shown with an unmarked 28-inch mask-faced Lucille Ball doll, missing her apron and head scarf. Circa 1952, she is valued at $1,000 up, complete. *Courtesy of Steve Malatinsky.*

Kellerman, Annette. Kellerman was a famous swimmer in films from 1909 until about 1921. She was in the Ziegfield Follies and swam in a tank as a mermaid.

Annette Kellerman as the Mermaid. Maker unknown. Circa 1920s. 38 inches. All cloth, painted features, mohair wig; dressed in a beautiful full-length gold gown with mermaid bottom, long ropes of pearls around her neck and arms. ....**$500-$750**

Annette Kellerman, in her mermaid costume, by an unknown maker. *Courtesy of Billie Nelson Tyrrell.*

Kelley, DeForest. Kelley, who appeared both in films and on television, is best known for his role as Dr. Leonard "Bones" McCoy on the NBC television series *Star Trek*, which aired from 1966 until 1969. He also played Dr. McCoy in the movie *Star Trek: The Motion Picture* in 1979.

1. Dr. McCoy (Bones) Mego. Hong Kong. #51200/3. 1974. 8 inches. All vinyl, fully jointed, painted hair and features; wearing Star Trek uniform. Copyright by Paramount Pictures Corporation. ....**$35-$50** (See Shatner, William for photograph.)

2. Dr. McCoy (Bones). Mego. Hong Kong. #91200/6. 1979. 3¾ inches. All vinyl, fully jointed, painted hair and features; painted clothing. Copyright by Paramount Pictures Corporation. ....**$15-$25**

1: DeForest Kelley as Dr. Leonard "Bones" McCoy from the television series *Star Trek*. By Mego.

Kelly, Emmett. Kelly was a full-time circus clown whose character was named Wearie Willie. He appeared in films, including *Fat Man* (1951) and *The Greatest Show on Earth* (1952).

1. Emmett Kelly. Baby Barry Toy. #713. Circa 1950s. 13 inches. Vinyl head, one-piece stuffed cloth body; dressed in "Wearie Willie" clown costume of blue pants with patch, brown jacket and tie with brown shoes and black hat. Head marked: "B.B.;" tag on jacket marked: "Exclusive Licensee//Baby Barry//Toy N.Y.C." ......**$75-$100**

2. Emmett Kelly. Baby Barry Toy. Circa 1950s. 21 inches. Vinyl hands and head, cloth body, rooted brown hair, green set-in eyes, wire inside arms and legs to change position; felt shoes. A variety of dolls were made, some with slightly different outfits, some with brown eyes. Head marked: "B.B.;" clothing marked: "Exclusive Licensee//Baby Barry//Toy N.Y.C." ....19- to 21-inch size, **$100-$125**; 24-inch size, **$125-$175**

3. Emmett Kelly. Juro. Circa 1970s. 29 inches. Vinyl head, cloth body, painted and molded hat, string to make mouth open and close, vinyl hands; dressed in "Wearie Willie" clown costume. Marked on neck: "EMMETT KELLY//TRADE MARK//WILLIE THE CLOWN//JURO NOVELTY CO. INC.//2." ....**$150-$225**

2A: Emmett Kelly in his clown costume by Baby Barry Toy. *Courtesy of Seaview Antique Dolls.*

2B: Another version of Emmett Kelly in his clown costume by Baby Barry Toy. *Courtesy of Lynnae Ramsey.*

Kelly, Emmett, Jr. The son of famous clown Emmett Kelly, Emmett Kelly, Jr., performed an act similar to that of his father. He starred in one film: *Emmett Kelly, Jr.—Circus.*

Emmett Kelly, Jr. Horsman. U.S.A. 1979. 24 inches. Vinyl head, painted features, moving mouth for "talking," cloth stuffed body; wears clown costume similar to Wearie Willie's. ....**$150-$200**

Kelly, Grace. Princess of Monaco. Actress Kelly played in many films, including *High Society* (1956), before marrying Prince Rainier of Monaco in 1956. She was mother to Caroline, Albert and Stephanie. She was killed in an automobile accident in 1982.

Grace Kelly Paper Dolls. Whitman Publishing Co. #94.1092. 1955. Shows picture of Grace Kelly on cover. Two paper dolls and various outfits. ....**$30-$40**

Kennedy (Schlossberg), Caroline.

Author Kennedy is the daughter of President John F.

Kennedy and Jacqueline Bouvier Kennedy Onassis. She co-authored two books, *The Right to Privacy* and *In Our Defense—The Bill of Rights in Action* with Ellen Alderman and edited *The Best-Loved Poems of Jacqueline Kennedy Onassis* (2001).

Though not advertised as Caroline Kennedy, the dolls produced by the Alexander Doll Company bear her likeness. In 1962, the name Caroline was registered as a trademark with the company. The doll was only made from 1961 to 1962.

1. Caroline. Alexander Doll Company. U.S.A. #4290. 1961 to 1962. 15 inches. Vinyl head, blue sleep eyes with real eyelashes, open/closed mouth, original rooted hair in original set, five-piece vinyl child body; wearing original tagged red/white dress, matching panties, socks and black strap shoes. Marked on back of head: "Alexander, 19©61"; marked on wrist tag: "Caroline"; marked "Caroline" on end label of original box; tag on dress also marked: "Madame Alexander, New York, All Rights Reserved." ....**$300-$400** (See photo on page 86.)

2. Caroline. Alexander Doll Company. U.S.A. #4290. 1961. 15 inches. Same as previous doll but wearing pink pants and jacket with matching pink hat. Hang tag on arm. ....$200-$300

The Alexander Doll Company's catalogs listed several different outfits for Caroline including the following: an organdy tea party dress with lace trim, satin sash, slip with matching panties, party slippers and socks, from 1961; a riding habit made with a suede-like cocoa brown and beige material, boots, from 1962; a checked cotton dress with white organdy lace-trimmed collar, from 1962; a play dress with polka dot collar and leotards made of cotton jersey, from 1962 ....$75-$100, in original box

1: Caroline with original box, by the Alexander Doll Company. *Courtesy of McMasters Doll Auctions.*

2: Alexander Doll Company's Caroline in a pink outfit. *Courtesy of Lynnae Ramsey.*

Kennedy (Onassis), Jacqueline Bouvier.

Wife of the thirty-fifth president of the United States, John F. Kennedy. Widowed after his assassination in 1963, she married Greek shipping tycoon Aristotle Onassis in 1968. A passionate supporter of the arts, she eventually had a career as a book editor until her death in 1994. She was mother to Caroline, Patrick, who died a few days after birth, and John Jr., who died in an airplane accident in 1998.

Although not originally advertised as "Jacqueline" dolls, the Alexander Doll Company trademarked the name Jacqueline in 1962.

1. Jacqueline. Alexander Doll Company. U.S.A. #2218. 1961. 21 inches. Vinyl and plastic, fully jointed, dark wig, brown sleep eyes with eyelashes; dressed in a three-piece brocade short coat. Head marked: "ALEXANDER//19©61." ....$600-$700

2. Jackie. Horsman. U.S.A. 1961. 25 inches. All vinyl, rooted hair, blue sleep eyes with long eyelashes, closed mouth, high-heeled feet, small waist. Marked: "HORSMAN//19©61// BC18." ....$75-$125

3. Jacqueline. Alexander Doll Company. U.S.A. #885. 1962. 10 inches. All hard plastic, fully jointed, dark wig, brown sleep eyes with eyelashes; dressed in a pink satin evening gown. ..$400-$500

4. Jacqueline. Alexander Doll Company. U.S.A. #865. 1962. 10 inches. All hard plastic, fully jointed, dark wig, brown sleep eyes with molded eyelashes; dressed in slacks, sweater and matching hat and leather jacket. ......$400-$500

5. Jacqueline. Alexander Doll Company. U.S.A. #886. 1962. 10 inches. All hard plastic, fully jointed, dark wig, brown sleep eyes with eyelashes; dressed in a satin evening gown with stole. Number 894 is the same doll dressed in a two-piece suit. Number 895 is the same doll wearing a sheath dress with a long matching coat. ....$400-$500 each

6. Jacqueline. Alexander Doll Company. U.S.A. #2125. 1962. 21 inches. Vinyl and plastic, fully jointed, dark wig, brown sleep eyes with eyelashes; dressed in a brocade satin side-panel gown. Head marked: "ALEXANDER//19©61." ....$650-$750

7. Jacqueline. Alexander Doll Company. U.S.A. #2130. 1962. 21 inches. Vinyl and plastic, fully jointed, dark wig, brown sleep eyes with eyelashes; dressed in a silver and white brocade evening gown. Head marked: "ALEXANDER//19©61." ....$650-$750

8. Jacqueline. Alexander Doll Company. U.S.A. #2140. 1962. 21 inches. Vinyl and plastic, fully jointed, dark wig, brown sleep eyes with eyelashes; dressed in a full-length ball gown with matching coat. Head marked: "ALEXANDER//19©61." ....**$650-$750**

9. Jacqueline. Alexander Doll Company. U.S.A. #2117. 1962. 21 inches. Vinyl and plastic, fully jointed, dark wig, brown sleep eyes with eyelashes; dressed in riding clothes. Head marked: "ALEXANDER//19©61." ..**$550-$650**

10. Jacqueline. Alexander Doll Company. U.S.A. #2130. 1962. 21 inches. Vinyl and plastic, fully jointed, dark wig, brown sleep eyes with eyelashes; dressed in a silver and white brocade evening gown. Head marked: "ALEXANDER//19©61." ....**$650-$750**

11. Jacqueline Kennedy. Peggy Nisbet. England. #P718. Circa 1970. 7 inches. All plastic; wearing white silk dress. ....**$150-$200**

12. Jackie. Alexander Doll Company. U.S.A. #45200. 1995. 10 inches. All vinyl, fully jointed, sleep eyes; wearing pink suit. Part of the Portfolio Series. ....**$75-$125**

13. Jackie. Alexander Doll Company. U.S.A. #17480. 1998. 10 inches. All vinyl, fully jointed, sleep eyes; wearing beaded cocktail dress. Part of the Portfolio Series. ....**$100-$150**

14. Jackie. Franklin Mint. China. Circa late 1990s. 15 inches. Vinyl, jointed at arms and legs. Several outfits were sold separately. ....**$100-$150**

15. Jackie. Franklin Mint. China. Circa late 1990s. 17 inches. Porcelain, hand-painted features, green eyes, brown wig; wearing a red dress, diamond drop earrings and pearl necklace. ....**$100-$150**

14: Franklin Mint's 15-inch Jackie, circa late 1990s.
Courtesy of McMasters Doll Auctions.

Kennedy, John F.
The thirty-fifth president of the United States, Kennedy served from 1961 until his assassination in 1963. Formerly the Senator from Massachusetts, Kennedy married Jacqueline Bouvier and had three children, Caroline, Patrick who died a few days after birth, and John, Jr., who died in an airplane accident in 1998.

1. John F. Kennedy. Kamar. Japan. Circa 1960s. 8 inches. Vinyl head, molded and painted features, body is cardboard with wire for the arms and legs, half arms and hands are vinyl; wearing brown suit with white shirt and blue/gray tie. Marked on pants: "TRADE-MARK// TKR//FANCY DOLL//JAPAN." Doll is sitting in a rocking chair. ....**$100-$150** (See photos on page 88.)

2. John F Kennedy. Peggy Nisbet. England. #P717. Circa 1970s. 8 inches. All plastic; dressed in suit. ....**$50-$75**

3. John. F. Kennedy. Effanbee Doll Company. China. 1986. 16 inches. All vinyl, painted features; wearing black suit with red tie and white shirt. Part of The Presidents Series. ....**$100-$150**

15: Franklin Mint's 17-inch Jackie, circa late 1990s.
Courtesy of McMasters Doll Auctions.

3: Effanbee's John F. Kennedy, part of The Presidents Series.
Courtesy of McMasters Doll Auctions.

1A: Close-up of Kamar's John F. Kennedy. *Courtesy of McMasters Doll Auctions.*

1B: John F. Kennedy by Kamar without the rocking chair. *Courtesy of McMasters Doll Auctions.*

4. John F. Kennedy as PT 109 Boat Commander (G.I. Joe). Hasbro. China. 2000. 12 inches. Likeness of JFK as G.I. Joe. Box shows picture of JFK on his boat. With many accessories. ....**$25-$40**

Khambatta, Persis. Actress and model

Khambatta was crowned Miss India before moving to the United States and starting a career in films and on television. She has appeared in more than half a dozen films, including the movie *Star Trek: the Motion Picture* (1979), in which she played the beautiful alien Ilia.

1. Ilia. Mego. Hong Kong. #91200/4. 1979. 3 inches. All vinyl, fully jointed, painted features; painted clothing. Sold on card. Copyright by Paramount Pictures Corporation. ....**$15-$20**

2. Ilia. Mego. Hong Kong. #91210/4. 1979. 12 inches. All vinyl, fully jointed, bald head, painted features; painted clothing; dressed in

2A: Ilia, by Mego, as portrayed by Persis Khambatta in *Star Trek: the Motion Picture.*

2B: The back of the box for Ilia sold in Italy.

white uniform from movie. Head marked: "©PPC;" marked on buttock: "© MEGO CORP. 1975//MADE IN HONG KONG." ......**$50-$75**

Kirkpatrick, Chris. (See N'Sync)

Kiss. The musical rock group of the 1970s was known for their black-and-white face paint. The group, whose records have sold millions of copies, consists of four members: Gene Simmons, Paul Stanley, Ace Frehley and Peter Criscoula (Peter Criss). In the late 1990s, the group reunited for touring, traveling the country to sell-out crowds.

1. Gene, Paul, Peter and Ace. Mego. Hong Kong. (Paul—#88000/1, Gene—#88000/2, Peter—#88000/3, Ace—#88000/4.) 1978. 12 inches. All vinyl, jointed, rooted hair, painted features and makeup. Head marked: "© 1978 AUCOIN//MGMT.INC;" marked on back: "©MEGO CORP 1077//MADE IN HONG KONG." Copyright by Aucoin Management, Inc. by agreement with KISS. ....**$75-$100** each

2. Gene, Paul, Peter and Ace. McFarlane Toys. China. 2000. 7 inches. All vinyl, painted and molded features; with guitar and speaker set. Each sold separately. ....**$15-$25** each

1A: Members of Kiss, the musical rock group by Mego: Paul, Ace, Gene and Peter. *Courtesy of McMasters Doll Auctions.*

1B: Members of Kiss, the musical rock group by Mego: Ace, Paul, Peter and Gene. *Courtesy of McMasters Doll Auctions.*

2A: Paul from the rock group Kiss by McFarlane Toys.

2B: The back of the package for Paul.

2C: Peter from the rock group Kiss, with his drum set, by McFarlane Toys.

2D: Ace from the rock group Kiss, by McFarlane Toys.

Knievel, Evel. Knievel's death-defying stunts have made him one of the greatest motorcycle stuntmen of all time. He has appeared in two films, *Seconds to Live* and *Viva Knievel!*, both filmed in 1977.

1. Evel Knievel. Ideal. Hong Kong. #3400-9. 1972. 7 inches. All vinyl, fully jointed, painted hair and features; wearing red jumpsuit, with helmet and swagger stick. Number 3401-9 is the same doll dressed in a white outfit. Number 3402-5 is the same doll dressed in a blue outfit. ....**$15-$25**, each

2. Evel Knievel. Ideal. Hong Kong. 1974 to 1977. #3403-3. 7 inches. All vinyl, molded brown hair, painted features; wearing jumpsuit of red, white and blue, with helmet and a red, white and blue stunt motorcycle with a picture of an eagle's head on the side. Marked: "© 1972 IDEAL/HONG KONG." ....**$20-$30**
(See photo on page 90.)

Marilyn
Knowlden by
Ideal, from
1935.
*Courtesy of
Patricia
Wood.*

Advertisement for the Evel Knievel doll by Ideal.

Knievel, Robbie. The son of Evel Knievel, Robbie followed in the footsteps of his famous father, performing death-defying stunts on his motorcycle.

Robbie Knievel. Ideal. Hong Kong. 1976. #3456-1. 6 inches. All vinyl, wire body for posing, painted hair and features. Unmarked. Portrays son of Evel Knievel at age 13 .... **$20-$30**

Knight, Jon. (See New Kids on the Block).

Knight, Jordan. (See New Kids on the Block).

Knowlden, Marilyn. Actress Knowlden starred in *Imitation of Life* (1935).

Marilyn Knowlden. Ideal Toy Corp. U.S.A. 1935. 13 inches. All composition, jointed, sleep eyes, mohair wig in long braids; wearing red and white dress with white apron top. Marked on back: "USA;" marked on head: "Ideal Doll USA." This doll was meant to be a Shirley Temple doll, but Shirley Temple did not authorize its release so it was renamed after Knowlden. .... **$400-$500**

Kopell, Bernie. Actor Kopell played on a variety of television shows, including *Get Smart* and *Bewitched*. He is best known for his role as Adam "Doc" Bricker on the hit television series *The Love Boat*, which aired from September 1977 to September 1986.

Doc. Mego. Hong Kong. #23005/3. 1982. 3 inch. All vinyl, fully jointed, painted hair and features; molded glasses and clothing. Copyright by Aaron Spelling Productions, Inc. Sold on card. Shows picture of cast on card. .... **$15-$25**

Kulp, Nancy. Actress Kulp is best known for her role as Jane Hathaway, the banker's secretary, from the 1960s television series *The Beverly Hillbillies*, which debuted in 1962.

Miss Hathaway. Maker unknown. Japan. 1969. 9 inches. Plastic, painted features, glued-on blonde wig; wearing green plastic skirt and jacket with yellow blouse and yellow shoes. The doll is unmarked and the only markings on the box are: "Jane Hathaway//of//The Beverly Hillbillies//Fame//1969 Japan." The box has a picture of the character. The doll is cheaply made. .... **$25-$75** (Price range varies due to uncertainty of date of manufacture.)

Miss Hathaway by an unknown Japanese maker. *Courtesy of David Spurgeon.*

L

Ladd, Cheryl. Actress and singer Ladd is best known for her role as Kris Munroe in the hit television series *Charlie's Angels*, which aired on ABC from September 1976 to August 1981. (See also Fawcett, Farrah and Jackson, Kate.)

1. Cheryl Ladd (Kris). Mattel, Inc. Korea. #2494. 1978. 11 inches. All vinyl, fully jointed, rooted blonde hair, painted eyes; wearing red pants under a pleated red skirt, with black and gold braid tied at her waist and across bodice, beauty mark on face. Marked on back of head: "© MATTEL INC. 1978 KOREA;" marked on rear: "©MATTEL INC., INC.//1966//KOREA;" box marked: "She's pretty. She's Clever. She's dynamite." Uses the Barbie body. ....**$40-$50**

2. Kris. Hasbro. Hong Kong. #4850. 1977. 8 inches. All vinyl, fully jointed, rooted blonde hair, painted brown eyes. Copyright by Spelling Goldberg Productions. ....**$25-$30**

3. Charlie's Angels Set. Hasbro. Hong Kong. 1977. 9 inches. Includes all three girls. ....**$175-$225**, set

Lahr, Bert. Actor Lahr began his career as a popular comic in vaudeville and burlesque. He then moved to work on stage and in films. His best-known role is that of the Cowardly Lion in the hit 1939 film *The Wizard of Oz*. (See Garland, Judy for photograph.)

1. Cowardly Lion. Mego. Hong Kong. #51500/3. 1974. 8 inches. All vinyl, jointed, painted features, molded head; wearing costume from the film. Copyright by Metro-Goldwyn-Mayer, Inc. ....**$40-$50**

2. Cowardly Lion from The Wizard of Oz. Ideal Toy Corp. 1984 to 1985. 9 inches. Vinyl, six-piece poseable body; wearing lion outfit from movie. ....**$30-$40**

3. Cowardly Lion. Mattel, Inc. China. 1995. 12 inches. All vinyl, jointed, painted features; wearing costume from movie. ....**$25-$35**

Lake, Veronica. Actress Lake's best-known films include two comedies —*Sullivan's Travels* (1941) and *I Married a Witch* (1942)—and three film-noirs with Alan Ladd (1942 to 1946). Her screen image was one of a cool yet sultry, tough yet vulnerable woman.

Veronica Lake. Film Star Creations, Inc. of Hollywood. U.S.A. 1945. 13 inches. All cloth, mohair wig; dressed in light pink pants with short top, beige shoes. Original tag reads: "Autographed//MOVIE STAR DOLLS," shows her autograph and continues: "POPULAR PARAMOUNT//MOTION PICTURE STAR//MADE IN CALIFORNIA//BY//Film Star Creations, Inc.//of HOLLYWOOD." ....**$450-$550**

A cloth Veronica Lake by Film Star Creations, Inc., from 1945. *Courtesy of Billie Nelson Tyrrell.*

Lamour, Dorothy. Actress Lamour acted in dozens of films from the early 1930s through the early 1950s. Some of her best-remembered roles were in *Thrill of a Lifetime* (1937), *Her Love Jungle* (1938) and *Man About Town* (1939).

Dorothy Lamour. Maker unknown. Circa 1930s. 14 inches. All cloth, mohair wig, painted features; wearing blue dress with flowers, red flower in hair. Original tag reads: "Autographed//MOVIE STAR DOLLS," shows her autograph and continues: "POPULAR PARAMOUNT// MOTION PICTURE STAR//MADE IN CALIFORNIA//BY//Film Star Creations, Inc.//of HOLLYWOOD." Another version is 13 inches, with a cotton yarn-type wig and wears a pink dress with flowers and a pink flower in her hair. ..**$500-$600** each

(See photo on page 92.)

Two all-cloth Dorothy Lamour dolls by Film Star Creations, Inc. *Courtesy of Billie Nelson Tyrrell.*

Lanchester, Elsa.
Actress Lanchester is best remembered for her dual roles in *The Bride of Frankenstein* (1935) as both the monster's mate and his creator, author Mary Shelley.

Bride of Frankenstein. Hasbro. China. #70952/70951 Asst. 1998. 13 inches. All vinyl, painted features on white face with red lips, jet black hair worn on top of head in large bun; wearing full-length white gown with white wrapping around arms and legs. Box marked: "© 1998 Hasbro, Inc." Part of Hasbro's Signature Series. ....**$15-$20**

Hasbro's Bride of Frankenstein, as portrayed by Elsa Lanchester, from the movie by the same name, in her original box. *Courtesy of David Spurgeon.*

Landau, Martin.
Actor Landau appeared with wife Barbara Bain on the television series *Mission Impossible* from 1966 to 1969. Both stars also appeared in *Space 1999*, which debuted in 1975.

1. Space 1999 Commander Koenig. Mattel, Inc. Taiwan. #9542. 1976. 9 inches. All vinyl, fully jointed, dark hair with painted features; wearing yellow uniform with shoes, with stun gun, holster, communicator-computer that clipped to belt. Marked on back of head: "© 1975 ATV LICENSING LTD. TAIWAN;" marked on back: "© 1973/MATTEL, INC./TAIWAN." ....**$50-$75**

2. Space 1999 Commander Koenig. ATV Licensing Ltd. #6347. 1976. 4 inches. Plastic. Called the "Official Space 1999 Parachutist." ....**$20-$30**

3. Eagle One Spaceship. Mattel, Inc. Taiwan. #9548. 1976. 2 feet long with living quarters. Includes 3-inch plastic figures of Professor Bergman, Doctor Russell and Commander Koenig. ......**$150-$200**, complete

Lander, David.
Actor Lander is best known for his role as Andrew "Squiggy" Squigman on the hit television show *Laverne & Shirley* which aired from January 1976 to May 1983.

Lenny and Squiggy. Mego. Hong Kong. #86500/2. 1977. 12 inches. All vinyl, fully jointed, painted features; Lenny wears red jacket with jeans, Squiggy wears black jacket, blue shirt and jeans. Copyright by Paramount Pictures Corporation. Boxed set contained both dolls. ....**$40-$50** each, loose; **$125-$150**, boxed set

David Lander as Squiggy, at right in photo, shown with Michael McKeon as Lenny, from the television series *Laverne and Shirley*. The 12-inch dolls are by Mego.

Lange, Ted.
Actor. Lange is best known for his role as Isaac Washington on the hit television series *The Love Boat* which aired from September 1977 to September 1986.

Isaac. Mego. Hong Kong. #23005/4. 1981. 3¾ inches. All vinyl, fully jointed, painted features; molded clothing. Copyright by Aaron Spelling Productions, Inc. Sold on card. Shows picture of cast on card. ....**$20-$25**

Isaac Washington, as portrayed by Ted Lange, from the television series *Love Boat*. By Mego.

Lansbury, Angela. Actress. Lansbury played the role of Miss Price in the film *Bedknobs and Broomsticks* (1971). Lansbury, the winner of four Tony Awards, found success with her own television series, *Murder She Wrote*, which aired from 1984 to 1996.

Miss Price. Horsman. Hong Kong. 1971. 6 inches. All vinyl, fully jointed, rooted blonde hair, painted blue eyes with long eyelashes; wearing short skirt with matching vest, long-sleeved blouse with tie scarf. Head marked: "HONG KONG." Sold with a metal bed with batteries to "fly." Dolls left over from production were also sold separately. ....**$30-$40**; **$75-$100**, with bed

The back of the box for Lisa Turtle. *Courtesy of David Spurgeon.*

Miss Price, as portrayed by Angela Lansbury, from the film *Bedknobs and Broomsticks.* *Courtesy of David Spurgeon.*

Lark (Lark Voorhies). Actress Lark played the role of Lisa Turtle on the television series *Saved by the Bell*, which aired from 1989 to 1993.

Lark. Tiger Toys. China. #6-115. Circa 1990s. 11 inches. All vinyl, jointed, black rooted hair, painted features; wearing yellow top and multi-colored flowered skirt, boxed with shoes, Bayside High School Yearbook and stamper with Lark's signature. ....**$10-$15**

Lark as Lisa Turtle by Tiger Toys, shown with her accessories. *Courtesy of David Spurgeon.*

Laurel, Stan. Actor Laurel was a successful comedian with his partner, Oliver Hardy. They performed in countless movies in the 1920s and 1930s. (See also Hardy, Oliver.)

1. Laurel and Hardy. Dakin. Circa 1970s. 5 inches. Vinyl wind-up dancing/skating dolls. **$45**

2. Laurel and Hardy. Lakeside Toys. Japan. Circa 1960s. Laurel, 5 inches; Hardy, 4 inches. One-piece vinyl, molded and painted features and clothing. ....**$50-$75**

3. Laurel and Hardy Dolls. Dell. 1962. 7 inches. One-piece vinyl, molded and painted features and clothing. Marked on back: "DELL//©LARRY HARMON PICTURES CORP. 1962//OLIVER LAUREL." (Or "HARDY.") ....**$50-$75**

4. Laurel and Hardy Dolls. Knickerbocker. Japan. Circa 1960s. Laurel, 9 inches; Hardy, 8 inches. Vinyl head, molded features and hat, painted features, cloth body with wire for posing. ......**$40-$60**

Lawless, Lucy. Actress Lawless starred in her own television series *Xena: Warrior Princess*, a spin-off of the popular show *Hercules: The Legendary Journeys*. The show ran for five years, ending in 2001.

1. Xena—Warrior Princess. Toy Biz, Inc. China. #42010. 1998. 12 inches. All vinyl, jointed, painted features, rooted black hair; wearing black and gold warrior mini dress with knee-high black and gold boots, with knife and circle weapon. ....**$15-$20** (See photo on page 94.)

2. Xena—Warrior Princess. Toy Biz, Inc. China. #41005. 1998. 6 inches. All vinyl, jointed, painted features, hair and clothing. Sold with weapons. On card. ....**$5-$10**

3. Xena. E Toys, a division of TNA Products. China. #98261. Circa 1990s. All vinyl, painted features; wearing Xena outfit. ..**$10-$15**

1: Xena–Warrior Princess by Toy Biz, Inc., played by Lucy Lawless. *Courtesy of David Spurgeon.*

Lawrence, Joey. Actor Lawrence starred in the television sitcom *Blossom*, which aired from January 1991 until June 1995, playing the role of Joey Russo, Blossom's teenage brother.

Joey Russo. Tyco Industries. People's Republic of China. #1905. 1993. 9 inches. All vinyl, jointed, painted features with smiling mouth and teeth, molded brown hair; dressed in jeans, white T-shirt, black jacket with red and black plaid shirt tied at waist, sold with two different outfits, shoes and microphone. Box marked: "©1993 Tyco Industries." ......**$20-$30**

Joey Russo, played by Joey Lawrence, from *Blossom*, with his extra clothes. *Author's collection.*

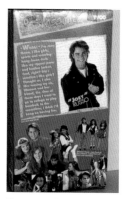

The back of the box for Joey Russo. *Author's collection.*

Learned, Michael. Actress Learned is best known for her role as the mother, Olivia Walton, on the television series *The Waltons*, which aired from September 1972 to August 1981. In 1981, Learned starred in her own series *Nurse*.

Mom. Mego. Hong Kong. #56000/2 (Mom and Pop) 1974. 8 inches. All vinyl, fully jointed, painted features, rooted blonde hair; wearing a blue-and-white dress with long white apron. Head marked: "© 1974//LORIMAR INC." Mom was sold singly and in a pack with Pop. ......**$15-$20**, loose; **$25-$30**, boxed, singly; **$40-$50**, boxed, pair

Mom from *The Waltons*, as portrayed by Michael Learned, shown with John Walton, played by Ralph Waite. (See Waite, Ralph for additional photograph.)

Lee, Brandon. The son of famous martial arts man Bruce Lee, Brandon Lee began a promising career as an actor. During the filming of the movie *The Crow* (1994), in which he starred, Lee was killed by an accidental gun shot.

Brandon Lee from The Crow. McFarlane Toys. China. 1999. 6 inches. All vinyl, long black hair with painted face and features; black vinyl painted outfit, came with guitar and stand. Part of the Movie Maniacs Collection. Sold on a card. ....**$20-$25**

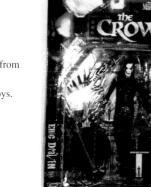

Brandon Lee from *The Crow* by McFarlane Toys. *Courtesy of David Cox.*

Lee, Bruce.
Lee was a martial arts dynamo who became popular showcasing his skills in many action films produced in Hong Kong. Among his early roles, Lee played Kato on the 1966-1967 television series *The Green Hornet.*

1. Kato. Largo. China. 7 inches. 1983. All vinyl, jointed. Available three ways including Tournament GI, Training GI and Nunchaku and staff. ....**$75-$100**

2. Kato. Playing Mantis. China. 1998. 11 inches. Includes Captain Action in Kato costume, brass knuckles, Ninja-style throwing stars, Nanchakus and micro-radar watch ....**$40-$50**

3. Bruce Lee. Medicom. Japan. 8 inches. All vinyl, jointed, painted features; wearing all black outfit of pants, long-sleeved shirt and shoes. Packaged on card. Sold in three styles. ..**$15-$20**

3: Bruce Lee by Medicom. *Courtesy of David Cox.*

Leick, Hudson.
Actress Leick is best known for her role as Callisto on the Warner Brothers television series *Xena: Warrior Princess.* The show ran for five years, ending in 2001.

Callisto. Toy Biz. China. #42013. 1998. 12 inches. All vinyl, painted features, rooted long blonde hair; wearing black and gold mini shorts, black and gold short top with black and gold boots, black and gold armbands, boxed with knife and sword. Box marked: "TM and © 1998 Toy Biz, Inc." ....**$15-$20**

Callisto from *Xena: Warrior Princess* as played by Hudson Leick. *Courtesy of David Spurgeon.*

Leigh, Janet.
Actress Leigh played the role of Meg in *Little Women* (1949). In 1960, she earned an Oscar nomination for best supporting actress for her role in Alfred Hitchcock's *Psycho*. The role won her a Golden Globe that same year.

Meg. Ideal Toy Corp. 1984 to 1988. 12 inches. Vinyl, jointed, sleep eyes with eyelashes, rooted hair; dressed as Meg from *Little Women.* Marked on head: "©1978 MGM/CBS INC/1438 IDEAL 1982." ....**$40-$50**

Leigh, Vivien.
Actress Leigh appeared in several films. She is best known for her role as Scarlett O'Hara in the film *Gone With the Wind* (1939), for which she won an Academy Award.

The Alexander Doll Company produced more than three dozen Scarlett O'Hara dolls.

1. Scarlett O'Hara. Alexander Doll Company. U.S.A. 1940. Various sizes. All composition, fully jointed, black wig, green sleep eyes; dressed in various costumes. ....11 inches, **$500-$600**, 14-16 inches, **$600-$700**; 18 inches, **$800-$1,000**; and 21 inches, **$1,000** up (See photo on page 96.)

2. Scarlett O'Hara. Alexander Doll Company. U.S.A. 1950. 14 inches. All hard plastic, fully jointed, black wig, sleep eyes; various costumes. ....**$1,200** up

3. Scarlett O'Hara. Alexander Doll Company. U.S.A. 1955. 8 inches. All hard plastic, sleep eyes; wearing print gown. ..**$1,000** up

4. Scarlett O'Hara. Alexander Doll Company. U.S.A. 1968. 21 inches. Vinyl, plastic, fully jointed, using the "Jacqueline" doll, dark wig, green sleep eyes with eyelashes; wearing white gown with print. ....**$800-$1,000**

5. Scarlett O'Hara. Alexander Doll Company. U.S.A. 1975. 21 inches. Vinyl, plastic, jointed, using the "Jacqueline" doll; wearing green velvet dress. ....**$350-$450**

6. Scarlett O'Hara. Peggy Nisbet. England. #P751. Circa 1977. 7 inch. Plastic; dressed in gown. ....**$100-$150**

7. Scarlett O'Hara. Ann Parker. England. 1982. 11 inches. Plastic, with attached doll stand, mohair wig, painted features; wearing Scarlett gown. ....**$150-$200**

8. Scarlett O'Hara. Franklin Mint. 1985 to 2000. Various dolls produced in different sizes. Porcelain with painted features; wearing off-the-shoulder green dress, with hat and shawl. Heirloom Doll. ....15 inches, **$75-$100**; 19 inches, **$100-$150**; 22 inches, **$150-$200**

Two Scarlett dolls by Alexander Doll Company in identical outfits. The 8-inch doll is hard plastic, while the 14-inch one is vinyl. *Courtesy of Sunnie Newell.*

All-original 17-inch composition Scarlett O'Hara by Alexander Doll Company. *Courtesy of McMasters Doll Auctions.*

All-original 14-inch composition Scarlett in her Southern Belle outfit, circa 1942, is valued at $700-$900. *Courtesy of Patricia Wood.*

A 14-inch composition Scarlett, in a very rare outfit, with her original box, made by Alexander Doll Company, is valued at $700-$900. *Courtesy of Patricia Wood.*

The Alexander Doll Company's 11-inch Scarlett O'Hara with original wrist tag and box is valued at $700-$900. *Courtesy of McMasters Doll Auctions.*

Lennon, John. (See Beatles, The)

Lewis, Shari. An actress, children's television show host and puppeteer, Lewis and her puppet, Lambchop, were a hit with children for years. Some of her television shows included *Facts 'N' Fun, Shari and Her Friends* and *The Shari Lewis Show*, which aired from 1960 until 1963 and again in 1975.

1. Shari Lewis. Alexander Doll Company. U.S.A. #1430. 1959 to 1960. 14 inches. All hard plastic, fully jointed, auburn wig, brown sleep eyes with eyelashes, high-heeled feet; dressed in gold lace short gown. This doll was also sold in a 21-inch version, #2430. ....14 inches, **$400-$600**; 21 inches, **$600-$800**.

2. Shari Lewis. Alexander Doll Company. U.S.A. #1433. 1959 to 1960. 14 inches. Same doll as above but wearing a green skirt with a rayon blouse. The 21-inch version of this doll is #2433. ....14 inches, **$400-$600**; 21 inches, **$600-$800**

3. Shari Lewis. Alexander Doll Company. U.S.A. #1440. 1959 to 1960. 14 inches. Same doll as above but wearing a costume of heavy satin with a lined coat. The 21-inch version of this doll is #2440. ....14 inches, **$400-$600**; 21 inches, **$600-$800**

4. Shari Lewis Paper Dolls. Whitman. U.S.A. Circa 1960s. ....**$40-$50**

4: Shari Lewis paper dolls by Whitman. *Courtesy of Steve Malatinsky.*

Liberace. The flamboyant singer and piano player was as well known for his elaborate outfits and trademark candelabra as for his musical talent.

Liberace. Effanbee Doll Company. China. 1986. 17 inches. Vinyl, painted features; wearing elaborate outfit. The Effanbee Doll Co. produced a variety of limited-edition dolls with numbered certificates. Many of the dolls could only be purchased through Effanbee's Limited Edition Doll Club or the secondary market. This doll is also known as "Mr. Showman." Part of the Legend Series. ....**$150-$200**

Lindbergh, Charles A. Nicknamed "Lucky Lindy," Aviator Lindbergh was the first person to fly non-stop over the Atlantic Ocean from New York to Paris in 1927.

1. Our Lindy. Regal Doll Co. Circa 1928. 28 inches. Sculpted by E. Peruggi. Composition, molded dark-blonde hair, painted features, cloth body; wearing flight suit with fur collar. Shoulder plate marked: "© REGAL DOLL CO//"SCULP" E. PERRUGGI//1928." ....**$500-$600**

2. Lucky Lindy. Uneeda Doll Co. U.S.A. 1927. 14 inches. Composition and cloth; wearing brown aviator suit. ....**$300-$400**

3. Lucky Lindy. Faith Wick. U.S.A. 1981. 20 inches. Porcelain head, painted brown hair, blue eyes, body is stuffed cloth with wire arms for posing; wearing one-piece tan aviator's outfit with brown fur-type collar, brown shoes, came with brown mitten-type gloves. Shoulder plate marked: "F.W." Produced for the UFDC National Convention in 1981. ....**$200-$300** (See photo on page 98.)

1: Our Lindy, Regal Doll Co.'s version of Charles Lindbergh. *Courtesy of Rosalie Whyel Museum of Doll Art.*

3: Faith Wick's Lucky Lindy, the UFDC Convention souvenir in 1981. *Author's collection.*

Lindros, Eric. Celebrated hockey player Lindros also co-authored *Fire on Ice* with Randy Starkman. Playing for the Philadelphia Flyers as #88, Lindros has won countless awards and is considered one of the greatest hockey players in the league.

Eric Lindros. McFarlane Toys. China. 2000. 6 inches. Part of a series of hockey players produced through McFarlane Toys. Other figures include Mark Messier, Patrick Roy and Steve Yzerman. ....$15-$25 each.

Hockey player Eric Lindros by McFarlane Toys.

Lithgow, John. Actor Lithgow has starred in dozens of films. One of his best-known roles was that of Roberta Muldoon, the transsexual football player in *The World According to Garp* (1982). Lithgow starred as George Henderson in the film *Harry and the Hendersons* (1987) and has enjoyed success on television with his hit series *3rd Rock From the Sun,* which began airing in 1996.

Harry and the Hendersons. JusToys. China. Circa 1987. #12023. 6 inches. All vinyl, painted and molded features, bendable poseable character figure. Sold on card. ....$10-$15

Little Colonel, The. (See Temple, Shirley)

Little Ricky. (See Keith, Richard)

Liu, Lucy. Actress Liu has starred on television and in films. She plays a regular on the current hit television series *Ally McBeal* and starred in the film *Molly* (1999). One of her more recent film roles was playing the part of Alex in the 2000 movie version of the 1970s television series *Charlie's Angels*. The movie also starred Drew Barrymore and Cameron Diaz.

Alex from Charlie's Angels. Jakks Pacific Inc. China. 2000. 11 inches. All vinyl, fully jointed, rooted black hair, painted features; wearing burgundy jacket with black pants, boxed with stand and clothes hanger, also sold dressed in a red one-piece jumpsuit with spaghetti straps. Box marked: "Action-Fashion Body I've got all the right poses! Charlie's Angels: TM & © 2000 Columbia Pictures Industries, Inc." ....$25-$40

The three new Charlie's Angels—Drew Barrymore, Lucy Liu and Cameron Diaz—from the 2000 *Charlie's Angels* movie.

Lugosi, Bela. Born near Transylvania, Actor Lugosi appeared in his first American film, *The Silent Command*, in 1923. Throughout the 1920s, he starred on stage and in films, including *Daughters Who Pay* (1925) and *How to Handle Women* (1928). In 1931, he played the bloodsucking Transylvanian Count Dracula, a role that turned him into a major star of the time and an American film legend.

1. Bela Lugosi as Dracula. Flatt World Manufacturing. 1999. 8 inches. All vinyl, painted hair and features; wearing black pants, a black jacket, and white shirt with red tie and emblem around his neck, holding candle; with coffin base. Designed by Moore Creations. **$150**

2. Dracula. Side Show Toys. China. 1999. 8 inches. Molded and painted vinyl with black plastic stand; heads are spring loaded and bob up and down (bobble-heads). The name of the character appears on the base. Part of the Universal Monsters Collection. ....**$20-$30**, each

1: Bela Lugosi as Dracula by Flatt World Manufacturing. *Courtesy of David Cox.*

2: Dracula by Side Show Toys, shown with Frankenstein, The Mummy and The Wolf Man. *Courtesy of David Cox.*

M

MacArthur, Douglas.
World War II hero MacArthur was a general in the United States Army who coined the phrase "Old soldiers never die, they just fade away."

1. General Douglas MacArthur. Freundlich Novelty Corp. 1940s. 18 inches. All composition, painted features; wearing khaki-green military uniform with molded hat. Unmarked except for paper tag on uniform which reads: "General MacArthur, Made in 1942." ....**$275-$375**

2. General Douglas MacArthur. Excel Toy. Corp. Hong Kong. 1974. 9 inches. All vinyl, fully jointed, painted hair and features; wearing military uniform. ....**$40-$60**

3. General Douglas MacArthur. Effanbee Doll Company. 1991. All vinyl, jointed, painted features; wearing military uniform. Part of the World's Greatest Heroes Series. ....**$75-$125**

1: General Douglas MacArthur by Freundlich Novelty Corp. *Author's collection.*

MacLeod, Gavin.
Actor MacLeod is best known for his role as Captain Merrill Stubing on the hit television series *The Love Boat,* which aired from September 1977 to September 1986.

Gavin MacLeod as Captain Stubing, by Mego.

Captain Stubing. Mego. Hong Kong. #23005/1. 1981. 3 inches. All vinyl, fully jointed, painted gray hair and features. Sold on card that shows picture of cast. Copyright by Aaron Spelling Productions, Inc. ....**$15-$20**

Madison, Dolley.
First lady Madison was the wife of President James Madison, the fourth president of the United States.

Dolley Madison. Alexander Doll Company. U.S.A. 1976 to 1978. 14 inches. All vinyl, fully jointed, rooted brown hair, sleep eyes with eyelashes; wearing a silver floral dress. Part of the First Ladies Series. ....**$100-$120**

Mahoney, Jerry.
Mahoney was ventriloquist Paul Winchell's dummy and was better known than the man who brought him to life.

Jerry Mahoney. Juro Novelty Co. U.S.A. Circa 1940s. 24 inches. Composition head, feet and hands with stuffed cloth ventriloquist body, molded hair, painted features; wearing a two-tone flannel and gabardine suit with red-and-white-dotted bow tie. He was advertised as an "Exact replica of the wise-cracking ventriloquist dummy with a movable head and mouth. He'll provide laughs galore for his friends." Originally sold for $6.49. ....**$200-$250**; **$300-$400**, with box

Paul Winchell's dummy, Jerry Mahoney, by Juro Novelty Co. with its box.

This nice example of a Jerry Mahoney dummy wearing a black-and-white checked outfit, by an unknown maker, is valued at $500 up. *Courtesy of Patricia Woods.*

Majors, Lee. Actor Majors is best known for his role as Steve Austin (The Bionic Man) on the television series *The Six Million Dollar Man*, which aired from October 1973 to February 1978. He was married to actress Farrah Fawcett.

1. Bionic Man—Maskatron, The Six Million Dollar Man's Enemy. Kenner. U.S.A. 1976. 12 inches. Kenner made the United States version while Denys Fisher made the United Kingdom version. The doll has three faces and can disguise itself as Colonel Steve Austin or Oscar Goldman or stay Maskatron. Box marked: "Kenner © 1976 General Mills Food Group, Inc. Character © 1973 Universal City Studios. Made in U.S.A." ....$30-$40, loose; $100-$150, boxed, U.S.A. version; $150-$200, boxed, U.K. version

2. Steve Austin. Lili Ledy. Mexico. 1974. All vinyl, jointed; shows Bionic Man in red outfit. ....$15-$20, loose; $75-$100, boxed

3. Steve Austin. Kenner. Various versions made between 1975 and 1978. All 12 inches. No. 1: dressed in red jogging suit with engine block (1975); No. 2: marked "New Bionic Grip," dressed in red jogging suit with a steel beam and a gripping right hand (1977); No. 3: marked "New Bionic Arm with bionic grip," dressed in jeans and red top with gripping right hand, karate action feature, blocks and boards (1978); No. 4: similar to No. 1 but packaged with outfits. ....No. 1 and No. 2 dolls: $20-$30, loose; $125-$150; No. 3 and No. 4 dolls: $250-$300

4. Dr. Kromedome. Steve Austin opponent. Mego. 1975. 12 inches. All vinyl, jointed except left leg and arm are chrome; dressed in purple jumpsuit with cape. Exclusive sold only through Montgomery Ward. ....$75-$100, loose; $350-$400, boxed

1A: Maskatron by Kenner, enemy of the Six Million Dollar Man. *Courtesy of Suellen Manning.*

1B: Close-up of Maskatron by Kenner. *Courtesy of Suellen Manning.*

3A: Lee Majors as Steve Austin, the Six Million Dollar Man, by Kenner, from 1977. *Courtesy of Suellen Manning.*

3B: The Six Million Dollar Man, Steve Austin, with a new biosonic arm, by Kenner, from 1978. *Courtesy of Suellen Manning.*

Malcolm X (Malcolm Little). African-American Muslim Leader Malcolm X, who led the Nation of Islam group and was known as "the angriest black man in America," was killed in the Audubon Ballroom in Harlem on February 21, 1965. With the help of author Alex Haley, he wrote *The Autobiography of Malcolm X.*

Malcolm X. Olmec Toys. China. 10026. 1994. 6 inches. All vinyl, molded and painted clothing and features; wearing plastic glasses, boxed with speaker's stand. Box marked "© Olmec Toys, Inc." ....$25-$35 (See photo on page 102.)

Malcolm X by Olmec Toys. *Courtesy of David Spurgeon.*

Mansfield, Jayne. Actress Mansfield starred in films in the 1950s and was considered a sex symbol.

Jayne Mansfield. Maker unknown. Circa 1950s. About 12 inches. Composition, molded figure and hair, molded and painted features; painted clothing. Since the doll is probably a one-of-a-kind, the value is not known.

Publicity photograph of Jayne Mansfield shown with the doll made in her likeness. *Author's collection.*

Mantle, Mickey. Legendary baseball player Mantle was an outfielder and first baseman for the New York Yankees, hitting 536 career home runs. He was inducted into the Baseball Hall of Fame in 1974.

Mickey Mantle Nodder. Company unknown. Japan. Circa 1960s. All composition, painted and molded features with hat; wearing Yankees uniform, copy of Mantle's signature at the bottom of stand. ....$50-$75

Margaret Rose (Princess). Margaret Rose is the sister of Queen Elizabeth the II.

1. H.R.H. Princess Margaret Rose. Chad Valley. England. 1938. 17 inches. Jointed cloth doll, pressed felt head, brown mohair wig, blue glass inset eyes, body is stuffed velveteen; wear-

ing pink felt coat with pink hat. Marked on right foot: "HYGENIC TOYS//MADE IN ENGLAND BY//CHAD VALLEY CO.LTD." ....$1,000 up

2. Margaret Rose. Alexander Doll Company. U.S.A. 1952. 14 inches. All hard plastic, fully jointed, blonde mohair wig, blue sleep eyes with eyelashes; wearing pink gown. Unmarked. ....$700-$800

3. Margaret Rose. Alexander Doll Company. U.S.A. #5023. 1952. 21 inches. All hard plastic, fully jointed, blonde mohair wig, blue sleep eyes; dressed in pink and white gown. Head marked: "A.L." ....$1,000 up

4. Margaret Rose. Tower Treasures Limited. England. 1979. 15 inches. Bisque head, painted features, synthetic wig, bisque arms and legs, stuffed body; wearing cotton dress with straw hat. ....$150-$250

Marie Antoinette. The 18th-century Queen of France was born November 2, 1755, in Vienna, Austria. She was the youngest daughter of Francis I and Maria Theresa, Emperor and Empress of the Holy Roman Empire. In 1792 the French royal family was arrested on suspicion of treason. Her husband, King Louis XVI, was convicted and executed. Antoinette was imprisoned and treated cruelly. On October 16, 1793, she too was executed.

1. Marie Antoinette. Alexander Doll Company. U.S.A. Circa 1940s. 21 inches. Composition, jointed; dressed in elaborate outfit. ....$1,200-$1,500

2. Marie Antoinette. Peggy Nisbet. England. #H215. Circa 1970s. 7 inches. Plastic. Part of the French Court Series, which included Madame Pompadour and Madame du Barry. ....$75-$100

3. Marie Antoinette. Peggy Nisbet. England. #P459. Circa 1970s. 7½ inches. Plastic ..$50-$75

4. Marie Antoinette. Alexander Doll Company. U.S.A. 1987 to 1988. 21 inches. All vinyl, jointed; wearing elaborate gown. ....$250-$300

Marshall, Penny. Actress and director Marshall is best known for her role as Laverne DeFazio on the hit television series *Laverne & Shirley*, which aired from January 1976 to May 1983. Marshall went behind the camera to become a successful director.

Laverne & Shirley. Mego. Hong Kong. #86500/1. 1977. 11 inches. All vinyl, fully jointed; both are wearing dresses, Laverne's is long-sleeved with the letter "L" on the left top part of dress. Boxed set with two dolls. .... $40-$50 each, loose; $125-$150, boxed set

Martin, Lori. Actress Martin played Velvet Brown on the television program *National Velvet*, which aired on NBC from 1960 until 1962.

Lori Martin. Ideal Toy Corp. U.S.A. 1961. 30 inches to 38 inches. Vinyl head, rooted brown hair, plastic body, fully jointed, twist waist and twist ankles, blue sleep eyes with eyelashes. Head marked: "METRO GOLDWYN MAYER INC//MFG BY//IDEAL TOY CORP.//38;" back marked: "© IDEAL TOY CORP//G-38." ....30 inches, **$400-$500**; 36-38 inches, **$500-$600**

Martin, Mary. Actress and singer Martin appeared in a variety of films. On Broadway, Martin starred in *South Pacific* (1949), *Peter Pan* (1954) and *The Sound of Music* (1959) . Her son is actor Larry Hagman, J.R. of *Dallas* fame.

1. Mary Martin. Alexander Doll Company. U.S.A. 1949. 14 inches. All hard plastic, fully jointed, curly wig, sleep eyes with eyelashes; dressed in sailor suit from South Pacific. ....**$700-$850**

2. Mary Martin. Alexander Doll Company. U.S.A. 1950. 14 inches. All hard plastic, fully jointed, curly wig, sleep eyes with eyelashes; dressed in white ball gown from South Pacific. ....**$700-$850**

3. Mary Martin. Alexander Doll Company. U.S.A. 1950. 17 inches. All hard plastic, fully jointed, curly wig, sleep eyes with eyelashes; dressed in white ball gown from South Pacific. ....**$700-$850**

Marx, Groucho. Comedian Marx had a successful vaudeville act with his brothers Harpo, Zeppo, Chico and Gummo. Their ensuing career in films lasted for more than twenty years. From 1950 until 1961, Marx hosted the NBC television show *You Bet Your Life*.

1. Groucho Marx. La Nina. Spain. 1979. 22 inches. All stuffed cloth, black yarn hair, button eyes, mustache; wearing a tuxedo with black felt coat with tails, black felt shoes, wire glasses, felt cigar. ....**$150-$200**

2. Groucho Marx. Juro. #30. 1981. 30 inches. Ventriloquist doll with vinyl head and hands, stuffed cloth body, painted black hair, painted brown eyes. Head marked: "GROUCHO MARX//©EEGEE CO. INC." ....**$50-$75**

3. Groucho Marx. Effanbee Doll Company. China. 1983. 17 inches. All vinyl, painted features; wearing black and white outfit. The Effanbee Doll Co. produced a variety of limited-edition dolls with numbered certificates. Many of the dolls

could only be purchased through Effanbee's Limited Edition Doll Club or the secondary market. Part of the Legend Series. ....**$100-$125**

4. Groucho Marx. Classic Headliners. Equity Marketing Inc. China. 2000. 6 inches. Molded vinyl, molded and painted features; wearing black striped pants, white shirt with black tie, black jacket and vinyl wire-rimmed glasses. Very realistic looking. Stands on base with his name engraved in base. Limited edition of 20,000. ....**$10-$15**

2B: Close-up of Groucho Marx ventriloquist doll by Juro. *Courtesy of David Spurgeon.*

2A: Groucho Marx ventriloquist doll by Juro. *Courtesy of David Spurgeon.*

4: Groucho Marx by Classic Headliners. *Courtesy of David Cox.*

Mary Poppins. (See Andrews, Julie)

Maxwell, Lois. Maxwell appeared in two James Bond films in the role of Miss Money Penny—*Dr. No* (1962) and *A View to a Kill* (1985). Other actresses played the role of Miss Money Penny in later films: Caroline Bliss (*The Living Daylights–1987* and *License to Kill–1989*) and Samantha Bond (*Golden Eye–1995*).

Miss Money Penny. Maker unknown. Japan. 1963. 9 inches. Cheaply made, plastic, painted features, glued-on brunette wig; wearing blue plastic dress with gold belt and silver shoes. The doll is unmarked and the only markings on the box are: "Miss Money Penny//of//James Bond//Fame//1963 Japan." The box shows a picture of the character. ....**$25-$75** (Price range varies due to uncertainty of date of manufacture.)

Lois Maxwell as Miss Money Penny by an unknown maker. *Courtesy of David Spurgeon.*

McCallum, David. McCallum is best known for his role in the hit television show *The Man from U.N.C.L.E.* (1964-1968) (See Vaughn, Robert for photo.)

David McCallum—The Man From U.N.C.L.E.—"Illya Kuryakin." Gilbert Company. U.S.A. 1965. 12 inches. All vinyl, fully jointed, painted molded blonde hair and features; wearing black turtleneck and black pants. Head marked with symbols. ....**$100-$150**

McCarthy, Charlie. Edgar Bergen's ventriloquist dummy was also his sidekick.

1. Charlie McCarthy. Effanbee. U.S.A. 1938. 20 inches. Composition head, hands and feet with stuffed body, mouth opens and closes, painted features; wears black pants, shoes and tweed jacket with white shirt and eyeglass. ....**$500-$600**

2. Charlie McCarthy. Effanbee. U.S.A. 1938. 20 inches. Composition head, hands and feet with stuffed body, mouth opens and closes, painted features; wears black tuxedo, monocle and top hat. Original box marked: "Edgar Bergen's Charlie McCarthy, an Effanbee Product." ....**$750-$850**

3. Charlie McCarthy. Ideal Toy Corp. 1938 to 1939. 8 inches. Hand puppet with composition head, cloth body, felt hands, molded hat, painted features, painted tuxedo. Marked on front: "Edgar Bergen's//©CHARLIE// McCARTHY//Made in U.S.A." ....**$75-$125**

4. Charlie McCarthy. Unmarked. Circa 1940s. 8 inches. All composition, open/closed

mouth, painted features; painted and molded clothing. ....**$50-$75**

5. Charlie McCarthy. Jamar Specialty Company. U.S.A. Circa 1940s. 5 inches. All wood, jointed, painted features; painted clothing, black wood top hat. Fun-E-Flex type arms. ..**$100-$150**

2: Charlie McCarthy, Edgar Bergen's ventriloquist dummy, by Effanbee. *Courtesy of McMasters Doll Auctions.*

3: Charlie McCarthy hand puppet by Ideal. *Author's collection.*

5: A wooden Charlie McCarthy by Jamar Specialty Company. *Courtesy of Ronnie Kauk.*

Charlie McCarthy in an advertisement for General Electric with Edgar Bergen. *Author's collection.*

McCartney, Paul. (See Beatles, The)

McIntyre, Joey. (See New Kids on the Block)

McKean, Michael. Actor McKean starred in the role of Lenny Kosnowski in the hit television show *Laverne & Shirley,* which aired from January 1976 to May 1983. (See Lander, David for photograph.)

Lenny and Squiggy. Mego. Hong Kong. 1977. Boxed set contains both dolls. Vinyl, painted features; Lenny wears red jacket with jeans, Squiggy wears black jacket, blue shirt and jeans. ....**$40-$50** each, loose; **$125-$150**, boxed set

McKeen, Sunny (Jim). As a baby in the late 1920s, actor McKeen played Baby Snookums in the silent comedy series *The Newlyweds and Their Baby.* He died at the age of eight.

Snookums. Madame Hendren. 1929. 12 inches and 14 inches. Composition head and arms, cloth body, painted hair and features, open/closed mouth with painted teeth. ....**$850-$1,000**

Sunny McKeen as Baby Snookums by Madame Hendren. *Courtesy of Billie Nelson Tyrrell.*

McNichol, Kristy. Actress McNichol is best known for her starring role as Buddy in the hit television series *Family,* which aired from 1976 to 1980.

1. Kristy McNichol. Mego. Hong Kong. #86400. 1978. 9 inches. All vinyl, poseable, rooted brown hair, painted eyes; wearing blue jeans, red sweater and white shirt. Head marked: "© MEGO CORP.//MADE IN HONG KONG;" back marked: "© 1977 MEGO CORP//MADE IN HONG KONG." Box shows picture of Kristy McNichol on the cover. ....**$50-$75**, boxed

2. Kristy McNichol as Buddy. Mattel, Inc. Philippines. #1013. 1978. 9 inches. All vinyl, fully jointed, rooted brown hair, painted brown eyes, painted teeth; wearing Buddy logo shirt, blue jeans and red shirt, extra clothing includes jacket, cap, shirt and sandals. Head marked: "© 1978//SPELLING-GOLDBERG//PROD." Box shows picture of Kristy McNichol with smaller photograph of the entire cast. ..**$40-$60**, boxed

2A: Kristy McNichol as Buddy from the television show *Family,* by Mattel. *Author's collection.*

2B: Kristy McNichol as Buddy, in her original box. *Author's collection.*

2C: The back of the box for Kristy McNichol. *Author's collection.*

Menzies, Heather. Actress Menzies starred as Louisa in the 1965 movie classic *The Sound of Music*. She later starred in various films and on television.

1. Louisa. Alexander Doll Company. U.S.A. #1004. 1965. 8 inches. All hard plastic, fully jointed, rooted blonde hair, sleep eyes; dressed in outfit from *The Sound of Music*. Part of set. ....**$150-$250**

2. Louisa. Alexander Doll Company. U.S.A. #1404. 1965 to 1970. 14 inches. All vinyl, fully jointed, rooted blonde hair, sleep eyes; wearing dress from *The Sound of Music*. Head marked: "ALEXANDER //19©65." Part of set. **$200-$250**

3. Louisa. Alexander Doll Company. U.S.A. #1404. 1966. 14 inches. All vinyl, fully jointed, rooted blonde hair, sleep eyes; dressed in school uniform/sailor outfit from *The Sound of Music*. Head marked: "ALEXANDER //19©65." Part of set. ....**$200-$250**

4. Louisa. Alexander Doll Company. U.S.A. #1104. 1971. 9 inches. All hard plastic, fully jointed, rooted blonde hair, sleep eyes; wearing dress from *The Sound of Music*. Head marked: "ALEXANDER//19©65." Part of set. ..**$250-$300**

Meredith, Burgess. Actor and director Meredith has appeared in films and on television, and is best known for his guest roles as the Penguin, Batman's rival, in the television series *Batman*, which ran from 1966 until 1968.

Penguin. Mego. Hong Kong. #1350. 1974. 8 inches. All vinyl, fully jointed, painted features. ....**$20-$30**

Meriwether, Lee. Actress Meriwether starred in the role of Cat Woman on the television series *Batman*, which aired from 1966 to 1968. She also appeared in the television series *Barnaby Jones* as Betty for eight years. Meriwether currently stars on the daytime soap opera *All My Children* in the role of Ruth Martin. She is also a former Miss America.

2: Mego's 8-inch Catwoman, as portrayed by Lee Meriwether, on the television series *Batman*.

1. Cat Woman. Mego. 1972. 5 inches. All vinyl, painted features; painted clothing. Super Hero Bendable series. ....**$100-$135**

2. Cat Woman. Mego. 1972. 8 inches. All vinyl, painted features. Super Hero Bendable series. ....**$400-$500**

3. Cat Woman. Kenner. China. 1992 to 1993. 11 inches. All vinyl, jointed; wearing Cat Woman outfit from show. From the Batman Returns series. ....**$15-$20**

Midler, Bette. Singer, actress and producer Midler has starred in a variety of feature films including *The First Wives Club* (1996) and *What Women Want* (2000). She received an Oscar nomination for Best Actress (1979) for her role in the film *The Rose*.

Bette Midler as Delores de Lago. Miss M. Productions. 1999. 12 inches. All vinyl, jointed, blonde hair with painted features; wearing mermaid outfit. These dolls were sold exclusively at Bette Midler's Divine Miss Millennium Tour and were limited to 5,000 pieces. Also known as The Divine Miss M doll. ....**$50-$75**

Bette Midler as Delores de Lago, 12 inches, from Miss M. Productions. *Author's collection.*

Mills, Hayley. Actress Mills, daughter of English actor Sir John Mills and writer Mary Hayley Bell, starred in more than two dozen films, but is best known for her role as Pollyanna in the Disney film *Pollyanna* (1960). The performance earned her an Academy Award.

Pollyanna. Uneeda. U.S.A. 1960. Various sizes. All vinyl, fully jointed, rooted blonde hair, sleep eyes with eyelashes, high-heeled feet; wearing a red-and-white-checked dress with panties and straw hat. Copyright by Walt Disney Productions. ....10 inches, **$40-$50**; 17 inches, **$100-$125**; 31 inches, **$125-$150**, 35 inches, **$150-$200**

Mills, Juliet. Actress Mills, sister of Hayley Mills, is best known for her role as Phoebe Figalilly, Nanny on the television series *Nanny and the Professor*, which aired from January 1970 to December 1971. From the 1960s to the early 1980s, Mills appeared in more than a dozen films.

Nanny Paper Dolls. Artcraft. 1971. Shows Nanny on the cover with the children in the background. ....**$15-$20**, cut; **$30-$40**, uncut

Mindy. (See Dawber, Pam)

Momsen, Taylor. Child actress Momsen starred in the 2000 film *How The Grinch Stole Christmas* in the role of Cindy Lou Who.

Cindy Lou Who. Playmates. China. Asst.#40310. Stock #40313. 2000. 14 inches. Vinyl and molded face, painted features, cloth body, hair is up high in braids (push her stomach and her hair flies around); wearing two-piece pink pajama outfit with white collar trim, pink furry slippers. Excellent likeness to actress. ....**$20-$30**

Monkees, The. This musical group was comprised of four members: Davy Jones, Mickey Dolenz, Mike Nesmith and Peter Tork. *The Monkees* television show aired from 1966 to 1968. Their albums produced a string of hits including "The Last Train to Clarksville."

1. Davy Jones of the Monkees. A Hasbro Show Biz Baby. Hong Kong. #8802. 1967. 4 inches. All vinyl, jointed at the head with wired vinyl poseable body, rooted brown hair, painted brown eyes; attached to a 33-1/3 rpm record cover. Copyright by Raybert Productions, Inc. Trademark of Screen Gems, Inc. ....**$20-$30**

2. Mike of the Monkees. A Hasbro Show Biz Baby. Hong Kong. #8804. 1967. 4 inches. All vinyl, jointed at the head with wired vinyl poseable body, rooted brown hair, painted brown eyes; came attached to a 33-1/3 rpm record cover. Copyright by Raybert Productions, Inc. Trademark of Screen Gems, Inc. ....**$20-$30** (See photo on page 108.)

3. Davy Jones. Remco. Hong Kong. 1975. 5 inches. Vinyl head, rooted black hair, painted features, movable arms, legs are cloth and made for a finger puppet. Marked on head: "2;" marked on back: "© 1970//REMCO// IND.INC.//HARRISON, N.J.//PAT. PEND.// HONG KONG." ....**$25-$35**

4. Mickey of the Monkees. A Hasbro Show Biz Baby. Hong Kong. #8803. 1967. 4 inches. All vinyl, painted features, brown rooted hair, jointed at head, open mouth with molded teeth; attached to a 33-1/3 rpm record. ....**$20-$30** (See photo on page 108.)

5. Mickey of the Monkees. Remco. Hong Kong. 1970. 5 inches. Finger puppet. Vinyl head, plastic arms and middle section, rooted curly brown hair, painted brown eyes; cloth pants with yellow vinyl boots for finger operation. Marked on back: "© 1970//REMCO IND. INC//HARRISON N.J.//PAT. PEND//HONG KONG. Copyright by Columbia Pictures Industries Inc." ....**$40-$50**

6. Monkees Hand Puppet. Mattel, Inc. Japan. 1967. #5373. Features the likeness of all four members. Advertised as the world's first "Four-headed Puppet." Pull string to hear voices of the performers. A sampling of phrases includes "Hi! I'm Mickey Monkee! Aw, shut up!," "Are you ready for this song? No!" and "I think I'm falling in love. Not again!" Marked: "QUALITY ORIGINALS BY MATTEL// MONKEES © 1966 Raybert Productions, Inc. Trademark of Screen Gems, Inc." ....**$250-$300** (See photo on page 108.)

1: Davy Jones of the Monkees, a Hasbro Show Biz Baby.

2, 3, 4: Hasbro Show Biz Baby's The Monkees. Seen here are Mike Nesmith, Mickey Dolenz and Davy Jones.

1A: Marilyn Monroe by Tristar from 1982. *Courtesy of David Spurgeon.*

6: Hand puppet by Mattel advertised as the world's first "four-headed puppet," circa 1967.

1B: The back of the box for the Tristar Marilyn Monroe shows the different outfits available. *Courtesy of David Spurgeon.*

Monroe, Marilyn. Marilyn Monroe's career as an actress spanned sixteen years. Regarded as a sex symbol, she made twenty-nine films, twenty-four of them in the first eight years of her career. She died in 1962 and is considered a Hollywood icon. Today she is more popular than at the time of her death.

1. Marilyn Monroe. Tristar. Hong Kong. #5017. 1982. 11 inches. All vinyl, painted features, blonde wig; sold in four different outfits. Box marked: "© 1982 20th Century Fox Corp." ....**$30-$40**

2. Marilyn Monroe. World Doll, Co. Inc. China. 1983. 18 inches. All vinyl, jointed, rooted blonde hair, painted features; wearing a red floor-length dress with white boa. ....**$75-$100**

3. Marilyn Monroe. DSI. China. #07406. 1993. 11 inches. All vinyl, jointed, blonde wig; wearing full-length black and gold dress with white fur type boa. Dolls sold in six different outfits. Box marked: "Design © 1993 The Estate of Marilyn Monroe." ....**$25-$40**

4. Marilyn Monroe. Christomas Corp. China. Circa 1990s. 6 inches. Spoof doll. All vinyl, molded nose and lips, blue inset eyes, blonde wig; wearing white dress with red shoes. Box marked: "© Celebrity Spoof Licensing Corp." ....**$15-$25**

3A: Marilyn Monroe by DSI from 1993. *Author's collection.*

3B: The back of the box for the DSI Marilyn Monroe shows the different outfits available. *Author's collection.*

4: A spoof doll of Marilyn Monroe by Celebrity Spoof Licensing Corp. *Courtesy of David Spurgeon.*

Montgomery, Elizabeth. Actress Montgomery
is best known for her role as Samantha Stevens in the hit television series *Bewitched*, which aired from September 1964 to July 1972. Montgomery also appeared in a variety of movies as both a character and dramatic actress.

1. Samantha. Ideal Toy Corp. U.S.A. 1965. 12 inches. Vinyl head, arms and legs with plastic torso, rooted blonde hair, brown side-glancing eyes; wearing long red dress, red witch's hat, came with a broom, also sold dressed in an identical black outfit. Marked on head: "IDEAL DOLL//M-12-E-2;. marked on body: "IDEAL" in oval shape with "1965." Box has window display and reads: "SAMANTHA is portrayed by Elizabeth Montgomery." ......**$400-$500**, loose, with broom; **$1,000-$1,500**, boxed

2. Samantha Paper Dolls. Magic Wand. 1965. Shows Samantha standing outside of house. ....**$75-$100**, cut; **$100-$150**, uncut

1: Ideal's Samantha, as portrayed by Elizabeth Montgomery from the television show *Bewitched*.

Montgomery, Peggy (Baby Peggy).
Known as Baby Peggy, Montgomery was a child star now referred to as the Shirley Temple of the 1920s. As Baby Peggy, she starred in a variety of movies, beginning when she was three years old and continuing until her mid-thirties. One of her early films was *April Fool* (1926).

1. Baby Peggy. Louis Amberg & Son. U.S.A. 1923. 19 inches. Composition head and shoulder plate, composition arms and legs, stuffed cloth body, painted brown hair with wig, brown eyes; dressed in different pink child's dresses. Some marked with cloth banner reading "BABY PEGGY" and other information. Also sold with a pin back with photograph of the child star. ....**$600-$700**

2. Baby Peggy. Louis Amberg & Son. U.S.A. 1923. Made by a German factory in various sizes. All bisque, jointed arms and legs, painted hair and features. ....3 inches, **$300-$325**; 4 inches with wig, **$450-$500**; 5 inches, **$450-$500**

1: Two 19-inch composition Baby Peggy dolls. *Courtesy of Billie Nelson Tyrrell.*

Moore, Clayton. Actor
Moore starred in several films but is best known for his role as The Lone Ranger, and those immortal words "Hi-Ho Silver!"

1. Lone Ranger and Tonto. Dollcraft. U.S.A. 1938. 20 inches each. Composition and cloth, painted features; each doll is dressed to represent its character and the Lone Ranger wears his mask. With their original lithographed boxes. ..**$1,000-$1,500**, pair; **$500-$800**, each individually (See photo on page 110.)

2. Lone Ranger. Kohner Brothers. U.S.A. #182. Circa 1950s. 4-inch push-up toy. Wood jointed horse with Lone Ranger atop. Horse is painted white with black shoes, Lone Ranger has black painted clothing with white hat....**$50-$75**

3. Lone Ranger. Ideal Toy Corp. U.S.A. Circa 1967. #3406-6. 12 inches. All vinyl, poseable arms and legs; wearing Lone Ranger outfit. Body marked: "1967//IDEAL TOY CORP;" head marked: "© 1966//IDEAL." ....**$100-$125**

4. Lone Ranger. Gabriel Inc. Hong Kong. 1973. 12 inches. All vinyl, poseable arms and legs; wearing Lone Ranger outfit. Body marked: "© 1973 Lone Ranger Tel. Inc. Made in Hong Kong. For Gabriel Ind. Inc." ....**$35-$50**

1: The Lone Ranger and Tonto by Dollcraft from 1938. *Courtesy of Annette's Antique Dolls.*

2: The Lone Ranger push-up toy by Kohner Brothers from the 1950s. *Courtesy of Ronnie Kauk.*

4: The Lone Ranger, as portrayed by Clayton Moore, shown with Tonto, by Gabriel Inc., from 1973. *Author's collection.*

Moore, Mandy. With the release of her debut album *So Real*, teenage singing star Moore has made a name for herself in the music industry. The album went platinum in just three months. Her next album, *I Wanna Be With You*, was also well accepted. In addition to being a teenage singing sensation, Moore is the national spokeswoman for Neutrogena products, appearing in the company's television and print advertising campaigns.

1. Mandy Moore. Play Along Toys, Inc. China. #78400. 2000. 11 inches. All vinyl, jointed, painted features, rooted blonde hair. A deluxe fashion doll, she was sold in three different outfits: a denim outfit, a candy T-shirt outfit and a pink snakeskin pants outfit. Different outfits have different style numbers. ....**$15-$25**

2. Mandy Moore Mini Doll. Play Along Toys, Inc. China. #78400. 2000. 6 inches. All vinyl, jointed, painted features, rooted blonde hair. Available in the same outfits as the 11-inch dolls. ....**$10-$15**

1: Mandy Moore by Play Along Toys in her original box, wearing the pink snakeskin pants outfit. *Author's collection.*

Moore, Roger. Actor Moore appeared in a variety of television shows including *The Alaskans* (1959), *Maverick* (1957) and *The Saint* (1962). In 1973, he took on the role of James Bond in several Bond films.

James Bond in Moonraker. Mego. Hong Kong. #96001. 1979. 12 inches. All vinyl, fully poseable, painted facial features, molded brown hair; wearing silver metallic cloth space suit, space helmet, backpack, cuff clips and laser gun. Created in 1979, coinciding with the release of the film *Moonraker* that same year. This was the eleventh Bond film, and the fourth to star Moore as secret agent James Bond. ..**$100-$150**, loose; **$300-$400**, mint-in-box

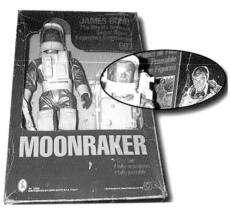

Mego's 1979 version of James Bond in *Moonraker*.

Mork & Mindy. (See Williams, Robin or Dawber, Pam)

Morse, Barry. Actor Morse is best known for his role as Professor Bergman on the television series *Space 1999*, which debuted in 1975. Morse also starred in the ABC television series *The Fugitive* as Lt. Gerard from 1963 until 1967.

1. Professor Bergman. Mattel, Inc. Taiwan. #9543. 1976. 9 inches. All vinyl, fully jointed, painted hair and features; wearing brown uniform and shoes, with stun gun, holster, communicator-computer that clips to belt. Copyright 1973 by ATV Licensing Limited. Copyright 1975 by Mattel, Inc. ....**$50-$75**

2. Eagle One Spaceship. Mattel, Inc. Taiwan. #9548. 1976. 2 feet long with living quarters. Includes 3-inch plastic figures of Professor Bergman, Doctor Russell and Commander Koenig. ......**$150-$200**, complete

1: Mattel's Professor Bergman as portrayed by Barry Morse, from the television series *Space 1999. Courtesy of Suellen Manning.*

Most, Donny. Actor Most starred in the role of Ralph Malph on the hit television series *Happy Days*, which aired from January 1974 to July 1984.

Ralph. Mego. Hong Kong. #63001/3. 1976. 8 inches. All vinyl, fully jointed, painted hair and features; wearing long-sleeved white shirt with dark pants. Head marked: "© 1976 PARAMOUNT// PICTURES CORP.;" back marked: "© MEGO CORP. 1974//REG. U.S. PAT. OFF // PAT. PEND-ING//HONG KONG." Sold on card. ....**$50-$60**

Mego's Ralph "the Mouth" Malph, as portrayed by Donny Most, from the television series *Happy Days.*

Murphy, Erin & Diane. Twin actresses Erin and Diane played little Tabatha on the hit television series *Bewitched*, which aired from September 1964 to July 1972. Previously, the role of Tabatha had been played by several other little actresses. The baby on the show was first played by Cynthia Black. Then twins Laura and Heidi Gentry took over. The next set of twins to play Tabatha was Tamar and Julie Young followed by the Murphy twins in 1967. After 1969, only Erin Murphy played Tabatha. Since the doll was produced in 1965, and the Murphy twins did not start with the show until 1967, the doll was not actually produced in their image. Most people, however, associate the Tabatha doll with Erin Murphy.

Tabatha. Ideal Toy Corp. 1966. #1150-2. 11 inches. All vinyl, fully jointed, rooted blonde hair, painted features; wearing two-piece pajamas. Head marked: "© 1965//SCREEN GEMS, INC//IDEAL TOY CORP//T.A. 18-6//H-25." Window box features photograph of Samantha, Darrin and Endora. ....**$200-$250**, loose; **$750-$1,000**, boxed

Murray, Mae. Actress Murray started her career as a beautiful Ziegfeld showgirl before moving on to Hollywood. Her first film was the hit *To Have and To Hold* (1916). Audiences loved the delicate blonde with the exquisite face, alabaster skin and kissable "bee-stung" lips. She starred in several films, including *The Delicious Little Devil* (1919) with Rudolph Valentino, and *The Big Little Person* (1919).

Mae Murray by an unknown maker, in wax, circa 1920s, shown with a wax John Gilbert. *Courtesy of Billie Nelson Tyrrell.* (See also Gilbert, John.)

Mae Murray. Maker unknown. Circa 1920s. 17 inches. Wax, painted features, white blonde wig; wearing full-length black gown with black boa, black feather hat. ....**$750-$1,000**

Myers, Mike. Actor and writer Myers appeared as a regular on the television comedy show *Saturday Night Live* from 1989 to 1994 before venturing into films. He created a starring role for his characters including Wayne in *Wayne's World* (1992) and Austin Powers in the films *Austin Powers, International Man of Mystery* (1997) and *Austin Powers: the Spy Who Shagged Me* (1999). He played several roles in the two films, including Fat Bastard (named later changed to Fatman) and Dr. Evil. Myers' voice can be heard in the lead role of the animated film *Shrek* (2001).

1. Austin Powers. McFarlane Toys. China. 1999. 6 inches. All vinyl, painted and molded features; painted and molded clothing; packaged with British flag, gun with hand and SEXY dictionary. Also has picture of Austin holding a champagne glass. The figures have different sayings, such as "Crikey, I've lost my mojo!" ....**$10-$15**

2. Austin (Danger) Powers. McFarlane Toys. China. 1999. 6 inches. All vinyl, painted and molded features, a very hairy chest; wearing red underwear, packaged with British flag, gun with hand and SEXY dictionary. Also has picture of Austin holding a champagne glass. The figures have with different sayings. ....**$10-$15**

1A: Austin Powers as portrayed by Mike Myers, by McFarlane Toys. *Author's collection.*

1B: The back of the box for Austin Powers. *Author's collection.*

N

Namath, Joe. Football player "Broadway Joe," as he is known, played quarterback for the New York Jets from 1965 until 1977 and for the Los Angeles Rams from 1977 until 1978. Namath has also appeared in films.

Broadway Joe Namath. Mego. Hong Kong. 1970. 12 inches. Soft vinyl head, hard vinyl body, painted hair and features, fully jointed; wearing green and white football uniform, with helmet and football. Wardrobe pieces sold separately. Marked on back: "BROADWAY JOE TM//©MEGO CORP MCMLXX//MADE IN HONG KONG." ....$75-$100

Broadway Joe Namath by Mego from 1970. *Courtesy of McMasters Doll Auctions.*

Naranjo, Ivan. Actor Naranjo is best known for his role as Lone Wolf on the popular ABC series *How the West Was Won* (1978).

Lone Wolf. Mattel, Inc. Hong Kong. #2369. 1978. 9 inches. All vinyl, fully jointed, rooted brown hair, painted black eyes, painted features; wears fringed pants with moccasins, bear claw necklace and headband, with rifle and knife. Marked on back of head: "©MATTEL INC. HONG KONG;" marked on back: "© 1971 MATTEL, INC.//HONG KONG US &//FOREIGN PATENDED." Copyright by MGM, Inc. ....$65-$85

Negri, Pola. Actress Negri was a star of the silver screen, seen in a number of films in the early 1920s, including *One Arabian Night* (1920) and *The Spanish Dancer* (1923).

Pola Negri. Bed Doll. Maker unknown. Circa 1920s. 32 inches. All cloth with silk type face, painted features, black silk hair; wearing full-length black gown with white and gold trim. ....$850-$1,000

A close-up of the Pola Negri bed doll shows her painted features in detail. *Courtesy of Billie Nelson Tyrrell.*

Pola Negri bed doll by an unknown maker, circa 1920s. *Courtesy of Billie Nelson Tyrrell.*

Nelson, Willie. One of singer Nelson's best-selling singles was the 1980 hit "On the Road Again." The song, which was used in the film *Honeysuckle Rose*, was nominated for an Oscar for Best Song. Nelson has won five Grammy Awards and is considered one of country music's greatest singers.

Willie Nelson. Catena Intl. China. #RN78213. 1989. 16 inches. All cloth, braided yarn hair; wearing blue pants, red shirt and red/black and white bandanna around head. Box marked: "© 1989 Willie Nelson & Family General Store." ....$20-$25

(See photo on page 114.)

A cloth Willie Nelson by Catena Intl. *Courtesy of David Spurgeon.*

Nesmith "Woolhat" Mike. (See The Monkees)

New Kids on the Block. This musical group of five young boys drove teenage girls wild with their pop music in the late 1980s to early 1990s. The group consisted of five members: Joey McIntyre, Donnie Wahlberg, Danny Wood, Jon Knight and Jordan Knight. Some of their biggest hit songs include "Please Don't Go Girl," "You Got It (The Right Stuff)," "I'll Be Loving You (Forever)" and "Hangin' Tough."

1. New Kids on the Block. Hasbro. China. 1990. 12 inches. Vinyl, jointed. Box marked: "© 1990 Big Step Productions, Inc." A separate doll was made for each of the boys in the band. ....**$15-$20** each

2. New Kids on the Block. Hasbro. China. 1990. 12 inches. Vinyl, jointed. Box marked: "© 1990 Big Step Productions, Inc." A separate doll was made for each of the boys in the band and each was packaged with a cassette tape and microphone. ....**$20-$25** each

3. New Kids on the Block. Hasbro. China. 1990. 18 inches. All cloth, nylon type hair, painted features; wearing a variety of outfits as shown on the back of the box. ..**$45-$65**, each; **$200-$250**, set of five

1A: One of the New Kids on the Block by Hasbro. *Courtesy of David Spurgeon.*

3A: Danny Wood of the New Kids on the Block, by Hasbro.

3B: Jonathan Knight of the New Kids on the Block, by Hasbro.

1B: The back of the box for one of the New Kids on the Block shows the others in the group. *Courtesy of David Spurgeon.*

3C: Joey McIntyre of the New Kids on the Block, by Hasbro.

3D: Donnie Wahlberg of the New Kids on the Block, by Hasbro.

3E: Jordan Knight of the New Kids on the Block, by Hasbro. *Photos 3A–3F Author's collection.*

3F: The back of the box from one of the cloth New Kids on the Block shows all five dolls.

2: One of the New Kids on the Block with cassette tape and microphone, by Hasbro. *Courtesy of David Spurgeon.*

Nichols, Nichelle.
Actress and author Nichols is best known for her role as Lieutenant Uhura on the hit television series *Star Trek*, which aired from 1966 until 1969. Her first book, *Saturn's Child*, is now in print.

    1. Lieutenant Uhura. Mego. Hong Kong. 1975 to 1977. #51200/4. 8 inches. All vinyl, fully jointed, black Afro-styled hair; wearing red Star Trek uniform top with brown tights and black boots. Sold on card. One of six figures sold. ....**$40-$50**

1: Lieutenant Uhura from *Star Trek*, portrayed by Nichelle Nichols, by Mego. *Courtesy of David Spurgeon.*

    2. Lieutenant Uhura. Playmates. China. #65532. 1999. 12 inches. All vinyl, jointed, painted features, black Afro-styled hair; wearing red Star Trek uniform top with brown tights and black boots. Box marked: "© 1999 Paramount Pictures." ....**$20-$30**

2A: Lieutenant Uhura from *Star Trek*, portrayed by Nichelle Nichols, by Playmates. *Author's collection.*

2B: The back of the box for Lieutenant Uhura by Playmates. *Author's collection.*

Nijinsky, Vaslay.
Nijinsky, a famous Russian ballet dancer and choreographer, was one of the premier ballet stars of the twentieth century. His last performance was on September 30, 1917.

Wax doll of Vaslay Nijinsky by an unknown maker, circa 1910-20. *Courtesy of Billie Nelson Tyrrell.*

Vaslay Nijinsky. Maker unknown. Circa 1910-1920. 21 inches. All wax, painted features; wearing turban, white silk outfit with black vest. Very rare. ....**$1,800-$2,000** (See photo on page 115.)

Nimoy, Leonard. Actor Nimoy is best known for his role as the pointed-eared Mr. Spock, a half-human and half-Vulcan personality on the hit television series *Star Trek*, which aired from 1966 until 1969. Nimoy also starred in the film version: *Star Trek the Motion Picture* (1979). (See Shatner, William for photograph.)

1. Mr. Spock. Mego. Hong Kong. #51200/2. 1974. 8 inches. All vinyl, fully jointed, painted hair and features; wearing Star Trek uniform. Copyright by Paramount Pictures Corporation. ....**$40-$50**

2. Mr. Spock. Mego. Hong Kong. #91200/2. 1979. 3 inches. All vinyl, painted hair and features. Copyright by Paramount Pictures Corporation. ....**$25-$35**

3. Mr. Spock. Mego. Hong Kong. #91210/2. 1979. 12 inches. All vinyl, fully jointed, painted hair and features. Head marked: "©PPC;" back marked; "©MEGO CORP. 1977//MADE IN HONG KONG." Copyright by Paramount Pictures Corporation. ....**$70-$85**

1A: Mego's 1974 Mr. Spock, as portrayed by Leonard Nimoy, on the television series *Star Trek.*

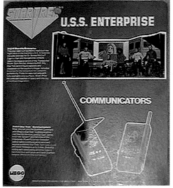

1B: Back of box for Mr. Spock as portrayed by Leonard Nimoy, by Mego, 1974.

Nisbet, Peggy. Dollmaker Peggy Nisbet created dolls from her factory in England. She is well known for her dolls that depict royalty.

Peggy Nisbet. Self Portrait. Peggy Nisbet Dolls. England. 1978. 8 inches. Plastic, painted features, white-blonde wig; wearing red dress with red cape, red feathers in hair. Limited-edition doll. ....**$100-$150**

Peggy Nisbet by Peggy Nisbet Dolls. *Courtesy of David Spurgeon.*

Norris, Chuck. Martial arts expert Norris has appeared in several high-action films including *Curse of the Dragon* (1993) and *Game of Death* (1978). Besides films, Norris starred in his own television series *Walker, Texas Ranger* (1993-2001).

Chuck Norris Ninja Figure. Kenner. Hong Kong. 1986. 4 inches. All vinyl, jointed; painted black ninja clothing. Sold on card. ......**$10-$15**

Chuck Norris Ninja Figure, 4 inches, by Kenner.

Norton-Taylor, Judy. Actress Norton-Taylor is best known for her role as Mary Ellen in the television series *The Waltons*, which aired from September 1972 to August 1981.

Mary Ellen. Mego. Hong Kong. #56000-1. 1974. 8 inches. All vinyl, fully jointed, rooted blonde hair, painted features; wearing a red plaid dress. Head marked: "©1974//LORIMAR INC." Mary Ellen was sold singly and in a pack with John Boy played by Richard Thomas....**$15-$20**, loose; **$25-$30**, boxed singly; **$40-$50**, boxed pair (See Thomas, Richard for photograph.)

'N Sync. Singing group 'N Sync is made up of five members: Lance Bass, Joey Fatone, Chris Kirkpatrick, JC Chasez and Justin Timberlake. In 1997, the quintet landed a contract with RCA Records. The group created a batch of crisp radio-friendly pop songs and issued the debut album exclusively in Europe, then released the music to American fans. The group's first two top 40 hits—"I Want You Back" and "Tearin' Up My Heart"—put 'N Sync on the road to stardom. Other hits followed along with merchandise items including dolls, T-shirts and lunch boxes.

1. 'N Sync Marionette Dolls. Living Toyz. China. 2000. 10 inches. All vinyl, jointed, painted and molded hair, painted features; came boxed with stand. Each doll in the group was sold separately. Box marked "© 2000 LIVING TOYZ, INC. Woodland Hills, CA 91367 USA. MADE IN CHINA." ....**$25-$35** each

2. 'N Sync Marionette Dolls. Living Toyz. China. 2001. 10 inches. All vinyl, jointed, painted and molded hair, painted features; came boxed with stand. Each doll in the group was sold separately ....**$20-$30**, each

1A: Marionette of Justin Timberlake, of the 'N Sync singing group. *Author's collection.*

1B: All 'N Sync members were made as 10-inch marionettes by Living Toyz in 2000.

2: The box holds 'N Sync members Lance Bass, Joey Fatone, Chris Kirkpatrick and JC Chasez wearing new outfits for 2001.

Oakley, Annie. Markswoman Oakley joined Buffalo Bill's Wild West Show in 1885. A musical was made based on her life entitled *Annie Get Your Gun.*

1. Annie Oakley. American Character. U.S.A. 1954. 17 inches. All hard plastic, fully jointed, blonde wig, blue sleep eyes with eyelashes; wearing a cowgirl outfit with fringed shirt, cowgirl boots and a holster with two guns, skirt is embroidered with the words "Annie Oakley." Usually unmarked. The doll used for Annie Oakley was a Sweet Sue. ......**$200-$250**

2. Annie Oakley. Excel Toy Corp. Hong Kong. 1974. 9 inches. All vinyl, fully jointed, painted blonde-yellow hair, painted features. ......**$50-$75**

3. Annie Oakley. Hallmark. Taiwan. #400DT113-3. 1979. 7 inches. All cloth, printed features and clothing; in box marked: "Buffalo Bill's Wild West." ....**$10-$15**

4. Annie Oakley. Annalee Mobilitee Doll Co. U.S.A. 1985. 10 inches. All cloth, painted features. ....**$300-$400**

O'Brien, Margaret.

Actress O'Brien appeared in several films including *Meet Me in St. Louis* (1944) and *Little Women* (1949). She also appeared on television shows.

There were a variety of dolls made in her likeness by the Alexander Doll Company in many sizes from 1946 until 1951, including composition and hard plastic versions.

1. Margaret O'Brien. Alexander Doll Company. U.S.A. 1946. 14 inches. All composition, fully jointed, brown or red mohair wig with center part in braids. Marked on dress tag: "Madame Alexander, New York, USA;" marked on wrist tag: "Margaret O'Brien, All Rights Reserved; A Madame Alexander Doll." Available in different outfits. ....**$700-$800**

2. Margaret O'Brien. Alexander Doll Company. U.S.A. 1946. 17 to 18 inches. All composition, fully jointed, brown or red mohair wig with center part in braids. Head marked: "Alexander." Available in different outfits. ....**$900-$1,000**

3. Margaret O'Brien. Alexander Doll Company. U.S.A. 1946. 18 inches. All composition, fully jointed, brown or red mohair wig with center part in braids; wearing dress with red skirt and white top, trimmed with blue ribbon sash and design in blue and white across bottom of dress. ....**$1,000-$1,200**

4. Margaret O'Brien. Alexander Doll Company. U.S.A. 1946. 21 inches. All composition, fully jointed, brown or red mohair wig with center part in braids. Available in different outfits. ....**$1,000-$1,200**

5. Margaret O'Brien. Alexander Doll Company. U.S.A. 1947 to 1951. 14 inches. All hard plastic, fully jointed, brown or red mohair wig with center part in braids. Available in different outfits. Hard-plastic Margaret O'Brien dolls are scarcer than the composition version. ....**$800-$900**

6. Margaret O'Brien. Alexander Doll Company. U.S.A. 1947 to 1951. 18 inches. All hard plastic, fully jointed, brown or red mohair wig with center part in braids. Available in different outfits. ....**$1,000-$1,200**

7. Margaret O'Brien. Alexander Doll Company. U.S.A. 1947 to 1951. 21 inches. All hard plastic, fully jointed, brown or red mohair wig with center part, in braids. Available in different outfits. ....**$1,200** up

8. Margaret O'Brien paper dolls. Whitman. U.S.A. Circa 1950s. ....**$40-$50**

9. Beth from the movie *Little Women.* Ideal Toy Corp. 1984 to 1988. 8 inches. Vinyl, jointed, sleep eyes with eyelashes, rooted hair; wearing *Little Women* Beth costume. Marked on head: "©1978 MGM/CBS INC/1438 IDEAL 1982." ....**$40-$50**

1: A 14-inch composition Margaret O'Brien by Alexander Doll Company wearing a red and green plaid dress. *Courtesy of Lynnae Ramsey.*

2: Margaret O'Brien with her original wrist tag. *Courtesy McMasters Doll Auction.*

O'Connor, Renee. Actress O'Connor recently starred in the television series *Xena: Warrior Princess*, in the role of Gabrielle. The series ran five years, ending in 2001.

    1. Gabrielle. Toy Biz, Inc. China. #42012. 1998. 12 inches. All vinyl, painted features, rooted blonde hair; wearing green and red full-length gown with gold stars, gold star headpiece. ....**$15-$25**

    2. Gabrielle. Toy Biz, Inc. China. 1998. 12 inches. All vinyl, painted features, rooted blonde hair; wearing boots, leather-look skirt and fringed top. ....**$15-$25**

3: An 18-inch composition Margaret O'Brien. *Courtesy of Lynnae Ramsey.*

1: Gabrielle, in a red and green gown, from the television series *Xena: Warrior Princess*, as portrayed by Renee O'Connor. *Courtesy of David Spurgeon.*

8: Margaret O'Brien paper dolls by Whitman.

2: Gabrielle, in a simple costume, from the television series *Xena: Warrior Princess*, as portrayed by Renee O'Connor. *Courtesy of David Spurgeon.*

7: An all-original 21-inch hard plastic Margaret O'Brien wearing a blue and white dress.

O'Connor, Tim. Actor O'Connor played the role of Dr. Huer in the NBC television series *Buck Rogers in the 25th Century*. The show aired from 1979 to 1981.

    1. Dr. Huer. Mego. Hong Kong. #85000/9. 1979. 3¾ inches. All vinyl, fully jointed, painted hair and features; painted clothing. Copyright by Robert C. Dille. ....**$5-$10**

    2. Dr. Huer. Mego. Hong Kong. #85001/6. 1979. 12 inches. All vinyl, fully jointed, painted gray hair, painted brown eyes. Head marked: "© 1978 ROBERT//C. DILLE;" back marked: "© MEGO CORP. 1977//MADE IN HONG KONG." ....**$30-$40**

O'Donnell, Rosie. Actress, comedian and talk show host O'Donnell has won countless Emmy awards for her daytime talk series *The Rosie O'Donnell Show.* She has appeared in several films, including *Harriet the Spy* (1996) and *A League of Their Own* (1992).

1. Rosie. Tyco. China. 1997. 20 inches. All cloth with sewn features; wearing bright blue sewn-on suit. Pull string to hear phrases. ....**$10-$15**

2. Rosie, Barbie's friend. Mattel, Inc. China. 12 inches. 1999. All vinyl, jointed, painted features, rooted brunette hair; dressed in red pants suit with black vest and white shirt. Holding microphone. ....**$15-$20**

2: Rosie, Barbie's Friend, by Mattel in original box.

O'Dowd, George. (See Boy George)

Olsen, Susan. Actress Olsen played the part of Cindy in the hit television series *The Brady Bunch,* which aired from 1969 to 1974.

Kitty-Karry All Doll. Remco. Hong Kong. 1969. 20 inches. All vinyl, blonde pigtails; wearing dress with lots of pockets which hold a variety of accessories. This doll does not represent Susan Olsen; it represents the doll that her

Kitty-Karry All by Remco, the doll Cindy Brady played with on the television series *The Brady Bunch.*

character, Cindy, played with on *The Brady Bunch.* Box shows photograph of doll with a small cast photograph, which features Cindy holding the doll. ....**$125-$150**, loose; **$300-$400**, boxed

O'Neal, Tatum. Actress O'Neal is the daughter of actor Ryan O'Neal and actress Joanna Moore. She won an Academy Award for her role in the film *Paper Moon* (1973) when she was nine years old. She also starred in the film *The Bad News Bears* (1976) and played the role of Sarah Velvet Brown in *International Velvet* (1978). She was married to tennis star John McEnroe from 1986 to 1994.

International Velvet. Kenner. Hong Kong. #44000. 1978. 11 inches. All vinyl, fully jointed, rooted blonde hair, painted blue eyes; wearing riding outfit with boots, jacket and hat. Head marked: "HONG KONG//© 1976 U.C.S.I.;" back marked: "© 1978 G.M.F.G.I. KENNER PROD.//CINCINNATI, OHIO 45202//MADE IN HONG KONG." Copyright by Metro-Goldwyn-Mayer, Inc. ....**$40-$50**

O'Neill, Kitty. Stuntwoman O'Neill performed stunts on various television shows in the 1970s.

Kitty O'Neill. Mattel, Inc. Taiwan. #2247. 1978. 11 inches. All vinyl, fully jointed; wearing yellow racing suit with red scarf, belt, boots and helmet. Marked on neck: "© ROCKET KAT 1978 TAIWAN;" back marked: "© MATTEL, INC. 1966//TAIWAN." The first-version box has a sticker over the words "Kitty O'Neill Story." The second edition has the words showing; a booklet is enclosed. ....**$50-$75**

Osmond, Donny. Singer, entertainer and talk show host Osmond had his own variety show on television with his sister Marie, which aired from 1976 to 1979, *The Donny and Marie Show.* Both were originally part of the family singing group The Osmonds. His single, "Puppy Love," was a huge hit in 1972. Recently, Donny and Marie had their own daytime talk show.

1. Donny & Marie Osmond doll pack. Includes both dolls. Mattel, Inc. Hong Kong. 1976. 12 inches, each; also sold separately. All vinyl, jointed with painted features; Marie is wearing a hot pink dress, Donny is wearing a hot pink and purple outfit. Both have microphones. ....**$40-$50**, boxed, individually; **$100-$125**, boxed set

2. Donny. Mattel, Inc. Hong Kong. 1977. #9767. 12 inches. Vinyl, poseable, one arm is permanently bent; wearing purple jumpsuit. First-edition box marked: "FOR AGES OVER 3;" second-edition box marked: "CONTAINS DONNY OSMOND DOLL//FOR AGES OVER 3;" doll marked on neck: "© Osbro Prod. 1976 HONG KONG, 1088-0500 4//©MAT-TEL//INC. 1968//HONG KONG." ......**$40-$50**

3. Donny Puppet. Osbro Productions, Inc. 1978. Sold separately or as gift pack with Marie Puppet. Lifelike features with cloth puppet bodies. ....**$50-$75** each; **$100-$150**, set

Osmond, Jimmy. Singer, entertainer. A member of the Osmond family of entertainers, Jimmy Osmond often appeared on the Osmonds' variety show, which aired from 1976 to 1979.

Jimmy Osmond. Mattel, Inc. 1978. Taiwan. #2200. 10 inches. All vinyl, fully jointed, left arm is permanently bent, painted brown hair, painted brown eyes, freckles, open smiling mouth with teeth; wearing silver jumpsuit with purple sleeves and holding microphone. Marked on back: "2200-2109 2//©MATTEL, INC.// 1968//TAIWAN." Also came in a Canadian version. ....**$50-$60**

vinyl, jointed with painted features; Marie is wearing a hot pink dress, Donny is wearing a hot pink and purple outfit. Both have microphones. Marked on Donny's neck same as 9767. Donny marked on back: "1088 0500 4//© MATTEL/INC. 1968//HONG KONG;" Marie marked on neck: "© OSBRO PROD 1976 KOREA;" marked on rear: "©MATTEL INC.//1966/8 KOREA." ....**$40-$50**, boxed, individually; **$100-$125**, boxed set

2. Marie. Mattel, Inc. U.S.A. 1977. 30 inches. Vinyl head, plastic jointed body, twist waist, rooted brown hair, painted brown eyes, smiling mouth with teeth; wearing long pink dress, with large tan-colored stand with the words "Marie Osmond." Marked on back of head: "©OSBRO PROD. 1976;" marked on neck: "© OSBRO PROD.//1976//USA." Fashion modeling doll with dress pattern. ....**$100-$150**, boxed

3. Marie. Mattel, Inc. China. 1977. #9768. 12 inches. Vinyl, jointed; wearing a tiered chiffon dress with satin trim, belt with six rhinestones and purple shoes. ....**$30-$50**

4. Marie Puppet. Osbro Productions, Inc. 1978. Sold separately or as gift pack with Donny Puppet. Lifelike features with cloth puppet bodies. ....**$50-$75**, each; **$100-$150**, set

Mattel's Jimmy Osmond from 1978. *Courtesy of Suellen Manning.*

3A: Mattel's Marie Osmond doll from 1977.

Osmond, Marie. Singer, entertainer, talk show host and doll designer, Marie had her own variety show on television, which aired from 1976 to 1979 with her brother, Donny, *The Donny and Marie Show*. Recently, the two had their own daytime talk show. She is also an active doll designer with her own successful line of dolls and author of the personal memoir, *Behind the Smile* (2001).

1. Donny & Marie Osmond doll pack. Included both dolls. Mattel, Inc. Korea. 1976. #9769. 12 inches, each; also sold separately. All

3B: The back of the Marie Osmond doll box.

P

Palillo, Ron. Actor Palillo is well known for his role as Arnold Horshack on the television series *Welcome Back Kotter*, which aired from 1975 until 1979. He currently works in stage productions in New York.

Horshack. Mattel, Inc. Taiwan. 1976. #9771. 9 inches. All vinyl, fully jointed, painted hair and features; dressed in dark pants, brown shirt, green jacket and hat. Marked on head: "©WOLPER//KOMACK;" marked on back: "©1973//MATTEL INC//TAIWAN." Each doll in this series is on a card with an accessory piece. ....**$15-$20**, loose; **$40-$50**, on card

Mattel's Horshack, as portrayed by Ron Palillo in the television series *Welcome Back, Kotter.*

Parker, Fess. Actor Parker starred in films and on television. He is best known for his roles as Davy Crockett in the Walt Disney television series about the frontiersman, and as Daniel Boone, appearing from 1964 until 1970 on NBC. (See also Crockett, Davy).

1. Fess Parker as Daniel Boone. Remco. Hong Kong. 1964. 5 inches. Vinyl jointed head, painted brown hair, painted black eyes, one-piece vinyl body. Head marked: "32;" body marked: "©AMERICAN//TRADITION CO.// 1964." ....**$20-$35**

2. Daniel Boone. SS. Kresge Company. Hong Kong. 1976. 7 inches. Vinyl head, painted hair and features. Marked on back: "MADE IN//HONG KONG." Part of a series called the Heroes of the American Revolution. The dolls in this series were distributed by Montgomery Ward & Co. Inc. ....**$20-$30**

3. Davy Crockett. Kohner Brothers. U.S.A. Circa 1960s. 6-inch push-up toy. Wood jointed on plastic base, painted features and clothing, wood gun and cloth cap. Label reads: "Walt Disney's//OFFICIAL DAVY CROCKETT// (FESS PARKER)//© Walt Disney Productions// Pat. No. 2,421,279 A KOHNER PRODUCT." ......**$50-$75**

1: Fess Parker as Daniel Boone by Remco, from 1964. *Author's collection.*

3: Davy Crockett, as portrayed by Fess Parker, push-up toy by Kohner Brothers from the 1960s. *Courtesy of Ronnie Kauk.*

Parton, Dolly. Actress and country-western singer Parton has appeared in a variety of films, including *Nine to Five* (1980) with Lily Tomlin. As a singer, Parton had her first solo hit with the song "Jolene." She continues to perform and started her own successful theme park—Dollywood—in Gatlinburg, Tennessee, near her hometown.

1. Dolly Parton. Goldberger Doll Mfg. Hong Kong. #DP12. 1978. 12 inches. All vinyl, fully jointed, rooted blonde hair, painted blue eyes; dressed in red satin-like jumpsuit with silver trim. Head marked: "DOLLY PARTON// ©EEGEE CO//HONG KONG;" box marked: "© Goldberger Doll Mfg. Co. Inc. Brooklyn, NY. 11237." ....**$30-$40**

2. Dolly Parton. Goldberger Doll. Mfg. (Eegee). Hong Kong. 1996. 12 inches. All

vinyl, fully jointed, rooted blonde hair, painted blue eyes; wearing red-and-white checked dress. ....$20-$30

3. Dolly Parton. Goldberger Doll. Mfg. (Eegee). Hong Kong. 1996. 12 inches. Vinyl, jointed with bendable knees; wearing full-length white gown. Marked on neck: "41190 EEGEE CO.;" marked on back: "Dolly Parton, © Eegee Co., Hong Kong." ....$30-$40

4. Dolly Parton. Goldberger Doll Mfg. Co. U.S.A. #5890. 17 inches. Wearing full-length gold dress. Box marked: "Goldberger Doll Mfg. Co Inc. Brooklyn, NY 11237." Licensed by Dolly Parton. ....$50-$75

5. Dolly Parton. Goldberger Doll. Mfg. (Eegee). Hong Kong. 19 inches. All vinyl, fully jointed, rooted blonde hair, painted blue eyes; wearing full-length red dress. Also sold in three different dress versions including two in white dresses. ....$50-$75

6. Dolly Parton outfit. Goldberger Doll Mfg. Co. U.S.A. Circa 1990s. Coat of Many Colors outfit. Came boxed. ....$15-$20

7. Dolly Parton. Christomas Corp. China. Circa 1990s. 6 inches. Spoof doll. All vinyl, molded lips and nose, blue inset eyes; wearing blue dress with gold trim, carrying a microphone and guitar. Box marked: "© Celebrity Spoof Licensing Corp." ....$20-$25

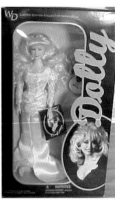

2 & 3A: Dolly Parton by Goldberger Doll, wearing checked dress (left) and white gown (right). In original boxes.

6A: The front of the box for Goldberger Doll Mfg.'s Dolly Parton outfit.

6B: The back of the box for the Goldberger Doll Mfg.'s Dolly Parton outfit.

2 & 3B: The back of the box for the Goldberger Doll Mfg.'s 1996 Dolly Parton dolls.

7: A spoof doll of Dolly Parton by Celebrity Spoof Licensing Corp. *Courtesy of David Spurgeon.*

1: Dolly Parton by Goldberger Doll Mfg. in original box, from 1978.

Patrick, Butch. Actor. Patrick is best known for his role as Eddie Munster on the hit television series *The Munsters*. The show aired from 1964 until 1966.

1. Woof Woof. This one-of-a-kind doll used as a show prop on *The Munsters* is shown at left, with Patrick.

2. Woof Woof. Produced by Jim Madden. Phoenix, Arizona. U.S.A. 1991. 24 inches. Cast in latex composition mold, all handmade taking six to eight weeks to complete, all hand-painted features, body was made with monkey fur body, molded cupped plastic hands; wearing pajamas and bathrobe. Comes with "Munster Goodies," which include old magazines, memorabilia, behind-the-scenes stories, two special personalized photographs, a handwritten letter and personal telephone call from Butch Patrick. Limited to 100. ....**$1,200-$1,400**

3. Eddie Munster. Side Show Toys. China. 1999. 4 inches. Little Big Head Figure. All vinyl, painted features; painted clothing. ....**$5-$10**

4. Eddie Munster. Side Show Toys. China. 1999. 3 inches. Little Big Head Figure. All vinyl, yellow in color, glows in the dark. ....**$5-$10**

5. Eddie Munster. Presents. China. 8 inches. All plastic, painted features; wearing a velvet short set with a high collar. Hang tag reads, on the outside: "THE MUNSTERS;" on the inside: "Eddie, His Lord Fauntleroy suit, widow's peak and pointed ears are not of the average 10 year old boy's appearance. Opening tin cans with his ears and sleeping in a coffin is an everyday occurrence for Edward ("Eddie") Wolfgang Munster. In the fifth grade, his school composi-

tion titled 'My Parents, an Average American Family' was written in blood ink."; on the back: "PRESENTS copyright 1964 Kayro-Vue Productions." ....**$25-$35**

5: Butch Patrick as Eddie Munster, by Presents, from the television series *The Munsters*. In original bag with hang tag.

2B: Another view of Woof Woof doll showing some of the associated "Munster Goodies." *Courtesy Butch Patrick and Jim Madden.*

2A: Woof Woof doll made by Jim Madden in 1991. *Courtesy Butch Patrick and Jim Madden.*

3: Butch Patrick as a 4-inch Eddie Munster by Side Show Toys.

4: This 3-inch Eddie Munster by Side Show Toys glows in the dark.

Perkins, Anthony. Actor Perkins won an Academy Award for best supporting actor for his role in the 1960 movie thriller *Psycho*. Perkins also played the role of Dr. Alex Durant in the film *The Black Hole* (1979).

1. Dr. Alex Durant from The Black Hole. Mego. Hong Kong. #95010. 1979. 3 inches. All vinyl, fully jointed, painted features; painted clothing. Copyright by Walt Disney Productions. ....**$15-$20**

2. Dr. Alex Durant from The Black Hole. Mego. Hong Kong. 1979. 12 inches. All vinyl, fully jointed, painted and molded hair, painted features; wearing long gray pants and jacket with white turtleneck. ....**$35-$50**

Perry, Luke. Actor Perry is best known for his role as Dylan McKay on the Fox hit television series *Beverly Hills, 90210*, which aired from 1990-2000.

Dylan. Mattel, Inc. China. 1991. 11 inches. All vinyl, jointed, painted features; wearing white pants, black shirt with red jacket, came with black shorts. ....**$15-$20**

Perry, Rod. Actor Perry played the role of Sgt. David "Deacon" Kay on ABC television's *S.W.A.T.*, which aired from February 1975 until July 1976.

1. Deacon from *S.W.A.T.* L.J.N. Toys Ltd. Hong Kong. #6600. 1975. 7 inches. All vinyl, fully jointed, painted hair and features; wearing all blue *S.W.A.T.* outfit. Copyright by Spelling-Goldberg Productions. ....$20-$30

2. Deacon from *S.W.A.T.* L.J.N. Toys Ltd. Hong Kong. #6850. 1976. 7½ inches. All vinyl, fully jointed, painted hair and features; wearing all blue *S.W.A.T.* outfit. Copyright by Spelling-Goldberg Productions. ....**$20-$30**

1: Deacon, from the television series *S.W.A.T.*, as portrayed by Rod Perry.

Peterson, Cassandra. Actress Peterson appeared on television and on films including *Cheech and Chong's Next Movie, Fantasy Island, Happy Days* and *St. Elsewhere*. She is perhaps best known by her character Elvira-Mistress of the Dark. Elvira has been featured in several shows including *Echo Park* (1986) and *Pee Wee's Big Adventure* (1985).

Elvira-Mistress of the Dark. Figures Toy Co. China. 1998. #00001. 7 inches. All vinyl, painted features, long black hair; wearing long black dress with low cut front and slit up the leg. Sold in four different variations including a figure with a chain saw and a snake and a figure

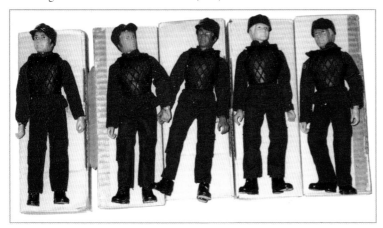

A group shot of *S.W.A.T.* team members. *Courtesy of Suellen Manning.*

with a witch hat and broom. All figures came with a vinyl knife. Two versions were limited to 5000 pieces and were glow-in-the-dark. A picture of Elvira is shown on the card. ....**$10-$15**

Two variations of glow-in-the-dark Elvira-Mistress of the Dark figures. *Author's collection.*

Philip (Prince). Husband of Queen Elizabeth II of England.

1. Prince Philip. Alexander Doll Company. U.S.A. Circa 1953. 17¾ inches. All hard plastic, fully jointed, dark brown wig, brown sleep eyes with eyelashes; dressed in royal outfit. Unmarked. ....**$650-$800**

2. H.R.H. Prince Philip. Peggy Nisbet. England. Circa #P403. 1970s. Plastic; dressed in Garter Robes. ....**$50-$75**

Pickford, Mary. Actress Pickford began her stage career in the early 1900s. She was known as the queen of the silent screen, starring in numerous films including, *Poor Little Rich Girl, Rebecca of Sunnybrook Farms* both 1917, and *Little Annie Rooney* (1925). She founded United Artists with Douglas Fairbanks and Charlie Chaplin so they could produce their own films.

Little Annie Rooney. Cameo Doll Company. U.S.A. 1926. All composition, painted features, long blonde braids; wearing plaid dress with hat. ....**$500-$700**

Advertisement from the January 1926 *Playthings* magazine for the Little Annie Rooney doll, which was distributed by Geo. Borgfeldt & Co. *Author's collection.*

Pine, Robert. Actor Pine played the role of Sergeant Joe "Sarge" Getraer on the NBC television series *CHiPs*, beginning in 1977.

1. Sarge. Mego. Hong Kong. #08010/3. 1981. 3 inches. All vinyl, painted features; painted clothing. Copyright by Metro-Goldwyn-Mayer Film Co. Sold on card. ....**$15-$20**

2. Sarge. Mego. Hong Kong. #87500/3. 1981. 8 inches. All vinyl, fully jointed, painted brown and gray hair, painted features; dressed in Sergeant's uniform, came with helmet and decals. Copyright by Metro-Goldwyn-Mayer Film Co. Sold on card. ....**$30-$40**

Presley, Elvis. Singer and actor Presley was known as the King of Rock 'n' Roll. He appeared in more than two dozen musical films. His records have sold millions of copies.

1. Elvis Presley. World Doll. China. Circa 1980s. 21 inches. All vinyl, painted and molded black hair, painted features; wearing white jumpsuit with red flared legs, yellow, red and blue eagle on chest, came with guitar with the words "Elvis Presley" on guitar. ......**$100-$150**

2. Elvis Presley. World Doll. China. 21 inches. #71950. 1984. All vinyl, painted and molded black hair, painted features; wearing black outfit with white shirt, came with guitar with the words "Elvis Presley" on guitar. Different dolls were sold in a variety of outfits. ......**$150-$200**

3. Elvis. Christmas Corp. China. Circa 1990s. 6 inches. Spoof doll. All vinyl, molded lips and nose, blue inset eyes; wearing white jumpsuit with cape, white shoes. Box marked: "© Celebrity Spoof Licensing Corp." ..**$20-$25**

3: A spoof doll of Elvis Presley by Celebrity Spoof Licensing Corp. *Courtesy of David Spurgeon.*

1: This 21-inch vinyl doll portraying Elvis Presley was made by World Doll in the mid 1980s. It was sold in a variety of outfits.

Priest, Pat. Actress Priest is best known for her role as Marilyn Munster on the television series *The Munsters*, which aired from 1964 until 1966.

Marilyn Munster. Maker unknown. Japan. 1964. 9 inches. Cheaply made, plastic, painted features, glued-on blonde wig; wearing red plastic dress and white shoes. The doll is unmarked and the only markings on the box are: "Marilyn Munster of The Munsters Fame 1964 Japan." The box has a picture of the character. ....**$25-$75**, depending on true age

Marilyn Munster from *The Munsters* television series, as portrayed by Pat Priest. *Courtesy of David Spurgeon.*

Priestley, Jason. Actor Priestley is best known for his role as Brandon on the Fox hit television series *Beverly Hills, 90210* which aired from 1990-2000.

1. Brandon. Mattel, Inc. China. 1991. 11 inches. All vinyl, jointed, painted and molded features; wearing jeans, green shirt and jean jacket, came with plaid shorts. ....**$15-$20**

2. Group pack with Brandon, Brenda and Dylan dolls. ....**$40-$50**

1: Brandon, as portrayed by Jason Priestly in the television series *Beverly Hills 90210*. By Mattel.

2: *Beverly Hills 90210* group pack with Brandon, Brenda and Dylon dolls, from Mattel.

Prowse, David. Actor Prowse played Darth Vader in the films *Star Wars* (1977) and *The Empire Strikes Back* (1980). The voice of Darth Vader, however, was that of actor James Earl Jones.

1. Darth Vader. Kenner. Hong Kong. #38230. 1978. 4 inches. All vinyl, fully jointed; painted Darth Vader costume. ....**$20-$30**

2. Darth Vader. Kenner. Hong Kong. #38610. 1978. 15 inches. Plastic and vinyl, fully jointed; black costume was molded onto doll. **$100-$150**

Pyle, Denver. Actor Pyle appeared in many films and on television. He was a regular on the *Andy Griffith Show* from 1960 to 1968. He also played Doris Day's father on *The Doris Day Show* (1968-1970) and starred as Uncle Jesse on *The Dukes of Hazzard*, which aired from 1979 until 1985.

Uncle Jesse. Mego. Hong Kong. #09010/6. 1982. 3 inches. All vinyl, fully jointed, painted features; painted clothing. Copyright by Warner Bros., Inc. ....**$15-$25**

Quigley, Juanita (Baby Jane).

Actress Quigley was known as Baby Jane. She performed in films from 1933 until 1936 under that name, then, from 1936 until 1944, under the name Juanita Quigley. Quigley left acting at the age of eighteen and went on to become a teacher.

Baby Jane. Alexander Doll Company. U.S.A. 1935. 17 inches. All composition, fully jointed, auburn mohair wig, brown sleep eyes with eyelashes, open mouth with teeth and tongue. Head marked: "BABY-JANE// REG//MME ALEXANDER." ....**$700-$800**

Quinn, Aileen.

Actress Quinn played the part of Annie in the 1982 film version of *Annie*, based on the comic strip "Little Orphan Annie," beating out more than 8,000 children who auditioned for the role.

1. Annie. Freundlich Novelty Corp. Circa 1940. 14 inches. All composition, molded and painted yellow hair, painted features, jointed at arms, legs and head; wearing red dress with white trim, white long socks and black shoes. ....**$300-$400**

2. Annie. Knickerbocker Toy Co. U.S.A. #3856. 1982. 6 inches. All vinyl, fully jointed, rooted bright-red hair, painted freckles across face, open/closed mouth; six different outfits were also sold for the doll. ....**$10-$20**

3. Annie. Knickerbocker Toy Co. U.S.A. #3851. 1982. 16 inches. All cloth doll, jointed arms and legs, red yarn hair, printed features; wearing bright-red dress with white socks and shoes. A plush dog, Sandy, is in her pocket. ....**$30-$50**

4. Annie. Knickerbocker Toy Co. U.S.A. #3852. 1982. 23 inches. All cloth, jointed arms and legs, red yarn hair, printed features; wearing bright-red dress with white socks and shoes. A plush dog, Sandy, is in her pocket. ......**$40-$60**

5. Annie. Maker unknown. China. 2000. 6 inches. All cloth, red hair; wearing red dress. Sold at the theater productions of Annie. ....**$5-$10**

1: Annie by Freundlich Novelty Corp., circa 1940. This early doll representing Little Orphan Annie was based on the original comic strip. *Author's collection.*

2: Knickerbocker's 6-inch Annie, as portrayed by Aileen Quinn, in the movie of the same name. Shown with Annie's friend Molly (center) and Miss Hannigan (right), played by Carol Burnett. *Author's collection.*

R

Reeve, Christopher. Actor Reeve played the role of Superman in the film *Superman*, released in 1978, and also starred in *Superman II* in 1981. A tragic horse riding accident in 1995 left him a quadriplegic, but he has continued to work in films.

Superman. Madel, S.A. Spain. #1300. 1979. 6 inches. All vinyl, fully jointed, painted hair and features. Unmarked. Copyright by D.C. Comics, Inc. ....**$25-$50**

Reeves, George. Actor Reeves is best known for his television role as Superman in the 1950s.

1. Superman. Ideal Toy Corp. U.S.A. 1945 to 1950. 13 inches. Composition head and upper torso, wood jointed arms and legs; blue and red painted costume with large "S" on chest. Designed by Joseph Kallus. Marked on belt: "DES. And COPYRIGHT BY SUPERMAN INC//MADE BY IDEAL NOVELTY and TOY CO." ....**$750-$1,000**; **$1,500-$2,000**, in original box

2. George Reeves Superman Hand Puppet. Ideal Toy Corp. U.S.A. 1965. Vinyl head, cloth body, painted and molded features. Trademarks: "©1965//NAT.PER.PUB.INC.//SM-P-HL3// IDEAL TOY CORP." ....**$100-$150**

3. Captain Action in Superman Outfit. Ideal Toy Corp. U.S.A. #3401-7. 1966 to 1970. 12 inches. Vinyl head, poseable arms and legs; wearing uniform. ....**$200-$250**

Reubens, Paul. Comedian Reubens hosted his own television series, *Pee Wee's Playhouse* (1986-1990). The show won a total of twenty-five Emmy Awards, three for acting. Reuben's character, Pee Wee, has entertained children for years.

1. Pee Wee Herman's sidekick Ricardo from Pee Wee's Playhouse. Matchbox. China. 1987 to 1988. 6 inches. All vinyl, painted features; painted clothing. Sold on card. Hard-to-find item. ....**$15-$25**

2. Pee Wee Herman. Matchbox. China. 1987. 18 inches. Vinyl and cloth talking doll, talks when you press doll. Four phrases include: "Aaaaaaaaagh! I'm Pee Wee Herman; I know I am, but what are you?" and "Ha-Ha" (Pee Wee's laugh). ....**$15-$30**

3. Pee Wee Herman. Matchbox. China. 1987. 26 inches. Vinyl and cloth doll; talks when you pull string. ....**$50-$75**

4. Pee Wee Herman Matchbox. China. 1988. 5 inches. All vinyl, painted features; painted clothing. Sold on card. ....**$15-$25**
(See photos of 1, 3, and 4 on page 130.)

2A: Close-up of the 18-inch Pee Wee Herman talking doll, by Matchbox. The character was played by Paul Reubens on the television series *Pee Wee's Playhouse*.

1: Ideal's Superman, dating from the late 1940s, designed by Joseph Kallus. *Author's collection.*

2B: The 18-inch Pee Wee Herman by Matchbox in its original box.

1: Pee Wee Herman's sidekick Ricardo, 6 inches, by Matchbox.

3: This 26-inch Pee Wee Herman talks when its string is pulled.

4: Pee Wee Herman, 5 inches, by Matchbox.

Paul Revere. S.S. Kresge Company. Hong Kong. 1976. 7 inches. Vinyl head, painted features and hair, fully jointed plastic body; wearing orange knickers, long jacket with white shirt in revolutionary style. Marked on back: "MADE IN//HONG KONG." Part of a series called the Heroes of the American Revolution. The dolls in this series were distributed by Montgomery Ward & Co. Inc. ....$15-$25

Paul Revere from the Heroes of the American Revolution series by the S.S. Kresge *Company. Courtesy of Suellen Manning.*

The back of the box for Paul Revere by the S.S. Kresge Company. Others offered in this series were Benjamin Franklin, John Paul Jones, Thomas Jefferson, George Washington, Patrick Henry and Nathan Hale. *Courtesy of Suellen Manning.*

Revere, Paul. American patriot and silversmith Paul Revere was born in Boston, January 1, 1735, and died May 10, 1818. He became a legendary hero at the start of the American Revolution, when he rode from Charlestown to Lexington Massachusetts, on the night of April 18, 1775, to warn the countryside of approaching British troops.

Rimes, Le Ann. By the age of eighteen, country singer Rimes had already won two Grammy Awards, three Academy of Country Music Awards, a CMA Horizon Award and four Billboard Music Awards. She has authored a book and starred in a syndicated television series and a movie. To date she has sold more than twenty million records.

Le Ann Rimes. Exclusive Toys, Inc. Signature Superstars. China. #18078. 1998. 9 inches. All vinyl, jointed, molded blonde hair, painted features; wearing black dress with black shoes. Box marked: "Manufactured by Exclusive Toy, Inc. Metuchen, N.J. 08840." ....**$25-$35**

Le Ann Rimes by Exclusive Toys, Inc. *Courtesy of David Spurgeon.*

Rippy, Rodney Allen. Child actor Rippy appeared in many television commercials and shows. He was best known for his Jack-in-the-Box commercials in the early 1970s.

Rodney Allen Rippy. Shindana Toys. Taiwan. 1973. 16 inches. All cloth, printed features, jointed arms and legs; printed clothing. Copyright by Target Marketing, Inc. and Shindana Toys. ....**$50-$75**

Robinson, Jackie. Baseball player Robinson was the first black player in the Major Leagues when he signed on with the Brooklyn Dodgers in 1947. He was inducted into the Baseball Hall of Fame in 1962.

Jackie Robinson by Allied Grand Mfg. Co., Inc., in his Brooklyn Dodgers uniform. *Courtesy of Annette's Antique Dolls.*

Jackie Robinson. Allied Grand Mfg. Co., Inc. 1950. 13 inches. Brown composition head and body, painted features, fully jointed; wearing Brooklyn Dodgers uniform in gray with blue jacket and cap, originally sold with a ball and bat and a Jackie Robinson comic book. ..**$600-$700**

Rogers, Roy. Actor and singer Rogers appeared in dozens of western films. He was married to Dale Evans and eventually had his own show *The Roy Rogers Show*, which ran from December 1951 until June 1957.

1. Roy Rogers. Dolls of Hollywood. 1948. 17 inches. All cloth, painted features. ..**$35-$50**

2. Roy Rogers. Duchess Doll Corp. 1948. 7 inches. All plastic, fully jointed, sleep eyes, mohair wig. ....**$25-$35**

3. Roy Rogers. Ideal Toy Corp. U.S.A. #RR7. 1949. 25 inches. Stuffed vinyl head, painted hair and features, cloth body with vinyl hands; cloth formed cowboy outfit and hat with guns in holster, "Roy Rogers" imprinted on hat. ....**$150-$200**

4. Roy Rogers. Zany Toys, Inc. 1952. Hand puppet with vinyl head, painted features. ....**$100-$125**

5. Roy Rogers with Trigger. Hartland Plastics, Inc., U.S.A. #806. 1955. 8 inches. ....**$250-$300**, mint-in-box

Cesar Romero in his role of The Joker on the television series *Batman.*

Romero, Cesar. Actor Romero starred in films in the early 1940s as the Cisco Kid. From January 1966 until March 1968, he played the Joker, Batman's rival, in the television series *Batman.*

Joker. Mego. Hong Kong. #1351. 1974. 8 inches. All vinyl, fully jointed, painted hair and features; wearing green and black Joker costume. ....**$40-$60**, mint-in-box

Roosevelt, Eleanor. First lady and wife of 32nd president Franklin D. Roosevelt, she was one of the most politically active first ladies in American history.

Eleanor Roosevelt. Effanbee Doll Company. China. 1985. #7642. 13 inches. All vinyl, painted features; wearing burgundy dress with jacket, came with matching hat, shoes and pearl necklace. Part of the Great Moments in History Series. ....**$50-$75**

Eleanor Roosevelt from Effanbee's Great Moments in History Series. *Courtesy of Marlene Grant.*

Roosevelt, Theodore. Roosevelt served as president of the United States from 1901 until 1909. The teddy bear was named after him after he refused to shoot a bear cub on a hunting trip.

1: Teddy Roosevelt Jack-in-the-Box by W.S. Reed Co. *Courtesy of Robert DeCenzo*

1. Teddy Roosevelt Jack-in-the-Box. W.S. Reed Co. U.S.A. Circa 1900. Composition head, molded hat; in wooden box. ....**$500** up

2. Teddy Roosevelt. Schoenhut. U.S.A. 1910. 9 inches. All wood, painted features, fully jointed; with removable wooden helmet. ....**$800-$1,000**

3. Teddy Roosevelt. Excel Toy Corp. Hong Kong. 1974. 9 inches. All vinyl, fully jointed, painted hair and features; wearing glasses, dressed as Lt. Col. ....**$25-$50**

4. Teddy Roosevelt. Peggy Nisbet. England. #P731. Circa 1970s. 8 inches. All hard plastic, jointed at arms, molded hair, painted features; dressed in trousers, shirt, long jacket and top hat. ......**$25-$50**

Ross, Betsy. Seamstress Ross is reputed to have sewn the first American flag.

1. Betsy Ross. Alexander Doll Company. U.S.A. #731. 1967 to 1974. 8 inches. All hard plastic, fully jointed, dark brown wig, sleep eyes with eyelashes; carries small flag. Was sold later as #431. ....**$75-$100**

2. Betsy Ross. Effanbee. China. #1152. 1976 to 1978. 11 inches. Vinyl head, arms, plastic legs and torso, rooted blonde hair, blue sleep eyes. Head marked: "EFFANBEE//©1976//1176." ....**$50-$75**

3. Betsy Ross. Hallmark. Taiwan. #250DT900-4. 1979. 7 inches. All cloth, printed features; printed clothing, in box shaped like a house. ....**$10-$15**

Ross, Diana. Singer and actress Ross was originally lead singer of the singing group Diana Ross and the Supremes, which at one point included Mary Wilson and Florence Ballard. She eventually became a successful soloist, and has starred in several major motion pictures, including *Lady Sings the Blues* (1972), for which she was nominated for an Academy Award.

1. Diana Ross. Ideal. U.S.A. #0920-9. 1969. 17 inches. Vinyl, fully jointed, rooted black hair, brown sleep eyes; in two versions: "On Stage" #0920-9, dressed in a gold dress with feathers and gold shoes, and "Off Stage" #0921-7, dressed in chartreuse knit mini dress with scarf and black shoes. Copyright by Motown, Inc. ....**$200-$300** each

2. Diana Ross. Mego. Hong Kong. #76000. 1977. 12 inches. Vinyl, fully jointed, rooted black hair, painted brown eyes with long eyelashes. Head marked: "© MOTOWN// RECORD CORPORATION;" box marked: "Fully Poseable Fashion Doll Includes; Posing stand, Diana's cut-out accessories, fully washable hair, (wash and blow dry on cool setting)." Manufactured in Hong Kong by Mego Corp. ....**$100-$125**

A 6-inch Snake Plissken from *Escape from LA*, as portrayed by Kurt Russell, by McFarlane Toys, 2000. *Author's collection.*

2: Diana Ross by Mego, from 1977. *Courtesy of Suellen Manning.*

Russell, Kurt. Actor Russell has starred in a variety of films, including *Soldier* (1998), *Breakdown* (1997), *Backdraft* (1991) and the 1996 film *Escape From LA*. He is the long-time partner of actress Goldie Hawn.

Snake Plissken from *Escape From LA*. McFarlane Toys, China. 2000. 6 inches. All vinyl, with painted and molded hair, painted features; painted and molded clothes, includes movie poster replica with backdrop and three guns. Box marked: "© 2000 Paramount Pictures." Part of the Feature Films Figures Series from the Movie Maniacs Collection. ....**$20-$30**

Ruth, George Herman (Babe Ruth).

Baseball player Ruth held more than fifty baseball records when he retired. His career home runs reached 714 and he was voted into the Baseball Hall of Fame in 1936. Ruth is considered by many one of the best baseball players of all time.

Babe Ruth. Hallmark. Taiwan. #400DT113-5. 1979. 7 inches. All cloth, printed features; printed clothing, in box shaped like a building. ....**$10-$15**

S

Sales, Soupy. Comedian Sales starred in several children's television shows. His own show aired on television from 1955 until 1962.

1. Soupy Sales. Ideal. U.S.A. 1965. 23 inches. Vinyl head, jointed cloth body, flocked black hair, painted blue eyes; wearing a bow tie and red sweatshirt. Head marked: "©1965//IDEAL TOY CORP//SOUPY SALES-WMC/H9." ....**$50-$70**

2. Soupy Sales. Knickerbocker. Japan. 1966. 13 inches. Vinyl head, molded and painted hair and features, stuffed cloth body made of corduroy; jacket and pants, felt collar sewn to shirt, large polka dotted bow tie glued to shirt. Head marked: "©1966 KNICK//JAPAN. Copyright by Soupy Sales, W.M.C." ....**$40-$50**

Savalas, Telly. Actor Savalas is best known for his role as Kojak, the detective, on the CBS television series of the same name. The show aired from 1973 until 1978.

1. Kojak. Excel Toy Corp. Hong Kong. #550. 1976. 8 inches. All vinyl, fully jointed, painted brown eyes; wearing black pants, shoes and long-sleeved jacket, with plastic gun, holster, hat, cigar and lollipops. Back marked: "© 1976 UNIVERSAL//CITY STUDIOS, INC//© 1976 EXCEL TOY CORP.//MADE IN HONG KONG." ....**$50-$75**

2. Kojak. Mego. Hong Kong. 1977. 9 inches. All vinyl, jointed, painted features; wearing dark pants and long-sleeved jacket. ....**$60-$75**

Schneider, John. Actor and singer Schneider is best known for his role as Bo Duke on the CBS television series *The Dukes of Hazzard*, which aired from 1979 until 1985.

1. Bo from Dukes of Hazzard. Mego. Hong Kong. #09060. 1981. 3 inches. All vinyl, fully jointed, painted yellow hair; molded clothing. Back marked: "© WB 1980//MADE IN HONG KONG." Part of a set with a car and Tom Wopat as Luke. ....**$10-$15**

2. Bo from Dukes of Hazzard. Mego. Hong Kong. #09050/1. 1981. 8 inches. All vinyl, fully jointed, painted yellow hair, blue painted eyes.

Head marked: "© WARNER BROS,// INC.1980." ....**$25-$35**

3. Bo from Dukes of Hazzard. Mego. Hong Kong. #09010/1. 1982. 3 inches. All vinyl, fully jointed, painted yellow hair; molded clothing. Back marked: "© WB 1980//MADE IN HONG KONG." Same as first doll but only sold individually. ....**$10-$15**

John Schneider (at right in photo) with Catherine Bach and Tom Wopat.

Schwarzenegger, Arnold. The Austrian bodybuilder came to the United States in 1968 to compete in the Mr. Universe competition. Schwarzenegger began his acting career in the 1977 film *Pumping Iron*. He went on to star in many blockbuster films, including *The Terminator* (1984). He is married to television news reporter and author Maria Shriver, who is also niece of the late John F. Kennedy. He actively works with many children's charities.

1. T2 Figure. China. #32200. Circa 1990s. 11 inches. Vinyl, painted and molded features, half of his face is painted silver; painted and molded clothing of black pants and jacket with silver shirt and brown boots. This is an unauthorized figure based on the movie *Terminator 2*. It is unmarked and the only markings on the box are: "Item No. 32200. MADE IN CHINA." ....**$30-$40**

2. The Terminator. Christomas Corp. China. Circa 1990s. 6 inches. All vinyl, painted and molded features, rooted black hair; painted and molded clothing. Celebrity spoof doll from the movie *The Terminator*. Box marked: "© Celebrity Spoof Licensing Corp." ....**$20-$30**

3. Terminator. Kenner. Hong Kong. 1992. 14 inches. All vinyl, jointed, painted features, eyes light up, moveable arms, five working action buttons on back (push buttons to hear Arnold speaking phrases including "Hasta La Vista Baby" and "I'll Be Back"); painted cloth-

ing, with machine guns and drums of destruction. ....**$15-$20**

1: Unauthorized figure representing Arnold Schwarzenegger from the movie *Terminator 2*. *Courtesy of David Spurgeon.*

2: A spoof doll of Arnold Schwarzenegger as the Terminator by Celebrity Spoof Licensing Corp. *Courtesy of David Spurgeon.*

Scott, Barbara Ann.
Scott, a Canadian ice skater, won the Women's European Figure Skating Championship and the Gold Medal in the Winter Olympics in 1947.

Barbara Ann Scott. Reliable Doll. Canada. 1949. 15 inches. All composition, fully jointed, brown mohair wig, blue sleep eyes with eyelashes, open mouth with teeth. Head marked: "RELIABLE DOLL//MADE IN CANADA." ....**$500-$600**

Scout, Dave Cub.
This fictional character represents the average American Cub Scout.

Dave Cub Scout. Kenner. Hong Kong. 1975. 8 inches. All vinyl, painted features; with Dave Cub Scout uniform, shoes, neckerchief, slide, scouting booklet. Box marked: "Dave Cub © 1975 General Mills Fun Group, Inc. Kenner." ....**$25-$40**

Dave Cub Scout by Kenner, in original box. *Courtesy of Suellen Manning.*

The back of the box for Dave Cub Scout. *Courtesy of Suellen Manning.*

Shanks, Don.
Actor Shanks is best known for his role as Nakoma on the television show *The Life and Times of Grizzly Adams*, which aired from February 1977 to July 1978.

Nakoma. Mattel, Inc. Hong Kong. 1978. #2381. 10 inches. Vinyl, jointed; wearing authentic brown leather Indian outfit with moccasins, with knife and spear. Marked on back of head: "© 1976 MATTEL INC.;" marked on back: "©1971 MATTEL. INC//U.S. & FOREIGN PATENTED//HONG KONG." ....**$20-$25**, loose; **$40-$50**, boxed

Shatner, William.
Actor Shatner starred on Broadway, in films and on television. He played Captain Kirk on the NBC television series *Star Trek*, which aired from September 1966 to September 1969 and is best known for his role on that series. Shatner also starred in the motion picture *Star Trek: the Motion Picture* (1979) and the television series *T.J. Hooker* (1982-1986)..

1. Captain Kirk. Mego. Hong Kong. #51200/1. 1974. 8 inches. All vinyl, fully jointed, painted hair and features. Copyright by Paramount Pictures. ....$40-$50

2. Captain Kirk. Mego. Hong Kong. #91200/1. 1979. 3 inches. All vinyl, painted features. ....$20-$30

3. Captain Kirk. Mego. Hong Kong. #91210/1. 1979. 12 inches. All vinyl, fully jointed, painted hair and features; wearing uniform from the Star Ship Enterprise. Head marked: "© PPC;" back marked: "© MEGO CORP. 1977//MADE IN HONG KONG." ......$40-$60

4. Captain Kirk. Knickerbocker. Haiti and U.S.A. #0599. 1980. 13 inches. Vinyl head, painted hair and features, cloth body with Velcro on hands so they stick together. Head marked: "1979 P.P.C.//K.T.C. Copyright by Paramount Pictures Corporation.". ....$25-$35

5. Captain Kirk. Applause. China. 1994. 10 inches. All vinyl, painted hair and features, movable arms; painted uniform. Copyright by Paramount Pictures Corporation. ....$10-$15

1: Captain Kirk from the *Star Trek* television series, portrayed by William Shatner, by Mego. He is in the middle, flanked by Dr. McCoy, portrayed by DeForest Kelly, and Mr. Spock, portrayed by Leonard Nimoy. *Courtesy of McMasters Doll Auctions.*

5: Captain Kirk, 10 inches, from the *Star Trek* television series, portrayed by William Shatner, by Applause. *Author's collection.*

Shera, Mark. Actor Shera is best known for his role as Luca on the ABC television series S.W.A.T., which aired from 1975 until 1977. (See Perry, Rod for group photograph.)

Luca from *S.W.A.T.* L.J.N. Toys, Ltd. Hong Kong. 1975. 7 inches. All vinyl, fully jointed, painted hair and features; dressed in S.W.A.T. gear. ....$20-$30

Luca from *S.W.A.T.*, as portrayed by Mark Shera, by L.J.N. Toys, Ltd. *Courtesy of Suellen Manning.*

Shields, Brooke. Actress and model Shields' acting career took off when she played a child prostitute in *Pretty Baby* (1978). She continued to appear in films and on television and starred in her own television series entitled *Suddenly Susan*, which aired from 1996 to 2000.

1. Brooke Shields. L.J.N. Toys, Ltd. Hong Kong. 1982. 11 inches. All vinyl, jointed, painted features, rooted brunette hair; dressed in sweater and leggings with white boots, sweaters in different colors. ....$20-$30

2. Brooke Shields. LJN Toys, Ltd. Hong Kong. 1983. 11 inches. All vinyl, jointed, painted features, rooted brunette hair; dressed in beautiful gown and holding flowers. Made to capitalize on the fact that Brooke was graduating from high school. Box marked: "© 1983 B.C.S. & Co. Inc." ....$20-$30

3. Brooke Shields Suntan Doll. L.J.N. Toys. Hong Kong. 1983. 11 inches. All vinyl, jointed, painted features, rooted brunette hair; dressed in short summer outfit with Brooke's picture on box. ....$20-$30

4. Brooke Shields Doll. L.J.N. Toys. Hong Kong. 1983. 11 inches. All vinyl, jointed, painted features, rooted brunette hair; basic doll with autographed picture. ....$15-$25

5. Prom Party Brooke. L.J.N. Toys. Hong Kong. 1983. 11 inches. All vinyl, jointed, painted features, rooted brunette hair, pulled back; wearing a beautiful gown. Very rare.

With 11-inch by 14-inch autographed color picture of Shields. Limited edition for Kay-Bee Toys. ....**$30-$40**

1A: Brooke Shields by L.J.N. Toys in the original box. *Courtesy of David Spurgeon.*

1B:The back of Brooke Shields' box. *Courtesy of David Spurgeon.*

5: Prom Party Brooke by L.J.N. Toys, a limited edition for Kay-Bee Toys.

Shirley, Anne.
Actress Shirley began acting in films by age four and, throughout her career, starred in nearly forty films, including *Anne of Green Gables* (1934). She retired from acting before the age of thirty, but not before winning an Academy Award nomination in 1937 for best supporting actress in the film *Stella Dallas*.

Effanbee used the Anne Shirley markings on many of the company's dolls, including Snow White and the Historical Series dolls. Anne Shirley dolls usually wore checked or flowered dresses but were also dressed in skating outfits, gowns and flower girl outfits.

1. Anne Shirley. Effanbee. U.S.A. Circa 1935. 11 inches. (Patricia-Kin) All composition, fully jointed, red human hair wig with pigtails, blue tin sleep eyes with eyelashes; dressed in pleated skirt with white blouse and jacket, matching hat. Head marked: "EFFANBEE// PATRICIA KIN;" back marked: "EFFAN-BEE//PATSY JR.//DOLL." ....**$300-$400**

2. Anne Shirley. Effanbee. U.S.A. Circa 1935. 14 inches. (Patricia) All composition, fully jointed, reddish mohair wig with pigtails, sleep eyes with eyelashes; wearing checked dress with matching hat. Back marked: "EFFANBEE//PATRICIA." ....**$275-$300**

3. Anne Shirley. Effanbee. U.S.A. 1935 to 1940. 15 inches. All composition, fully jointed, reddish mohair or human-hair wig with pigtails, sleep eyes with eyelashes; wearing dress with straw hat. Back marked: "EFFANBEE//ANNE SHIRLEY." ....**$275-$300**

4. Anne Shirley. Effanbee. U.S.A. Circa 1935. 16 inches. (Mary Lee) All composition, fully jointed, red wig with pigtails, sleep eyes with eyelashes; wearing checked dress. Head marked: "© MARY LEE;" back marked:

5: Effanbee's Anne Shirley in an 18-inch size, circa late 1940s. She has been re-dressed. *Courtesy of Sunnie Newell.*

7: Black version of Effanbee's Anne Shirley in a 21-inch size. *Author's collection*

"EFFANBEE//PATSY-JOAN;" came with tag that reads: "I am Anne Shirley. Inspired by Anne Shirley in RKO Pictures, 'Anne of Green Gables' An Effanbee Doll." ....$300-$350

5. Anne Shirley. Effanbee. U.S.A. Circa late 1940s. 18 inches. (Also called Little Lady.) All composition, fully jointed, yarn hair; re-dressed. ....$300-$375

6. Anne Shirley. Effanbee. U.S.A. Circa late 1940s. 21 inch. (Also called Little Lady) All composition, fully jointed, red wig, blue sleep eyes with eyelashes; wearing in satin gown. Back marked: "EFFANBEE//ANNE SHIRLEY." ....$400-$450

7. Anne Shirley. Effanbee. U.S.A. Circa 1940s. 21 inches. Black version, dark composi-tion, black mohair wig. ....$600-$700

8. Anne Shirley. Effanbee. U.S.A. Circa 1940s. 24 inches. All composition, fully jointed, all original. ....$500-$600
(See photos 5 and 7 on page 137.)

8: Effanbee's Anne Shirley, circa 1940s, in a 24-inch size, all original. *Courtesy of Patricia Wood.*

Silla, Felix. Actor Silla played the role of Twiki the Robot in the NBC television series *Buck Rogers in the 25th Century*, which aired from 1979 to 1981. The character was voiced by Mel Blanc.

1. Twiki from Buck Rogers in the 25th Century. Mego. Hong Kong. #85000/2. 1979. 2 inches. Vinyl, fully jointed; in robot outfit. Copyright by Robert C. Dille. ....$10-$15

2. Twiki from Buck Rogers in the 25th Century. Mego. Hong Kong. #85016. 1979. 7 inches. All plastic, fully jointed; in robot outfit. Copyright by Robert C. Dille. .... $25-$35

Simmons, Gene. (See KISS)

Silva, Henry. Actor Silva played the role of Killer Kane in the NBC television series *Buck Rogers in the 25th Century*, which aired from 1979 to 1981.

1. Killer Kane from *Buck Rogers in the 25th Century*. Mego. Hong Kong. #85000/4. 1979. 3 inches. All vinyl, fully jointed, painted hair and features; painted clothing. Copyright by Robert C. Dille. ....$5-$10

2. Killer Kane from *Buck Rogers in the 25th Century*. Mego. Hong Kong. #85001/3. 1979. 12 inches. All vinyl, fully jointed, painted hair and features; wearing all black outfit. Copyright by Robert C. Dille. ....$30-$40

Simms, Lu Ann. Singer Simms sang on the CBS show *Arthur Godfrey and His Friends* from 1952 until 1955.

1. Lu Ann Simms. Roberta Doll Company, Inc. U.S.A. 1953. 14 inches. All hard plastic, fully jointed, dark-brown saran wig pulled back into ponytail with bangs, blue sleep eyes with eyelashes, open mouth with teeth and felt tongue; wearing a cotton dress with green trim, black vinyl shoes, with green vinyl purse and hair curlers. Head marked: "180;" sometimes marked: "U.S.A." ....$200-$250

2. Lu Ann Simms. Horsman. U.S.A. 1953. 18 inches. All hard plastic, fully joint-ed, dark-brown saran wig pulled back into ponytail with bangs, blue sleep eyes with eyelashes, open mouth with teeth and felt tongue; wearing a cotton dress with black vinyl shoes. Head marked: "180." Also sold in 21 inches. ....14 inches, **$200-$300**; 18 inches, **$300-$400**; 21 inches, **$400-$500**

Simpson, O. J. Football player and actor, Simpson, "The Juice," was a running back for the Buffalo Bills from 1969 to 1977. He was then with the San Francisco 49ers until 1979. Simpson held the NFL rushing record with 2,003 yards. He played small roles in films and was the spokesperson for Hertz Rental Cars. In the late 1990s, Simpson was charged with murdering his wife, Nicole Brown Simpson, and a friend of hers, and was acquitted.

O.J. Simpson. Shindana Toys. Hong Kong. #9005. 1975. 9 inches. All vinyl, fully jointed, paint-ed hair and features; with 26 pieces of sports equip-ment, also sold with helmet and football only. Head marked: "SHINDANA TOYS//©1975." Copyright by O.J. Simpson Enterprises Inc. ......**$50-$60**, doll with helmet/football; **$150-$200**; doll with sports equipment

O.J. Simpson by Shindana Toys, from 1975.

The back of the box for Shindana Toys' O.J. Simpson.

Close-up of the box for O.J. Simpson showing the stats.

Slater, Christian.

Actor Slater began his career in 1985 on the television series *Ryan's Hope* before moving on to stage and film work. He performed in several films including *Robin Hood–Prince of Thieves* (1991) with actor-director Kevin Costner.

Christian Slater as Will Scarlett, made by Kenner in 1991.

Will Scarlett-Prince of Thieves. Kenner. Hong Kong. 1991. 4 inches. All plastic, poseable, painted hair and features; painted clothing with fabric and vinyl clothing. Marked: "©MCP&WBI 91." Sold on card with picture of star. Copyright by Warner Brothers. ....**$15-$20**

Smith, Jaclyn.

Actress and clothing designer Smith is best known for her role as Kelly Garrett in the hit television series *Charlie's Angels*, which aired from 1976 to 1981. She continues to act while working on her own line of clothing, which is sold nationally through K-Mart department stores. (See also Fawcett, Farrah)

1. Jaclyn Smith. Mego. Hong Kong. 1977. 12 inches. All vinyl, fully jointed, painted features; dressed in jumpsuit. ....**$35-$45**, loose

2. Kelly. Hasbro. Hong Kong. #4862. 1977. 8 inches. All vinyl, fully jointed, rooted dark brown hair, painted brown eyes; dressed in jumpsuit with boots. Copyright by Spelling-Goldberg Productions. ....**$20-$30**, loose

3. Charlie's Angels Set. Included all three girls. Hasbro. Hong Kong. 1977. 8 inches. ....**$175-$225**, each set

4. Kelly. Raynal. Belgium. 1977. 8 inches. All vinyl, painted features. ..**$100-$125**, boxed

Smith, Kevin.

Actor Smith was a regular cast member on the Warner Brothers television series *Xena: Warrior Princess*, which aired for five years ending in 2001. Smith played the role of Aires.

1. Aires. Toy Biz, Inc. China. #42025. 1998. 12 inches. All vinyl, painted features, molded

1: Aires from the television series *Xena: Warrior Princess*, as portrayed by Kevin Smith, by Toy Biz, Inc. *Courtesy of David Spurgeon.*

black hair, painted beard and mustache; wearing one-piece black leather styled jumpsuit with silver spikes. ....**$15-$25**

2. Aires. Toy Biz, Inc. China. #42028. 1999. 12 inches. All vinyl, painted features, molded black hair, painted beard and mustache. ....**$10-$20**

Somers, Suzanne. Actress, entrepreneur and author Somers is best known for her role as Chrissy Snow on the television series *Three's Company*, which aired from March 1977 to September 1984. A fitness enthusiast, Somers also markets her own exercise equipment and has written several books on food and fitness.

Chrissy. Mego. Hong Kong. #76300. 1978. 12 inches. All vinyl, fully jointed, rooted blonde hair, painted blue eyes with long eyelashes; wearing long pink dress. Head marked: "©THREE'S//COMPANY." Box shows fellow cast members Joyce DeWitt (Janet Wood) and John Ritter (Jack Tripper). ....**$50-$60**

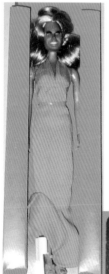

Chrissy from the television series *Three's Company*, as portrayed by Suzanne Somers, by Mego. *Courtesy of Suellen Manning.*

The front of the box for Mego's Chrissy. *Courtesy of Suellen Manning.*

The back of the box for Mego's Chrissy shows the other cast members from the television show *Three's Company*. *Courtesy of Suellen Manning.*

Sorbo, Kevin. Actor Sorbo is best known for his role on the hit television series *Hercules*. With his great looks and muscular build, Sorbo had no problem playing the series lead as Hercules.

1. Hercules. E toys a division of TNA Products. China. #98261. Circa 1990s. 12 inches. All vinyl, jointed; wearing brown Hercules outfit. ....**$20-$30**

2. Hercules. Maker unknown. China. #98281. Circa 1990s. 8 inches. Cheap plastic, painted and molded features. A copy (knockoff) of licensed Hercules doll. Shown with matching Xena look-alike doll. ....**$10-$15**, each

2: A knockoff of a licensed Hercules doll, from the television series of the same name. A look-alike Xena doll is shown with him. *Courtesy of David Spurgeon.*

Soul, David. Actor Soul is best known for his role as Detective Ken "Hutch" Hutchinson on the television series *Starsky & Hutch*, which aired from September 1975 to August 1979. (See Glaser, Paul for photograph.)

1. Hutch. Mego. Hong Kong. 62800/2. 1975. 7 inches. All vinyl, fully jointed, painted yellow hair. First issue doll is on a card with a picture of a car on it and shows two photographs on the back. ..**$15-$20**, loose; **$40-$50**, on card

2. Hutch. Mego. Hong Kong. 1976. 8 inches. All vinyl, jointed, painted featues, molded blonde hair; wearing blue jeans, yellow sweater with tan vest. Second issue doll is on a card with a picture of a car on card and shows five photographs on the back. ....**$15-$20**, loose; **$30-$40**, on card.

3. Hutch Doll. Palitoy. United Kingdom. 1977. 8 inches. Vinyl, painted features. Sold on card with illustrations. Looks like Mego type dolls. ....**$20-$30**, loose; **$75-$100**, on card

4. Starsky and Hutch. Palitoy. United Kingdom. 1977. 8 inches. Vinyl, painted features. Sold in pack with both dolls. Looks like Mego-type dolls. ....**$150-$200**, boxed

2: The box for Mego's Hutch, as portrayed by David Soul, from the television series *Starsky and Hutch*.

Spears, Britney. Singer Spears began her career in the early 1990s with the Disney Channel's *Mickey Mouse Club* (MMC). After the show was canceled, Spears pursued her singing career. In 1998, her first album, *Baby. . . One More Time*, was a huge success, hitting number one on the charts and turning Spears into one of the hottest teen singers in the country.

1. Britney Spears. Play Along Toys, Inc. China. #20000. 1999. 11 inches. All vinyl, jointed, rooted blonde hair, painted brown eyes and features; wearing outfit from "Baby...One More Time" video. Copyright by Britney Brands, Inc. First doll in series. ....**$25-$30**

2. Britney Spears. Play Along Toys, Inc. China. #20100. 1999. 11 inches. All vinyl, jointed, rooted blonde hair, painted brown eyes and features; wearing outfit from her performance of the song "Sometimes." Copyright by Britney Brands, Inc. The deluxe sets include additional accessories and show Britney in outfits from her concert performances. ....**$30-$35**

1: Britney Spears by Play Along Toys, Inc., in the costume from her "Baby...One More Time" video. This is the first doll in the series. *Courtesy of Play Along Toys, Inc.*

2: Britney Spears by Play Along Toys, Inc., in the costume she wore performing the song "Sometimes." *Courtesy of Play Along Toys, Inc.*

3. Britney Spears. Play Along Toys, Inc. China. #20000. 2000. 11 inches. All vinyl, jointed, rooted blonde hair, painted brown eyes and features; wearing MTV fashion in silver and charcoal gray. Copyright by Britney Brands, Inc. ..$15-$20

4. Britney Spears. Play Along Toys, Inc. China. #20000. 2000. 11 inches. All vinyl, jointed, rooted blonde hair, painted brown eyes and features; wearing one of three outfits from the "Oops I Did it Again" collection: a black and white outfit from "Oops" video, a white leather top and skirt from "Oops" video and a red cat suit from "Oops" video. ....$25-$30

5. Britney Spears. Play Along Toys, Inc. China. #90000. 2000. 11 inches. All vinyl, jointed, rooted blonde hair, painted brown eyes and features; wearing outfit from her concert "Baby...One More Time," came boxed with CD single. Copyright by Britney Brands, Inc. ....$30-$40

6. Britney Spears. Play Along Toys, Inc. China. 2001. 11 inches. All vinyl, jointed, rooted blonde hair, painted brown eyes and features. Same dolls as described in 4 plus newest doll style from "Lucky" video, wearing blue top with black pants. ....$20-$30

7. Britney Spears. Play Along Toys, Inc. China. #20100. 2001. 11 inches. All vinyl, jointed, rooted blonde hair, painted brown eyes and features; wearing one of many new outfits, including a red top with white skirt, a purple jumpsuit and a turquoise fringed outfit. Deluxe set includes updated packaging, much different from the 1999 to 2000 production run. ..$25-$30

8. Britney Spears. Play Along Toys, Inc. China. #20100. 2000. 11 inches. All vinyl, jointed, rooted blonde hair, painted brown eyes and features. Assortment of three styles released in Fall 2000 includes a white outfit with extra outfit, a gold pastel tulle outfit with bear and a turquoise fringed outfit with bracelet. ..$30-$40

9. Britney Spears Mini Dolls. Play Along Toys, Inc. China. #23500 (Boxed version; also came in blister package.) 1999 to 2000. 6 inches. All vinyl, jointed, rooted blonde hair, painted brown eyes and features; wearing original "Baby...One More Time Outfit" worn by Britney in her first video. ....$10-$15

10. Britney Spears Mini Doll. Play Along Toys, Inc. China. #23000 (Blister package version; also came boxed.) 1999 to 2000. 6 inches. All vinyl, jointed, rooted blonde hair, painted brown eyes and features; wearing MTV outfit. ..$10-$15

3: Britney Spears by Play Along Toys, Inc., wearing an MTV fashion in silver and charcoal gray. *Courtesy of Play Along Toys, Inc.*

4: Britney Spears dolls by Play Along Toys, Inc., wearing outfits from the "Oops I Did it Again" collection. *Courtesy of Play Along Toys, Inc.*

5: Britney Spears by Play Along Toys, Inc., wearing outfit from "Baby...One More Time" concert. *Courtesy of Play Along Toys, Inc.*

8: Assortment of 11-inch Britney Spears dolls wearing three different outfits, 2000. *Courtesy of Play Along Toys, Inc.*

9: Play Along Toys produced these 6-inch Britney Spears Mini Dolls in 1999-2000. *Courtesy of Play Along Toys, Inc.*

Spelling, Tori. Actress Spelling was cast by her father, Aaron Spelling, as Donna Martin in the Fox hit series *Beverly Hills 90210*. Besides her hit television series, Spelling has appeared in half a dozen films including *Scream 2* (1997).

Donna. Mattel, Inc. China. 1991. 11 inches. All vinyl, jointed, painted features; wearing black-and-white flowered mini dress, with red and pink two-piece bathing suit. ....$15-$20

Tori Spelling as Donna in *Beverly Hills 90210* by Mattel.

Spencer, Lady Diana. (See Diana, Princess)

Spice Girls. A very popular singing band of the late 1990s from the United Kingdom, The Spice Girls consisted of five girls until one, Geraldine Halliwell, dropped out after the first few years. The original group was made up of: Victoria Addams (Posh Spice), Melanie Brown (Mel B/Scary Spice), Emma Bunton (Baby Spice), Melanie Chisholm (Mel C/Sporty Spice) and Geraldine Halliwell (Geri/Ginger Spice). Their song, "Wannabe," hit number one and was followed by many more big hits.

1. Geri. Galoob Toys, Inc. China. #23504. 1997. 11 inches. All vinyl, jointed, painted features; wearing United-Kingdom-style dress with flag. Sold with booklet. ....$20-$30
2. Emma. Galoob Toys, Inc. China. #23502. 1997. 11 inches. All vinyl, jointed, painted features; wearing pink mini dress and holding white dog. ....$25-$35
3. Mel C. Galoob Toys, Inc. China. #23503. 1997. 11 inches. All vinyl, jointed, painted features; wearing black spandex styled legging and top and holding microphone. ....$25-$35

1-5: The Spice Girls by Galoob Toys, Inc. Top row, from left: Victoria, Mel B; bottom row, from left: Mel C, Emma and Geri. *Courtesy of David Spurgeon.*

4. Mel B. Galoob Toys, Inc. China. #23505. 1997. 11 inches. All vinyl, jointed, painted features; wearing two-piece leopard print outfit and holding microphone, also came with player. ....**$25-$35**

5. Victoria. Galoob Toys, Inc. China. #23501. 1997. 11 inches. All vinyl, jointed, painted features; wearing black mini skirt and top, holding microphone and came with two bags. ....**$25-$35** (See photos of 1-5 on page 143.)

6. Mel C. Street Life Limited. China. #62012. 1999. 12 inches. All vinyl, jointed, painted features; wearing orange pants with striped short top, came with white platform shoes. Box marked: "© 1999 Virgin Records LTD. U.S. Patent #5,607,336. © 1999 Spice Girls LTD. All Rights Reserved. © 1999 Toymax Inc. Plainview, NY 11803." ..**$15-$20**

7. Victoria. Street Life Limited. China. #62013. 12 inches. All vinyl, jointed, painted features; wearing red lace dress with black trim, came with black high heels. Box marked: "© 1999 Virgin Records LTD. U.S. Patent #5,607,336. © 1999 Spice Girls LTD. All Rights Reserved. © 1999 Toymax Inc. Plainview, NY 11803." ....**$15-$20**

8. Mel B. Street Life Limited. China. #62011. 12 inches. All vinyl, jointed, painted features; wearing rainbow colored pants and short top, came with orange platform shoes. Box marked: "© 1999 Virgin Records LTD. U.S. Patent #5,607,336. © 1999 Spice Girls LTD. All Rights Reserved. © 1999 Toymax Inc. Plainview, NY 11803." ....**$15-$20**

9. Emma. Street Life Limited. China. #62009. 1999. 12 inches. All vinyl, jointed, painted features; wearing blue mini dress, came with blue high heels. Box marked: "© 1999 Virgin Records LTD. U.S. Patent #5,607,336. © 1999 Spice Girls LTD. All Rights Reserved. © 1999 Toymax Inc. Plainview, NY 11803."......**$15-$20**

10. Spice Girls. Toy Concepts. China. Circa 1990s. Cheap plastic, painted features and rooted hair. These dolls are what are called "knock-offs," copies of licensed Spice Girl dolls. They were sold in two sizes and could be found in discount stores. The original retail price was $1.99 to $2.99. ....**$5-$10**

7: Victoria by Street Life Limited, wearing red lace dress.

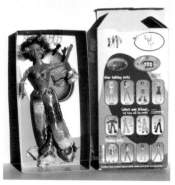

8: Mel B by Street Life Limited, wearing rainbow colored pants and short top.

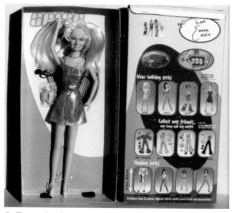

9: Emma by Street Life Limited, wearing a blue mini dress.

6: Mel C by Street Life Limited, wearing orange pants with striped short top.

10A: "Knockoff" versions of two Spice Girls in the 11-inch size.

10E: "Knockoff" version of a Spice Girl in the 15-inch size.

10B: "Knockoff" version of a Spice Girl in the 11-inch size.

10F: "Knockoff" versions of the Spice Girls in the 15-inch size.

10C: "Knockoff" versions of two Spice Girls in the 11-inch size.

10D: "Knockoff" versions of the Spice Girls in the 15-inch size.

Springer, Jerry. Talk-show host Springer is best known for his syndicated talk show, which brings together people who are usually not on the best of terms and encourages confrontations. Guests have been known to "punch each other out." The show has been on the air since 1991 on NBC.

Jerry Springer. Studios U.S.A. Made in China. #06298. 1998. 11 inches. All vinyl, jointed, painted features; wearing gray pants, black jacket, white shirt with yellow tie and glasses, with microphone. Box marked: "© 1998 Studios U.S.A. Television Distribution LLC." ....$20-$25

Stanley, Paul. (See KISS)

Starr, Ringo. (See Beatles, The)

Stevenson, Parker. Actor Stevenson played the role of Frank Hardy on the ABC television series *The Hardy Boys Mysteries*, which aired from 1977 until 1979.

Parker Stevenson as Frank Hardy. Kenner. Hong Kong. #45020. 1978. 12 inches. All vinyl, fully jointed, painted brown hair and brown eyes. Head marked: "© 1978 U.C.S.I. Copyright by Universal City Studios." ....$25-$40

Stimson, Sara. Actress Stimson was a child star who appeared in the Universal Pictures 1980 remake of the movie *Little Miss Marker*.

Little Miss Marker. Ideal. Hong Kong. #1382-1. 1980. 11 inches. Vinyl head and body, rooted brown hair, painted eyes; wearing blue cap with red and white trim, blue dress with white collar with red and blue trim, blue sweater, brown high-top shoes. Marked on back: "IDEAL//HONG KONG//P;" marked on head: "©1979//UNIV.STUDIOS//IDEAL//H390// HONG KONG." Box shows scenes from the movie and a picture of Sara Stimson. ......$35-$50

Jerry Springer by Studios U.S.A. *Author's collection.*

Box for Studio U.S.A.'s 11-inch Jerry Springer.

Sara Stimson from the remake of *Little Miss Marker,* by Ideal. *Courtesy of Suellen Manning.*

The side of the box for Sara Stimson shows scenes from the movie. *Courtesy of Suellen Manning.*

The original Little Miss Marker was played by Shirley Temple. The 1980 Ideal catalog shows both Sara Stimson and Shirley Temple as dolls.

Stooges, Three. (See Three Stooges)

Superman. (See Reeve, Christopher and Reeves, George)

Swit, Loretta. Actress Swit is best known for her role as Major Margaret "Hot Lips" Houlihan on the television series *M*A*S*H*, which aired on CBS from 1972 until 1983.

"M*A*S*H" Nurse. Distributed by F.W. Woolworth. Hong Kong. 1976. 8 inches. All vinyl, molded yellow hair. Copyright by Aspen Productions Inc. and Twentieth Century Fox Productions. ....**$20-$30**

2. Hot Lips. Tristar International, Ltd. #4100. 1982. 3 inches. All vinyl, fully jointed, painted hair and features; painted clothing. ....**$15-$25**

The back of the box for Sara Stimson shows a photograph of the child star from the movie. *Courtesy of Suellen Manning.*

Tabatha. (See Murphy, Erin)

Taylor, Elizabeth. Actress Taylor, an Academy Award winner, starred in a variety of films, including *Who's Afraid of Virginia Woolf* (1966) and *Cleopatra* (1963). She has also made headlines by the number of marriages she has had (eight to date). Taylor is an advocate for AIDS awareness.

1. Elizabeth Taylor paper dolls. Whitman Publishing Co. #94.1093. 1956. Shows two pictures of Elizabeth Taylor on cover. ......**$50-$75**

2. Elizabeth Taylor in *Father of the Bride*. Peggy Nisbet. England. #P758. 1970s. 7½ inches. All hard plastic, jointed at arms, mohair wig, painted features. ....**$50-$75**

3. Elizabeth Taylor in *The Blue Bird*. Horsman. U.S.A. #9921. 1976. 11 inches. Vinyl head, plastic body, rooted black hair, painted blue eyes, same doll that was used for Mary Poppins. ....**$40-$50**

4. Elizabeth Taylor as Amy in the movie *Little Women*. Ideal Toy Corp. 1984 to 1988. 12 inches. Vinyl, jointed, sleep eyes with eyelashes, rooted hair; dressed as Amy from *Little Women*. Marked on head: "©1978 MGM//CBS INC//1438 IDEAL 1982." ....**$40-$50**

5. Elizabeth Taylor White Diamonds. Timeless Treasures for Mattel, Inc. China. 2000. 12 inches. All vinyl, jointed, painted features, rooted black hair; wearing a violet gown with Swarovski necklace. ....**$75-$100**

5: Elizabeth Taylor White Diamonds, 12 inches, from Timeless Treasures for Mattel.

Temple, Shirley. Actress, singer and ambassador, curly-topped Shirley Temple was a beloved child star of the 1930s. She appeared in a great number of films and won a special miniature Academy Award for her work. After her career in the movies, she moved into politics, using her full married name of Shirley Temple Black. Her many accomplishments include being a delegate to the United Nations, serving as a delegate to numerous international conferences and summits on cooperative treaties, and becoming the first female Chief of Protocol of the United States. She also served as ambassador to the Republic of Ghana and then to the Czech and Slovak Federal Republics.

Only Ideal was authorized to produce Shirley Temple dolls in the United States. General values for composition dolls in mint, all-original condition are as follows: 11 inches, $700-$800; 13 inches, $500-$600; 15 inches, $500-$600; 16 inches, $600-$700; 18 inches, $800-$900; 20 inches, $1,000-$1,200; 22 inches, $1,000-$1,200; 25 inches, $1,200-$1,500; 27 inches, $1,500-$2,000.

3: Elizabeth Taylor from *The Blue Bird*, by Horsman. *Author's collection.*

Shirley Temple with one of Ideal's Shirley Temple dolls.

The vinyl and plastic Shirley Temple dolls went into production in 1957. (The dolls made in the 1970s and afterwards are valued at approximately half of the prices listed below, depending on doll.) They came in a variety of sizes including the following: 12 inches, $150-$200; 15 inches, $250-$300; 17 inches, $300-$375; 19 inches, $400-$450; 36 inches, $1,200-$1,400.

1. Shirley Temple. Ideal Toy Corp. U.S.A. 1930s. 13 inches to 22 inches. Composition. All original; wearing outfit from the movie *The Little Colonel*. ....13 inches, **$500-$600**; 22 inches, **$1,000-$1,200**

2. Shirley Temple. Ideal Toy Corp. U.S.A. Circa 1930s. 13 inches. Composition, all original, with a variety of outfits. ....**$1,000** up

3. Shirley Temple Ranger. Ideal Toy Corp. U.S.A. Circa 1930s. 17 inches. Composition, wearing a cowboy (Ranger) outfit, with box, outfit is all original with holster and silver gun marked "G Man." Head is marked: "Shirley Temple, Cop Ideal N & T Co." Shirley Temple tag on red bandanna with original Shirley Temple button. ....**$2,000-$3,000**

4. Shirley Temple look-alike. Maker unknown. Circa 1930s. 18 inches. Composition and jointed with tin sleep eyes, open mouth with teeth, black mohair wig. A black unauthorized Shirley Temple look-alike. ....**$400-$500**

5. Shirley Temple. Ideal Toy Corp. U.S.A. Circa 1930s. 18 inches. Composition, wearing outfit from the movie *Wee Willie Winkie*. ..**$1,000** up

6. Shirley Temple Baby. Ideal Toy Corp. U.S.A. Circa 1930s. 18 inches. Composition, all original, with flirty eyes; wearing yellow baby dress with ruffled bonnet. ....**$1,000** up

7. Shirley Temple. Ideal Toy Corp. U.S.A. Circa 1930s. 18 inches. Brown composition, wearing Hawaiian outfit. ....**$800-$1,000** (See photos of 5-7 on page 150.)

8. Shirley Temple. Reliable Doll Company. Canada. Circa 1940s. 29 inches. All composition, jointed at arm, legs and head, sleep eyes, mohair wig; wearing original dress. ....**$800-$1,000**

9. Shirley Temple. Ideal Toy Corp. U.S.A. 1957. 12 inches. Vinyl character head, hazel sleep eyes with molded eyelashes, single-stroke eyebrows, painted lower eyelashes, open/closed

1: Two composition Shirley Temples, 13 inches and 22 inches, both in original outfits from the movie *The Little Colonel*.

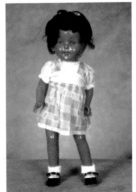

3: This all-original composition Shirley Temple Ranger, circa 1930s, sold at a McMasters Doll Auction for $5,000. *Courtesy of McMasters Doll Auctions.*

2: All-original 13-inch composition Shirley Temple with trunk and variety of outfits, circa 1930s. *Courtesy of Patricia Wood.*

4: An 18-inch black unauthorized composition Shirley Temple look-alike by an unknown maker, circa 1930s. *Author's collection.*

5: An 18-inch composition Shirley Temple in her outfit from the movie *Wee Willie Winkie. Courtesy of Susan Killoran.*

6: An 18-inch composition Shirley Temple baby, all original, with flirty eyes. *Courtesy of Patricia Wood.*

mouth with six teeth, original rooted hair in original set, five-piece vinyl child body; wearing original blue-and-white print playsuit, red felt coat, original socks and black plastic shoes. Marked: "Ideal Doll, ST-12" on head; "ST A-N" on back; "Shirley Temple Doll" on paper wrist tag; "Shirley Temple" in script on pin. ....**$150-$300**

10. Shirley Temple. Ideal Toy Corp. U.S.A. 1957. 12 inches. Vinyl character head, hazel sleep eyes with real eyelashes, single-stroke eyebrows, painted lower eyelashes, open/closed mouth with six upper teeth, dimples, rooted blonde hair in original set, five-piece vinyl body; wearing original pink nylon dress with black ribbon trim, pink slip and matching panties, original socks and black plastic shoes, extra clothing includes a red taffeta coat, orange print dress, red-and-white dress with Scotty dog, yellow dress with red rickrack, red-and-white checked dress, red straw hat, two extra pairs of black shoes, three extra original pairs of socks, two pairs of red tights, two pairs of panties, green vinyl raincoat, hat and purse, five red-and-white vinyl Shirley Temple purses, one black-

and-white Shirley Temple purse, one extra Shirley Temple script pin, a pair of brown pajamas. Marked: "Ideal Doll, ST-12" on back of head; "Shirley Temple" on script pin. This set with all the extra clothing sold at McMasters Doll Auctions in 1996. ....**$550**

11. Shirley Temple. Ideal Toy Corp. U.S.A. 1957. 12 inches. Vinyl head, blue sleep eyes with molded eyelashes, painted lower eyelashes, open/closed smiling mouth, six upper teeth, original rooted hair in its original set, five-piece vinyl child body; wearing original outfit from the movie *Wee Willie Winkie*, panties, socks and shoes. Marked: "Ideal Doll, ST-12" on back of head; "Shirley Temple, made by Ideal Toy corp." on tag on skirt; "Shirley Temple" in script on pin; "Ideal Shirley Temple Doll" in box lid. In original well-marked box. ....**$225-$275**

12. Shirley Temple. Ideal Toy Corp. U.S.A. 1957. 17 inches; 19 inches. Vinyl; flirty eyes, rooted hair in factory set; wearing a tagged yellow nylon dress with name tag at waist, double side-snap black leatherette shoes. ....**$450-$500**

13. Shirley Temple. Ideal Toy Corp. U.S.A. 1957. 36 inches. Shirley Temple Playpal. All vinyl, character head, hazel sleep eyes with real eyelashes, open/closed smiling mouth with six upper teeth, original rooted hair in its original set, child body jointed at shoulders, wrists and hips; wearing original yellow nylon dress with attached slip, white nylon panties, white socks, black one-strap shoes, with an 8-inch by 10-inch promotional picture of Shirley dating circa 1930s-1940s .

7: An 18-inch brown composition Shirley Temple in a Hawaiian outfit.

Marked: "Ideal Doll, ST-35-38-2" on back of head; "Ideal, 28-5" on back; "Shirley Temple" in script on pin; paper wrist tag reads: "Shirley Temple Playpal, 3 years old, She's a wonderful doll...she's Ideal." .... **$1,200-$1,400**

14. Shirley Temple. Ideal Toy Corp. U.S.A. 1958. 17 inches. All vinyl, rooted hair in its original factory set; wearing a tagged dress and black leatherette shoes, her Shirley Temple photo pin is attached at the waist......**$350-$400**

15. Shirley Temple Paper dolls. Circa 1950s. ....**$40-$50** (See photos 11-15 on page 152.)

16. Shirley Temple. Ideal. Hong Kong. 1972. 15 inches. Vinyl, fully jointed, sleep eyes; wearing flower-print dance dress. Marked on body: "IDEAL ST-15//HONG KONG;" marked on head: "IDEAL DOLL//ST-19-1." Reissued doll offered exclusively by Montgomery Ward. ......**$125-$150**

17. Shirley Temple. Ideal. Hong Kong. 1973 to 1975. 16 inches. Vinyl head, plastic body, rooted blonde hair with curls, brown painted eyes, open mouth with teeth; wearing dotted dress from the movie *Stand Up and Cheer*. Marked on back: "1972//2M-5534-2;" marked on head: "1972//IDEAL TOY CORP.//ST-14-H-213//Hong Kong." Box shows different scenes from various movies. ....**$150-$200**

18. Shirley Temple. Ideal. #14456. 1983 to 1985. 16 inches. Porcelain, painted features, wig with curls; wearing pink dress and white shoes. Limited edition of 10,000, with signed, numbered certificate of authenticity. The retail price at issue was $400. ....**$250-$300**

19. Bright Eyes. 1934. 22 inches. Wearing aviator jacket and helmet; rare. .... **$1500** up

20. Captain January. 1936. 16 inches to 20 inches. Flirty eyes; wearing organdy dress with blue and white flowers. ....16 inches, **$800-$900**; 18 inches, **$900-$1,000**; 20 inches, **$1,000** up.

21. Curly Top. 1935. 22 inches. Wearing velveteen coat and hat, white organdy pleated dress. .... **$1,000** up; with trunk and skates, **$1,500**

22. Now & Forever. 1934. 18 inches. Wearing green, lavender, orange and red dress ..**$1,000** up

23. Our Little Girl. 1935. 13 inches and 18 inches. Wearing Scotty dog dress. ......13 inches, **$800-$900**; 18 inches, **$1,000** up

24. Poor Little Rich Girl. 1936. 20 inches. Wearing sailor suit. ....**$1,000** up

A 12-inch vinyl Shirley Temple shown with her original box. *Courtesy of McMasters Doll Auctions.*

10: A 12-inch vinyl Shirley Temple with additional outfits, circa 1957, brought $550 at auction in 1996. *Courtesy of McMasters Doll Auctions.*

This 12-inch vinyl Shirley Temple with her original box and extra outfits, circa 1957, sold for $1,800 in 2000 at McMasters Doll Auctions. *Courtesy of McMasters Doll Auctions.*

11: A 12-inch vinyl Shirley Temple in her original outfit from the movie *Wee Willie Winkie*, in her original box, circa 1957. *Courtesy of McMasters Doll Auctions.*

15: Shirley Temple paper dolls, circa 1950s. *Courtesy of Steve Malatinsky.*

12B: A 19-inch vinyl Shirley Temple, nearly identical to the previous one except she is taller by two inches, the upper portion of the dress is different and she has her Shirley Temple tin photo button pinned on her waist ribbon. Her value is $500-$550. *Courtesy of Patricia Wood.*

Tennille, Toni. Singer Tennille is part of a musical duet with her husband, Daryl "The Captain" Dragon. They were known as The Captain and Tennille. Their television show, *The Captain and Tennille,* ran on ABC from 1976 until 1977.

Tennille. Mego. Hong Kong. #75000. 1977. 12 inches. All vinyl, fully jointed, rooted brown hair, painted brown eyes with eyelashes. Head marked: "© MOONLIGHT & //MAGNOLIAS INC.;'" box marked: "1977 MOONLIGHT AND MAGNOLIAS INC." ....$50-$60

13: A 36-inch vinyl Shirley Temple Playpal in her original outfit. *Courtesy of McMasters Doll Auctions.*

Toni Tennille from the duo The Captain and Tennille, by Mego.

Box for Mego's Toni Tenille.

14: A 17-inch vinyl Shirley Temple in an original tagged dress. *Courtesy of Patricia Wood.*

Tewes, Lauren. Actress Tewes is best known for her role as Julie McCoy on the hit television series *The Love Boat,* which aired from September 1977 to September 1986.

Julie. Mego. Hong Kong. #23005/2. 1981. 3 inches. All vinyl, fully jointed, painted red hair, painted blue eyes; painted and molded clothing. Sold on card showing picture of cast. ..**$15-$20**

Julie McCoy, as portrayed by Lauren Tewes, from the television series *Love Boat*. By Mego, on original card.

Thomas, Marlo.

Actress Thomas is best known for her role as Ann Marie in the television series *That Girl*, which aired from September 1966 to September 1971. The wife of former talk show host Phil Donahue, she is active with St. Jude's Children Hospital, a charity that was started by her father, actor Danny Thomas.

1. Marlo Thomas Paper Dolls. Saalfield. 1966. 6-inch by 15-inch box with paper dolls, coloring book, crayons, sticker book and travel game. ....**$30-$40**, cut; **$75-$100**, uncut

2. Marlo Thomas Paper Doll Box. Saalfield. 1967. 11-inch by 14-inch box with 13 outfits. ....**$30-$40**, cut; **$75-$85**, uncut

3. Marlo Thomas Paper Dolls Booklet. Artcraft. 1967. Shows illustration of Ann Marie with color photo. Green background. ....**$20-$25**, cut; **$35-$45**, uncut

4. That Girl—Marlo. Alexander Doll Co. U.S.A. #1789. 1967. 17 inches. Vinyl, plastic, fully jointed, rooted dark-brown hair, black sleep eyes with eyelashes; wearing green and blue jersey dress, white stockings and high white boots. Head marked: "ALEXAN-DER//19©66." ....**$600-$700**

5. That Girl—Marlo. Alexander Doll Co. U.S.A. #1793. 1967. 17 inches. All vinyl, fully jointed, rooted dark-brown hair, black sleep eyes with eyelashes; wearing red velvet gown. Head marked: "ALEXANDER//19©66." ....**$600-$700**

Thomas, Richard. Actor Thomas is best known for his role as John Boy Walton on the television series *The Waltons*, which aired from September 1972 to August 1981.

John Boy. Mego. Hong Kong. #56000/1. 1974. 8 inches. All vinyl, fully jointed, painted hair and features; wearing blue overalls with blue cap and plaid shirt. Head marked: "© 1974 LORIMAR//PROD.INC.;" back marked: "© MEGO CORP. 1974//REG. U.S. PAT. OFF// PAT. PENDING//HONG KONG." Sold singly and in a pack with Mary Ellen, who was played by Judy Norton-Taylor. ....**$15-$20**, loose; **$25-$30**, boxed, single; **$40-$50**, boxed pair

Mary Ellen and John Boy Walton by Mego, from the television series *The Waltons*. *Courtesy of McMasters Doll Auctions.*

The back of the box for Mary Ellen and John Boy Walton showing the farmhouse and truck that were also available. *Courtesy of McMasters Doll Auctions.*

Thorson, Linda. Actress Thorson's career was launched at the age of twenty, when she replaced Diana Rigg as Steed's partner in the television series *The Avengers* (1968-1969), selecting the name of Tara King for herself. After *The Avengers*, Thorson worked on stage as well as in films and on television before being cast in *Star Trek: The Next Generation* (1987), in the role of a Cardassian.

• **153**

Tara King. Maker unknown. Japan. 1968. 9 inches. Cheaply made plastic doll, painted features, glued-on brunette wig; wearing silver plastic top with red pants and silver shoes. The doll is unmarked and the only markings on the box are: "Tara Kins [marked incorrectly]//of// The Avengers Fame// 1968 Japan." The bottom of the box is marked "Tara King." The box has a picture of the character on it. ....$25-$75 (Price range varies due to uncertainty of date of manufacture.)

Tara King as portrayed by Linda Thorson by an unknown maker. Her name is spelled incorrectly on the box. *Courtesy of David Spurgeon.*

Three Stooges: (Moe, Curly, Larry.)

This comedic trio's antics would bring audiences to tears with laughter. They appeared in several films throughout their careers. Three were real-life brothers—Curly Howard, Moe Howard and the oldest, Shemp Howard; Larry Fine, known as the middleman, was eventually also one of the Stooges.

1. The Three Stooges. Exclusive Toy Products, Inc. China. 1997. 9 inches. All vinyl, painted features; wearing football outfits of tan pants and striped shirts. Larry's shirt is black-and-white and marked "½," Curly's shirt is black-and-white with "?" and Moe's shirt is red

and white and marked "H2O2." From the Limited Edition Collector's Series. **$125-$135**, set of three

2. Curly. Play-by-Play ACME. China. 1999. 14 inches. All vinyl, painted features ..**$15-$20**

3. Moe, Larry, Curly and Shemp. Figures Toy Co. China. 1999. 7 inches. All vinyl, painted features; all wearing identical outfits of red sleep gown with red sleep hat. Three Stooges Pajamas Set, limited to 5,000 pieces. ....**$60-$80**, set

4. Stooges. Highlight Starz. Sun Times Enterprises, Inc. China. 1999. 9 inches. All cloth with sewn-on clothes and features; wearing gray baseball uniforms with red letters that say "Stooges," also wearing gray hat with the initial "S." Part of the 1999 Baseball Collection. ..**$20-$30**, set

5. Curly. Figures Toy Co. China. 1999. 7 inches. All vinyl, painted features, wearing blue jeans with black tie and black-and-white checked shirt. Box marked: "The Three Stooges—Curly Joe 7 inch Action Figure." ....**$10-$15**

6. The Three Stooges. Classic Headliners. Equity Marketing Inc. China. 2000. 6 inches. Molded vinyl, molded and painted features; wearing molded clothing of black and white striped shirts with black knickers. They are each standing on a base on which their names— Larry, Moe, Curly—have been engraved. Limited edition of 20,000. ....**$10-$15** each

3: The Three Stooges—Moe, Larry, Curly and Shemp—by Figures Toy Co. *Courtesy of David Cox.*

1: The Three Stooges by Exclusive Toy Products, Inc.: Moe, Larry and Curly. *Courtesy of David Cox.*

4: The 1999 Baseball Collection Stooges. *Courtesy of David Cox.*

6: The Three Stooges Classic Headliners. *Courtesy of David Cox.*

5: Curly by Figures Toy Co., one of the Three Stooges. *Courtesy of David Cox.*

Timberlake, Justin. (See N'Sync)

Tork, Peter. (See Monkees, The)

Trang, Thuy. Actress Trang, a Vietnamese beauty, has appeared on television and in films. She played the role of Yellow Power Ranger Trini Kwan in *Mighty Morphin Power Rangers*, which aired from 1993 to 1996. (See Johnson, Amy Jo for photograph.)

Trini. Ban Dai. China. #2222. 1994. 9 inches. Power Rangers for Girls. All vinyl, jointed, painted features, long dark-brown hair; dressed in jean shorts with multicolored trim, yellow T-shirt with multicolored vest. Box marked: "© Bandai America, Inc." Came in boxed set with Pink Power Ranger and was also sold separately. ......**$25-$35** set; **$15-$20**, singly

Travis, Randy. Country-western singer Travis is one of America's best-loved country artists. He released seven consecutive number-one singles during one stretch. He won the CMA's Horizon Award in 1986 and was the association's Male Vocalist of the Year in 1987 and 1988.

Randy Travis. Exclusive Toy Products, Inc.

China. #18077. 1998. 9 inches. All vinyl, jointed; wearing jeans with blue shirt and belt. Boxed with stand and guitar. Box marked: "© Randy Travis." ....**$20-$30**

Randy Travis by Exclusive Toy Products, Inc.

Travolta, John. Actor Travolta's career blossomed when he played the role of Vinnie Barbarino on the television series *Welcome Back, Kotter*, which aired from 1975 until 1979. After the series ended, Travolta began a film career. He was nominated for Academy Awards for *Saturday Night Fever* (1977) and for *Pulp Fiction* (1994). Some of his other film credits include *Phenomenon* (1996), *Michael* (1996), *A Civil Action* (1998) and *Battlefield Earth* (2000).

1. Barbarino. Mattel, Inc. Taiwan. #9772. 1976. 9 inches. All vinyl, fully jointed, painted black hair, painted blue eyes; dressed in brown pants and jacket with T-shirt. Marked on back of head: "©WOLPER//KOMACK;" marked on back: "©1973//MATTEL INC//TAIWAN." Each doll in this series was sold on a card with an accessory piece. ....**$40-$50**

2. Barbarino Paper Dolls. Toy Factory. 1976. Shows illustration of Barbarino on cover. ....**$10-$15**, cut; **$30-$40**, uncut

4: Terl from *Battlefield Earth*, as portrayed by John Travolta, by Trendmasters Inc. *Author's collection.*

3. John Travolta. Chemtoy. #610. 1977. 12 inches. All vinyl, fully jointed, painted blue eyes, molded black hair; dressed in blue jeans with blue shirt and black belt. Box marked: "On Stage John Travolta Superstar 12" doll, can wear clothes of Ken, Donnie and all other 12" dolls. Made by Chemtoy Corp., Illinois, 1977." The box has a large photo of Travolta on the back. ....**$30-$40**, loose; **$60-$80**, boxed

4. Terl from *Battlefield Earth*. Trendmasters Inc., China. 1999. 11 inches. All vinyl, fully jointed, molded and painted hair and features, fully articulated with lights and sound. (When a button is pressed, one of six phrases from the movie is heard, including: "destroy all humans and animals.") Accessories include Gold Bricks, Radiation Detector, and Mining Gun that lights up. Box marked: "© 1999 Franchise Pictures LLC © Battlefield Productions LLC." With stand. ....**$20-$30** (See photo on page 155.)

Troyer, Verne. Actor and stuntman Troyer played Dr. Evil's silent midget clone, Mini Me, in the film *Austin Powers: the Spy who Shagged Me* (1999).

1. Mini Me. McFarlane Toys. China. 1999. 6 inches. All vinyl, painted features. Sitting on chair and sold on card. ....**$20-$25**

2. Mini Me. McFarlane Toys. China. 1999. 18 inches. All vinyl, painted features; dressed in gray suit. Push button to hear phrases. ....**$30-$40**

3. Mini Me (Moon Mission). McFarlane Toys. China. 1999. 18 inches. All vinyl, painted features; dressed in space suit. Push button to hear phrases. ....**$50-$60**

2: Vern Troyer as Mini Me, from the film *Austin Powers: The Spy Who Shagged Me*. By McFarlane Toys, in original box.

3: John Travolta from Chemtoy. Box marked "On Stage John Travolta Superstar 12" doll."

3: Mini Me as portrayed by Verne Troyer, by McFarlane Toys. *Author's collection.*

Truly Scrumptious. (See Howes, Sally Ann)

Turner, Debbie. Actress Turner played the role of Marta in the 1965 film classic *The Sound of Music*.

1. Marta. Alexander Doll Company. U.S.A. #1002. 1965. 8 inches. All hard plastic, fully jointed, dark brown wig, blue sleep eyes with molded eyelashes; wearing outfit from film. Part of set. ....**$200-$250**

2. Marta. Alexander Doll Company. U.S.A. #1102. 1965 to 1970. 11 inches. All vinyl, fully jointed, rooted dark brown wig, blue sleep eyes; wearing outfit from film. Part of set. ....**$200-$250**

3. Marta. Alexander Doll Company. U.S.A. #802. 1971 to 1973. 8 inches. All hard plastic, fully jointed, dark brown wig, blue sleep eyes with molded eyelashes; wearing outfit from film. Back marked: "ALEX." Part of set. ....**$175-$200**

Twiggy. (Leslie Hornby).

Twiggy was London's top teen model in the late 1960s, known for her big eyes and thin body. She arrived in the United States in 1967, causing a media frenzy.

1. Twiggy. Mattel, Inc. Japan. #1185. 1967. 11 inches. Vinyl, rooted eyelashes, heavy eye makeup, twist 'n turn waist, bendable legs; wearing a blue, yellow and green striped dress with panties and yellow boots, with orange and silver wrist tag and clear stand. Marked on rear: "© 1966//MATTEL, INC//U.S. PATENT-ED// U.S. PAT. PEND.//MADE IN JAPAN." Mattel's first fashion doll modeled after a living celebrity. ....**$75-$150**, loose; **$350-$400**, mint-in-box

1B: Close-up of Mattel's Twiggy. *Courtesy of McMasters Doll Auctions.*

2. Mint-in-box Twiggy outfits. Number 1725: made in 1968, a short yellow dress with green stripes and matching yellow socks, shoes, purse and necklace. Number 1728: made in 1968, a tank top with white pants, belt, hat, shoes and camera. Number 1726: made in 1968, includes a silver one-piece dress with belt, bra, panties and boots. Number 1727: made in 1968, includes an orange and yellow dress with matching scarf and shoes, orange cosmetic case, powder puff, mirror, eyelash brush, brush, pencil and comb. ....**$150-$200** each

Tyson, Mike. Tyson is a former Heavyweight Boxing Champion who was jailed from 1992-1995 following a trial for rape.

Mike Tyson. Maker Unknown. Korea. 12 inches. Vinyl head, cloth body, painted hair and features; wearing black-and-white prison outfit with red boxing gloves. ....**$15-$20**

1A: Twiggy from 1967, Mattel's first fashion doll modeled after a living celebrity. *Courtesy of McMasters Doll Auctions.*

Boxer Mike Tyson by an unknown maker. *Courtesy of David Spurgeon.*

Urich, Robert.

Actor Urich has starred both on television and in films. He played the role of Officer James Street on ABC's television series *S.W.A.T.*, which aired from 1975 until 1977. He also starred in *The Love Boat—The Next Wave* (1998).

1. Street from *S.W.A.T.* L.J.N. Toys, Ltd. Hong Kong. #6600. 1975. 7 inches. All vinyl, fully jointed, painted hair and features; dressed in S.W.A.T. gear. ....**$20-$30**

2. Street from *S.W.A.T.* L.J.N. Toys, Ltd. Hong Kong. #6850. 1976. 7 inches. All vinyl, fully jointed, painted hair and features; dressed in *S.W.A.T.* gear. ....**$20-$30**

Valentino, Rudolph.

Born May 6, 1895, in Castellaneta, Italy, actor Valentino came to America in 1913. Originally a stage actor, Valentino moved into film work with his first project, *Alimony*, in 1917. He starred in fourteen films, usually playing a suave lover, before his death from peritonitis at the age of thirty-one.

1. Valentino. LaRosa Company. Milana Croso Venezia. Italy. Circa 1920s. All felt, painted and molded features; wearing long cream cape, cream pants, bright red and multicolored belt and vest and turban. ....**$10,000-$12,000**

2. Valentino. Lenci. Italy. Circa 1920s. 29 inches. All felt, brown mohair wig, painted brown eyes; wearing leather boots and brightly colored felt outfit with long cape. ......**$10,000-$20,000**, depending on condition

3. Valentino. Unmarked and undated. 17 inches. Bisque head, hands and boots, cloth body. Bought in Italy. ....**$500-$700**

1: Street from *S.W.A.T.*, as portrayed by Robert Urich, by L.J.N. Toys., Ltd. *Courtesy of Suellen Manning.*

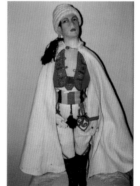

1: Rudolph Valentino by LaRosa Company, circa 1920s. *Courtesy of Billie Nelson Tyrrell.*

3: Unmarked 17-inch Valentino with bisque head, hands and boots. *Courtesy of Billie Nelson Tyrrell.*

Van Dyke, Dick. Actor Van Dyke is known for both his comedic and dramatic roles. He starred in his own television series, *The Dick Van Dyke Show* (1961-1966), as well as in many movies and television shows. Some of his best-known roles were in *Mary Poppins* (1964) and *Chitty Chitty Bang Bang* (1968) where he appeared as Mr. Potts. Van Dyke starred in the television series *Diagnosis Murder* (1993-2001).

1. Mr. Potts Talking Doll. Mattel, Inc. Mexico. 1969. #5235. 24 inches. Soft plush, pull string on side, screen-printed face with likeness of Dick Van Dyke; wears tan corduroy jacket with metal buttons, shirt collar, paisley tie, blue slacks and black boots. Pull the string to activate talking mechanism to hear one of ten different phrases. Marked: "Quality Originals by//MATTEL R//MR. POTTS TM//© 1968 GLIDROSE//PRODUCTIONS, LTD.//and WARFIELD//PRODUCTIONS, LTD.//© 1968 Mattel, Inc.//Hawthorne, Calif.//Made in Mexico." ....**$125-$150**

2. Chitty Chitty Bang Bang Miraculous Movie Car. Mattel, Inc. 1968 to 1969. #6150. Contains molded passengers in car depicting Mr. Potts, Truly Scrumptious and the two children. Car rolls and has an inflatable raft for floating on water. ....**$175-$200**

3. Chitty Chitty Bang Bang Paper Dolls. Whitman Paper Doll. #1982:59. Shows all the members of the principal cast. ....**$10-$15**, cut; **$30-$40** uncut

4. Chitty Chitty Bang Bang Liddle Kiddles. Mattel, Inc. 1969. #3597. Tiny doll versions of Mr. Potts and Truly Scrumptious with the two children. Adults are 2 inches tall, the children are 1 inch tall. ....**$300-$350**, mint-in-package set

Varney, Jim. Comedian Varney was famous for his big nose and exaggerated facial expressions. His character, Ernest, became well known and was cast in everything from television shows to car commercials.

Ernest Talking Doll. Kenner. China. 1989. 16 inches. All vinyl, with pull string in back, painted hair and features, molded head; wearing short-sleeved gray T-shirt with "ERNEST" on front, and blue vest. Pull the string to activate the talking mechanism to hear different phrases. Marked on tag: "© 1989 CARDEN AND CHERRY ADVERTISING AGENCY INC. Made in China. Kenner. Cincinnati, Ohio 45202;" box reads: "Hey Vern, IT'S ERNEST! Hey Vern, I TALK." ....**$40-$60**

3: Chitty Chitty Bang Bang Paper Dolls from Whitman. Include all members of the principal cast.

Ernest Talking Doll, Jim Varney's character, from Kenner.

4: Chitty Chitty Bang Bang Liddle Kiddles, from Mattel include Mr. Potts, as portrayed by Dick Van Dyke.

Kenner's 16-inch Ernest Talking Doll (Jim Varney) shown in original box.

Illya Kuryakin, as portrayed by David McCallum, and Napoleon Solo, as portrayed by Robert Vaughn—both from the television series *The Man From U.N.C.L.E.*—are shown with Honey West as portrayed by Anne Francis. They are all made by Gilbert. *Courtesy of McMasters Doll Auctions.*

Vaughn, Robert.
Actor Vaughn received a nomination for an Academy Award for his role in the film *The Young Philadelphians* (1959). From 1964 until 1968, he played the role of super-agent Napoleon Solo in the NBC television series *The Man From U.N.C.L.E.*

Napoleon Solo. Gilbert. Hong Kong, Japan and U.S.A. #16120. 1965. Vinyl head, painted hair and features, heavy vinyl arms, plastic legs and torso; wearing black pants with white shirt. Head marked: "K 4 5;" lower torso marked: "Copyright by Metro-Goldwyn-Mayer, Inc." ....**$75-$100**

Von Oy, Jenna.
Actress Von Oy played the role of Six LeMuere on the television series *Blossom*, which aired from January 1991 until June 1995.

Six LeMuere. Tyco Industries. People's Republic of China. #1915. 1993. 9 inches. All vinyl, jointed, painted features, smiling mouth with teeth, rooted dark brown hair; came dressed in black and gold shorts and top with red fishnet style skirt over top of shorts, black hat with red flower, with two different outfits, shoes and mirror. Box marked: "© 1993 Tyco Industries." ....**$20-$30**

Six LeMuere, as portrayed by Jenna Von Oy, from the television series *Blossom. Courtesy of David Spurgeon.*

The back of the box for Six LeMuere. *Courtesy of David Spurgeon.*

W

Waggoner, Lyle. Actor Waggoner is best known for his role as Steve Trevor on the television series *Wonder Woman*, which aired from March 1976 to September 1979.

Steve Trevor. Mego. Hong Kong. 1978. 12 inches. All vinyl, fully jointed, painted hair and features; wearing off-white top and pants. Shows a picture of Lynda Carter on the box. ....**$40-$50**, loose; **$100-$150**, boxed

Wagner, Lindsay. Actress Wagner is best known for her role as Jaime Sommers in the hit television series *The Bionic Woman*, which aired from January 1976 to September 1978.

1. Fembot. Kenner. Hong Kong. 1977. 12 inches. All vinyl, fully jointed with "bionic modules" in right arm, legs and ear, rooted blonde hair, painted olive eyes. Shows Fembot in disguise as mystery lady on box. Fembot was The Bionic Woman's Enemy. ..**$50-$75**, loose; **$150-$200**, boxed

2. Jaime Fashion Doll. Denys Fisher. United Kingdom. 1977. 18 inches. Came with gold gown and jewelry. Released only in the United Kingdom. Hard-to-find doll. ....**$200-$250**, loose; **$500-$600**, boxed

1A: Fembot, Jaime Sommers' enemy, by Kenner. Fembot could disguise herself as Jaime or as the Mystery Lady. *Courtesy of Marlene Grant.*

3. Jaime Sommers. Kenner. Hong Kong. 1976. 12 inches. All vinyl, fully jointed. There were three different dolls issued the same year. Issue No. 1 was dressed in a jogging suit, Issue No. 2 was dressed in a blue jumpsuit with mission and Issue No. 3 includes three different fashions. Canadian versions with French titles were also produced. .... Issue No. 1: **$30-$40**, loose; **$100-$125**; boxed. Issue No: 2: **$40-$50**, loose; **$150-$175**, boxed. Issue No. 3: **$50-$60**, loose; **$175-$200**, boxed

4. The Bionic Woman Paper Dolls. Children's Books. Italy. 1978. Shows picture of Lindsay Wagner on cover. ....**$30-$40**

1B: The back of the box for Fembot. *Courtesy of Marlene Grant.*

3A: Jaime Sommers, as portrayed by Lindsay Wagner, the Bionic Woman by Kenner. Her mission purse accessory and its contents are shown on the front. *Courtesy of Marlene Grant.*

3B: The back of the box for Jaime Sommers as the Bionic Woman. Details of her accessories and additional clothing are shown. *Courtesy of Marlene Grant.*

Wahlberg, Donnie. (See New Kids on the Block)

Waite, Ralph. Actor. Waite was cast as the father, John Walton, on the television series *The Waltons*, which aired from September 1972 to August 1981.

Pop from The Waltons. Mego. Hong Kong. #56000/2 (Mom and Pop). 1974. 8 inches. All vinyl, fully jointed, painted hair and features; wearing pants with plaid shirt and overalls. Head marked: "© 1974 LORIMAR// PROD.INC." Pop was sold singly and in a pack with Mom. ....**$15-$20**, loose; **$25-$30**, boxed, single; **$40-$50**, boxed, pair

John "Pop" Walton, from *The Waltons*, as portrayed by Ralph Waite, shown with Olivia "Mom" Walton, played by Michael Learned. *Courtesy of Marlene Grant.*

Walken, Christopher. Actor Walken made his stage debut at the age of sixteen, and has since starred in a variety of television shows and films, including *Dogs of War* (1980) and *The Deer Hunter* (1978), which earned him a Best Supporting Actor Oscar. Walken also played the role of the Headless Horseman in the film *Sleepy Hollow* (1999).

Headless Horseman. Todd McFarlane Toys. China. 1999. 6 inches. Vinyl, painted and molded hair, painted features, with head and skull that snap on neck; painted and molded clothing including cape, with axe and instruction booklet.

Christopher Walken as the Headless Horseman from *Sleepy Hollow* by Todd McFarlane Toys.

Package marked: "SLEEPY HOLLOW is TM Paramount Pictures and Mandalay Pictures LLC. © 1999 Todd McFarlane Productions, Inc." Part of "Feature Film Figures Series." ....**$25-$35**

Walker, Jimmie (J.J.). Actor Walker is best known for his role as James J.J. Evans, Jr., on the hit television series *Good Times*, which aired from February 1974 to August 1979.

1. J.J.–Talking J.J. Shindana Toys. Taiwan, U.S.A. 1975. 23 inches. Cloth doll with a pull string; wearing red shirt with the word "DYN-O-MITE!" and blue hat. Pull the string to hear nine different phrases. Tag reads: ©1975//TANDEM//PRODUCTIONS//INC.//SHINDANA TOYS." ....**$50-$75**, boxed

2. J.J. Shindana Toys. Taiwan. 1975. 15 inches. Cloth doll, printed features, "DYN-O-MITE" is written across his chest. Head marked: "© 1975//SHINDANA TOYS. Copyright by Tandem Productions, Inc." In window box. ....**$40-$50**, boxed

1A: Talking J.J., by Shindana Toys, based on the character played by Jimmie Walker in Good Times. *Courtesy of Suellen Manning.*

1B: Close-up of Talking J.J. by Shindana Toys. *Courtesy of Suellen Manning.*

Washington, George. Washington was the first president of the United States of America. His likeness is shown on the one dollar bill.

George Washington. S.S. Kresge Company. Hong Kong. 1970s. 7 inches. Vinyl head, painted features and hair, fully jointed plastic body; wearing blue jacket with orange suit and white shirt in revolutionary style. Marked on back "MADE IN//HONG KONG." Part of a series called the Heroes of the American Revolution, distributed by Montgomery Ward & Co. ....**$15-$25**

George Washington from the Heroes of the American Revolution series by the S.S. Kresge Company. *Courtesy of Suellen Manning.*

Wayne, John. Actor Wayne is best known for his many film roles as a cowboy and soldier. He appeared in more than 250 films, winning an Academy Award for his role in the film *True Grit.*

1. John Wayne Soldier (Cavalry). Effanbee Doll Company. China. 18 inches. 1982. All vinyl, fully jointed, painted features, painted blue eyes; dressed in soldier's uniform, with plastic

1B: Close-up of John Wayne Soldier. *Courtesy of Larry Rossiter, Jr.*

1A: John Wayne Soldier by Effanbee, the second in the Legend Series. *Courtesy of Larry Rossiter, Jr.*

gun and felt hat. Head and back marked: "WAYNE//ENT.//19©81;" tag reads: "JOHN WAYNE, AMERICAN Symbol of the West." The Effanbee Doll Co. produced a variety of limited-edition dolls with numbered certificates. Many of the dolls could only be purchased through Effanbee's Limited Edition Doll Club or the secondary market. Second in the Legend Series. ....**$200-$225**

2. John Wayne Cowboy. Same as previous doll but dressed in cowboy outfit and made one year earlier, in 1981. ....**$200-$225**

2A: John Wayne Cowboy by Effanbee, from 1981. *Courtesy of Larry Rossiter, Jr.*

2B: Close-up of a mint-in-box John Wayne Cowboy. *Courtesy of Marlene Grant.*

Weller, Peter. Actor Weller has performed both on stage and in films. He was the Robo Cop in the film of the same name.

1. Robo Cop. Kenner, Hong Kong. 1989. 4 inches. All vinyl, painted features and clothing; came with Gatlin Blaster. Sold on card. ..**$5-$10**

2. Robo Cop. Maker unknown. China. #32100. Circa 1990. 11 inches. All vinyl, poseable, molded and painted metal type clothing with helmet. This is an unauthorized figure and is unmarked. The only marking on the box is: "ROBOCOP FIGURE. Item No. 32100. MADE IN CHINA." ....**$20-$30** (See photos 1 and 2 on page 164.)

3. Robert Cop. China. #1201. Circa 1990. 11 inches. All vinyl, poseable with molded and painted metal type clothing with helmet. This is an unauthorized figure and is unmarked. Made to look like the Robo Cop figures, it is nearly identical to the previous figure except for a

slight difference in size and the shine on the black paint. Note the box with this figure is marked "ROBERT" not Robo. The only marking on the box is: "ROBERT COP 2. Item No. 1201. MADE IN CHINA." ....$20-$30

1: Peter Weller as Robo Cop, from the movie of the same name. By Kenner.

2: Unmarked and unauthorized version of Robo Cop from the movie of the same name. *Courtesy of David Spurgeon.*

3A: Unmarked and unauthorized version of Robo Cop, in a box marked "Robert Cop." *Courtesy of David Spurgeon.*

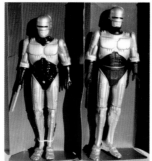

3B: A comparison of the two unmarked and unauthorized versions of Robo Cop. *Courtesy of David Spurgeon.*

Wells, Dawn. Actress Wells is best known for her role as Mary Ann Summers on the hit television series *Gilligan's Island*, which aired from September 1964 to September 1967.

1. Mary Ann. Maker unknown. Japan. Circa 1960s. 9 inches. Cheap plastic, painted features, glued-on hair. The doll is unmarked and the only markings on the box reads: "Mary Ann//of Gilligan's Isle//Fame//1965 Japan." A picture of the character appears on the box also ..$25-$75 (Price range varies due to uncertainty of date of manufacture.)

2. Mary Ann. Playskool. 1977. 3 inches. Soft rubber, painted features; from the cartoon series. Companion dolls were Gilligan and Skipper. ....$10-$15, each

1: Mary Ann from the television series *Gilligan's Island*, as portrayed by Dawn Wells, by an unknown maker. *Courtesy of David Spurgeon.*

West, Adam. Actor. West is best known for his role as Batman in the hit television series of the same name, which aired on ABC from 1966 until 1968.

1. Batman and Robin hand puppets. Ideal Toy Corp. U.S.A. 1966. 12 inches. Soft vinyl, cloth body. Trademarks: "©1966//NAT'L PERIODICALS." ....$50-$75

2. Batman. Ideal Toy Corp. U.S.A. Circa 1967. #3402-5. 12 inches. All vinyl, poseable arms and legs; dressed in Batman outfit. Body marked: "1967//IDEAL TOY CORP;" head marked: "© 1966//IDEAL." ....$100-$125

1: Batman hand puppet by Ideal, 1966.

3. Batman. Mego. Hong Kong. #51301. 1973. 8 inches. All vinyl, fully jointed, painted features; wearing Batman outfit. ....**$75-$85**

4. Batman. Mego. Hong Kong. 12 inches. 1978. All vinyl, fully jointed, painted features; wearing Batman outfit. ....**$75-$100**

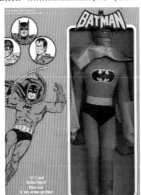

4: Batman, as portrayed by Adam West, from Mego. This is the 12-inch, 1978 version in original box.

3: Batman by Mego from 1973. *Courtesy of David Spurgeon.*

West, Mae. Actress West appeared in several films, often with W.C. Fields. Known as a sex symbol, West starred in *She Done Him Wrong* (1933) and *My Little Chickadee* (1940). She worked in the entertainment business from childhood until her late eighties.

1. Mae West. Effanbee Doll Company. China. U.S.A. #1982. 1982. 18 inches. All vinyl, fully jointed, rooted blonde hair, painted blue eyes; wearing black dress with hat and boa, large hat with feathers and walking stick. The Effanbee Doll Co. produced a variety of limited-edition dolls with numbered certificates. Many of the dolls could only be purchased through Effanbee's Limited Edition Doll Club or the secondary market. Part of the Legend Series. ....**$125-$150**

2. Mae West. Hamilton Gifts Ltd. Inc. China. #945056. 1991. 18 inches. All vinyl, painted features; wearing long black dress and hat. Box marked: "© 1991 Receivership Estate of Mae West." ....**$10-$25**

2: Mae West by Hamilton Gifts Ltd. Inc. from 1991. *Courtesy of David Spurgeon.*

Whelan, Jill. Actress Whelan is best known for her role as Vicki Stubing in the hit television series *The Love Boat*, which aired from September 1977 to September 1986.

Vicki. Mego. Hong Kong. #23005/6. 1981. 3 inches. All vinyl, fully jointed, painted red hair, painted blue eyes; painted clothing. Copyright by Aaron Spelling Productions, Inc. Sold on card that shows picture of cast. ....**$15-$20**

Mego's Vicki Stubing, as portrayed by Jill Whelan, from the television series *The Love Boat*. Three inches, on original card.

Whitaker, Forest. Actor Whitaker has starred on television and in films. He was a football player in the film *Fast Times at Ridgemont High* (1982) and he appeared as KER in John Travolta's film *Battlefield Earth* (2000).

KER. Trendmasters. China. #81627. 1999. 6 inches. All vinyl, molded and painted features; molded and painted clothing, with Psychlo Blaster and Dead Rats. Package marked: "©

1999 Trendmasters, Inc. St. Louis Mo. 63101
U.S.A." ....**$10-$15**

KER, as portrayed
by Forest Whitaker,
from the movie
Battlefield Earth by
Trendmasters.
Author's collection.

Janice Rand from the
television series *Star
Trek*, as portrayed by
Grace Lee Whitney,
by an unknown
maker. *Courtesy of
David Spurgeon.*

The back of the
box for KER. *Author's
collection.*

White, Vanna.
Television personality White is
the Letter Turner on the popular game show *Wheel
of Fortune.*

Vanna. Totsy Manufacturing Co. Inc. China.
HSN #92/975. 1998. 11 inches. All vinyl, fully
jointed, painted features, rooted blonde hair;
wearing black jumpsuit with metallic trim.
Exclusive for Home Shopping Network.
Limited edition. ....**$15-$25**

Whitney, Grace Lee.
Actress Whitney is best
known for her role as Yeoman Janice Rand on the television series *Star Trek*, which aired from 1966 until 1969.

Janice Rand. Maker unknown. Japan. 1966.
9 inches. Cheaply made, plastic, painted features, glued-on blonde wig; wearing yellow
plastic top with Star Trek logo, black plastic
pants and black shoes. The doll is unmarked and
the only markings on the box are: "Janice
Rand//of Star Trek//Fame//1966 Japan." The
box has a picture of the character. ......**$25-$75**
(Price range varies due to uncertainty of date of
manufacture.)

Wilcox, Larry.
Actor. Wilcox is best known for
his role as Officer Jon Baker on the NBC television
series *CHiPs*, which aired from September 1977 until
July 1983. He is currently working as a successful
businessman.

1. Jon from *CHiPs*. Mego. Hong Kong.
#08010/2. 1981. 3 inches. All vinyl, fully jointed,
painted yellow hair; painted uniform. ....**$10-$15**

2. Jon from *CHiPs*. Mego. Hong Kong.
#87500/1. 1981. 8 inches. All vinyl, fully joint-
ed, painted yellow hair and features; wearing
uniform with black boots. ....**$20-$25**

Wild, Jack.
Actor Wild is best known for his role
as the Artful Dodger in the film version of *Oliver*. He
also played Jimmy in the television series *H.R.
Pufnstuf*, which aired from 1969 to 1971.

Jimmy Hand Puppet. Remco. Hong Kong.
1971. 11 inches. Lifelike vinyl head, cloth puppet
body. ....**$100-$125**, loose; **$200-$300**, boxed

William (Prince).
Son of Prince Charles and
Princess Diana, William was born on June 21, 1982,
and is second in line to the British throne, after his
father, Prince Charles.

The back of the
box for Prince
William. *Courtesy
of David
Spurgeon.*

H.R.H. Prince William. House of Nisbet. England. #3181. 1982. 18 inches. Vinyl, jointed, blue sleep eyes, blonde rooted hair; wearing blue-and-white romper outfit with matching hat and red shoes with white socks. ....**$50-$75**

Prince William by House of Nisbet from 1982. *Courtesy of David Spurgeon.*

Williams, Anson. Actor and singer Williams appeared as Warren "Potsie" Weber on the hit television series *Happy Days*, which aired from January 1974 to July 1984. (See Howard, Ron for photograph.)

Potsie. Mego. Hong Kong. #63001/2. 1976. 8 inches. All vinyl, fully jointed, painted features, painted teeth; wearing pants, white shirt with jacket. Sold on card. ......**$50-$60**, on card

Williams, Barry.

Actor Williams is best known for his role as the oldest son, Greg Brady, on the hit television series *The Brady Bunch*, which aired from September 1969 to August 1974. Williams went on to work on the stage when the television show ended and has appeared in more than seventy-five stage productions.

1. Greg Brady. Exclusive Toy Products, Inc. China. #16052. 1998. 9 inches. All vinyl, jointed, painted and molded hair, painted features; wearing a groovy 1970s outfit from one of the show's episodes (in which he wants to be a singer), with guitar and stand. Copyright by Paramount Pictures. ....**$30-$40**

2. Brady Bunch Paper Dolls. Whitman. #4784/7418 in 1972, #4320/7209 in 1973 and #4340/7420 in 1974. Includes the cast of Robert Reed, Florence Henderson, Barry Williams, Maureen McCormick, Chris Knight, Eve Plumb, Mike Lookinland, Susan Olsen and Ann B. Davis. ....**$40-$50**, each, loose; **$60-$75** each, uncut

2: Brady Bunch Paper Dolls by Whitman.

1A: Greg Brady from the television series *The Brady Bunch*, as portrayed by Barry Williams, by Exclusive Toy Products, Inc. *Author's collection.*

1B: The back of the box for Greg Brady, autographed by Barry Williams. *Author's collection.*

Williams, Billy Dee. Actor Williams has appeared on stage and in films and played Lando Calrissian in the 1980 film *The Empire Strikes Back*.

1. Lando Calrissian. Kenner. Hong Kong. #39800. 1980. 3 inches. All vinyl, fully jointed, painted hair and features; painted clothing, wearing gray cape made of vinyl. Marked on left leg: "© 1980 L.F.L.//HONG KONG." ....**$25-$35**

2. Lando Calrissian. Hasbro. 1996. 12 inches. All vinyl, jointed, painted features; wearing long pants, blue shirt with blue and beige cape. ....**$20-$30**

2B: The back of the box for Lando Calrissian. *Author's collection.*

2A: Lando Calrissian, as portrayed by Billy Dee Williams, by Hasbro, from the film *The Empire Strikes Back. Author's collection.*

Williams, Cindy. After her big break in the film *American Graffiti* in 1973, Williams went on to star as Shirley Feeney on the hit television series *Laverne & Shirley*. The show aired from January 1976 to May 1983.

Laverne & Shirley. Mego. Hong Kong. #86500/1. 1977. 11 inches. All vinyl, fully jointed, rooted brown hair, painted blue eyes; both are wearing dresses. Boxed set with two dolls. **$40-$50**, each, loose; **$125-$150**, boxed set

Williams, Guinn, Jr. (Also known as "Big Boy.") A child star of the 1920s on the silent screen, Williams appeared in a variety of films into the 1950s. He was usually cast in westerns such as the film *Big Boy*, and had supporting roles in comedies such as *Bachelor Father* (1931) and dramas such as *The Glass Key* (1935), *A Star Is Born* (1937) and *Thirty Seconds Over Tokyo* (1943).

Big Boy. Maker unknown. U.S.A. 1929. Distributed by Educational Films. 18 inches. All composition, molded hair, painted features; wearing oversized pants, white shirt and black boots, with pin back with picture of Big Boy and the words "BIG BOY." ....**$750-$1,000**

Big Boy, as portrayed in the film of the same name by Guinn Williams, Jr., by an unknown maker, distributed by Educational Films. *Courtesy of Billie Nelson Tyrrell.*

Williams, Robin. Actor and comedian Williams first came to the attention of the public with his role as Mork in the hit television series *Mork & Mindy*, which aired from September 1978 to August 1982. He went on to star in a variety of feature films.

1. Mork. Mattel, Inc. Taiwan. #1276. 1979. 9 inches. All vinyl, fully jointed, painted hair and features; wearing a red and silver outfit, has backpack with talking mechanism that says eight different phrases. Copyright by Paramount Pictures Corporation. Shows Mork upside down in box. ....**$20-$25**, loose; **$45-$50**, boxed

2. Mork. Mattel, Inc. Hong Kong. #1275. 1979. 4 inches. All vinyl, fully jointed, painted hair and features; painted clothing. Sold on card with white egg-shaped space ship. ......**$25-$30**

1: Mork, as portrayed by Robin Williams from the television series *Mork & Mindy*, by Mattel, Inc., shown upside down in box.

3. Mork Talking Rag Doll. Mattel, Inc. Taiwan. #1279. 1979. 16 inches. Printed likeness of Robin Williams on cloth head with cloth printed body. Pull string to hear: "NA-NOO, NA-NOO." ....**$15-$20**, loose; **$35-$40**, boxed

3A:Mattel's Mork Talking Rag Doll based on the character portrayed by Robin Williams in the television series *Mork & Mindy*. *Author's collection.*

3B: The back of the box for Mattel's Mork Talking Rag Doll. *Author's collection.*

Williams, Serena. Professional tennis star Williams is the younger sister of professional tennis player Venus Williams. In her young career, she has already won two Grand Slam mixed doubles titles, two Grand Slam doubles titles and her first Grand Slam Singles Title (1999). In 2000, Williams became a Wimbledon Champion. (See also Williams, Venus.)

Serena Williams by Play Along Toys, Inc. *Courtesy of Play Along Toys, Inc.*

Serena Williams. Play Along Toys, Inc. China. #77000. 2000. 11 inches. All vinyl, jointed, painted features, smiling mouth and teeth, rooted and braided long black hair pulled back in ponytail; boxed with certificate of authenticity, blue gym bag with "Serena" on it, tennis racket, tennis balls, water bottle, shoes and headband. Box marked: "© 2000 Play Along (Hong Kong) Ltd. Copyright © 2000 by Serena Williams." ....**$25-$30**

Williams, Van. Williams starred as the Green Hornet in the 1966 television series of the same name.

1. Captain Action as the Green Hornet. Ideal Toy Corp. #3413-2. Circa 1966 to 1970. 12 inches. All vinyl, fully jointed; wearing the Green Hornet costume, the Green Hornet's sting cane, gas pistol and shoulder holster, gas mask, television set and telephone. Body marked: "1967//IDEAL TOY CORP;" head marked: "© 1966//IDEAL." ....**$100-$125**

2. Captain Action as the Green Hornet. Playing Mantis. China 1998. 11 inches. All vinyl, jointed; wearing traditional Green Hornet outfit, with accessories including sting cane, gas pistol, shoulder holster, gas mask, television set and telephone. Kay Bee Toys Exclusive. ....**$20-$30**

2: Captain Action as the Green Hornet as portrayed by Van Williams, by Playing Mantis. *Author's collection.*

Williams, Venus. Professional tennis star Williams made her professional tennis debut at the age of fourteen in Oakland, Calif. She is six feet, two inches tall and has a serve that has been clocked at 110 mph. She wears her signature beaded braids when playing. She won her first singles title, the IGA Tennis Classic on March 1, 1998, and is a Grand Slam and Wimbledon Champion. Williams signed an endorsement contract with Reebok reported to be worth twelve million dollars. Her sister is Serena Williams. (See also Williams, Serena.)

Venus Williams. Play Along Toys, Inc. China. #77000. 2000. 11 inches. All vinyl, jointed, painted features, smiling mouth and teeth, rooted and braided long black hair pulled back in ponytail; came boxed with certificate of authenticity, yellow gym bag with "Venus" on it, tennis racket, tennis balls, water bottle, shoes and headband. Box marked: "© 2000 Play Along (Hong Kong) Ltd. Copyright © 2000 by Venus Williams." ....**$25-$30**

Venus Williams by Play Along Toys, Inc. *Courtesy of Play Along Toys, Inc.*

Wilson, Flip. Comedian Wilson starred in his own NBC variety show *The Flip Wilson Show*, which aired from 1970 until 1974. He created a group of characters that he himself played, including the opinionated female Geraldine.

These photos of the Flip Wilson doll by Shindana show both the Flip Wilson side and the Geraldine side.

Flip Wilson. Shindana. Taiwan and U.S.A. Circa 1970. 15 inches. All cloth talking doll, printed differently on the two sides, one side showing Flip Wilson and the other side showing one of his characters, Geraldine. Copyright by Street Corner Productions, Inc. ....**$25-$35**

The box for the Flip Wilson doll.

Winkler, Henry. Actor and director Winkler is best known for his role as Arthur "Fonzie" Fonzerelli in the hit television series *Happy Days*, which aired from January 1974 to July 1984. He then moved behind the camera and became a successful director.

1. Fonzie Cloth Doll. Samet and Wells, Inc. Taiwan. 1976. 16 inches. All cloth, lifelike screened features and clothing. Tag marked: "© 1976 Paramount Pictures." ....**$25-$35**

2. Fonzie. Mego. Hong Kong. #63000. 1976. 8 inches. All vinyl, fully jointed, painted hair and features; wearing blue jeans, white T-shirt and black leather looking jacket. Copyright by Paramount Pictures Corporation. ....**$50-$60**

3. Fonzie Paper Dolls. Toy Factory. 1976. Cover shows Fonzie with black leather jacket. ....**$20-$30**, uncut

1A: Cloth Fonzie doll based on the character played by Henry Winkler in the television series *Happy Days*, by Samet and Wells, Inc. *Author's collection.*

1B: The back of the cloth Fonzie doll. *Author's collection.*

2A: Fonzie, as portrayed by Henry Winkler, from the television series *Happy Days*, by Mego Toys.

2B: Fonzie, by Mego, shown in original packaging. *Courtesy of Suellen Manning.*

Winslet, Kate. Actress Winslet has appeared in a variety of roles, but is best known for her portrayal of Rose in the blockbuster 1997 film *Titanic*.

Rose. Wayout Toys. China. #40304A. Circa 1990s. 11 inches. Cheaply made, vinyl, jointed at arms and legs, twist waist, painted features, rooted hair; wearing full-length burgundy dress with sash, with purse and famous Titanic jewel necklace. Unauthorized versions of the characters Jack, played by Leonardo Di Caprio, and

Rose from the film *Titanic*. Sold in set with Jack (also 11 inches). ....**$10-$15**, individually; **$25-$40**, pair

Rose as portrayed by Kate Winslet and Jack as portrayed by Leonardo DiCaprio, in the film *Titanic*, by Wayout Toys.

Wiseman, Joseph. Actor Wiseman appeared as Draco in the NBC television series *Buck Rogers in the 25th Century*, which aired from 1979 to 1981.

1. Draco. Mego. Hong Kong. #85000/5. 1979. 3 inches. All vinyl, fully jointed, painted gray hair, painted brown eyes; painted clothing. Copyright by Robert C. Dille. ....**$5-$10**

2. Draco. Mego. Hong Kong. #85001/4. 1979. 12 inches. All vinyl, fully jointed, painted gray hair, painted brown eyes; wearing long coat with boots. Copyright by Robert C. Dille. ......**$30-$40**

Withers, Jane. Actress Withers was a child actress who starred with Shirley Temple in the film *Bright Eyes* (1934). She continued to play small roles as an adult actress.

Jane Withers. Alexander Doll Company. U.S.A. 1937. 17 inches. Composition, fully jointed, brown or blue sleep eyes, open mouth with teeth (others were made with closed mouths), dark red mohair wig; wearing white straw hat with blue trim, pink dress with blue flowers and matching panties, also sold in a variety of outfits including pink dress with flowers. Pin reads: "Jane Withers;"

dress tagged: "Jane Withers All Rights Reserved, Madame Alexander, NY." ....**$1,000-$1,200**

Jane Withers by Alexander Doll Company, wearing pin and tagged dress. *Courtesy of McMasters Doll Auctions.*

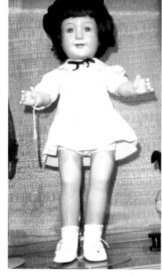

A 15-inch Alexander Jane Withers doll wearing her original white dress. *Courtesy of Annette's Antique Dolls.*

Witt, Katarina. A professional ice skater and actress, Witt competed in the Winter Olympics. Her titles include: two-time Gold Medal winner at the Olympics; four-time World Figure Skating Champion; six-time European Figure Skating Champion; and the 1995 Jim Thorpe Pro Sports Award. Witt also won an Emmy Award for her role in the 1990 film *Carmen on Ice*. A talented ice skater, Witt performs for Stars on Ice, a traveling ice-skating show that visits more than sixty cities across the United States.

Katarina. Playmates. China. Asst. #52500. Stock #52507. 1998. 11 inches. All vinyl, jointed, rooted black hair, painted blue eyes, painted features, smiling mouth and teeth; wearing one-piece black ice-skating skirt with halter style top covered with silver mesh, white sparkle-tone hose and white ice skates, with stand and "Stars on Ice" medal. Box marked: "© 1998 Playmates toys Inc. STARS ON ICE is a trademark of IMG." ....**$20-$30**

Katarina Witt by Playmates, shown with the back of her box. *Author's collection.*

Wood, Danny. (See New Kids on the Block)

Wopat, Tom. Actor Wopat is best known for his role as Luke Duke on the CBS television series *The Dukes of Hazzard*, which aired from 1979 until 1985.

1. Luke. Mego. Hong Kong. #09060. 1981. 3 inches. All vinyl, fully jointed, painted features, sold with two different head molds. Was part of a set with car and Bo (John Schneider). **$20-$30**

2. Luke. Mego. Hong Kong. #0950/2. 1981. 8 inches. All vinyl, fully jointed, painted dark hair and features. Head marked: "© WARNER BROS.//INC.1980;" back marked: "© MEGO CORP. 1974//REG U.S. PAT OFF//PAT.PEND-ING//HONG KONG." ....**$20-$30**

3. Luke. Mego. Hong Kong. #09010/2. 1982. 3¾ inches. Same as the first doll, but packaged separately. ....**$10-$15**

X

Xuxa. Originally from Brazil, Xuxa is a singer and entertainer who has appeared in movies and on television.

Xuxa. Rose Art Industries, Inc. China. 1993. #21000. 12 inches. All vinyl, painted blue eyes, painted features, rooted long blonde hair; wearing full-length pants suit with hot pink on the bottom and teal on the top, also sold wearing long white and black pants with multi-colored top with the letter "X" on front. Boxed with 25 Jewels 'N' Gems and silver and pink glitter glue to design your own sparkling fashions. Box marked: "© 1993 Rose Art Industries, Inc. Orange, NC. © 1993 Xuxa International Corp." ....**$40-$50**

Xuxa in white-and-black pants with multicolored top, by Rose Art Industries, Inc. *Courtesy of David Spurgeon.*

Xuxa in hot pink and teal pants suit, by Rose Art Industries, Inc. *Courtesy of David Spurgeon.*

The back of one of the boxes for Xuxa. *Courtesy of David Spurgeon.*

Y

Yamaguchi, Kristi. Professional ice skater Yamaguchi competed in the Winter Olympics and many championships. Her wins have included: Olympic Gold Medalist—1992; World Champion—1991, 1992; World Pro Figure Skating Champion—1992, 1994, 1996, 1997. Yamaguchi performs for Stars on Ice, a traveling ice-skating show that visits more than sixty cities across the United States.

Kristi. Playmates. China. Asst. #52500. Stock #52508. 1998. 11 inches. All vinyl, jointed, rooted black hair, painted brown eyes, painted features, smiling mouth and teeth; wearing one-piece black ice-skating skirt with halter style top trimmed with rhinestones, white sparkle-tone hose and white ice skates, came with stand and Stars on Ice medal. Box marked: "© 1998 Playmates Toys Inc. STARS ON ICE is a trademark of IMG." ....$20-$30

Kristi Yamaguchi by Playmates, shown with the back of her box. *Author's collection.*

Yeoh, Michelle. Actress Yeoh starred as the mysterious Wai Lin, a James Bond woman with a distinctly 1990s twist, who becomes 007's (Pierce Brosnan) most formidable female ally in the James Bond film *Tomorrow Never Dies* (1997). The Hong Kong-based action star is known to her fans as the female Jackie Chan.

Wai Lin. Exclusive Toy Products, Inc. China. #28014. 1997. 6 inches. Box marked: "© 1962 Danjaq, LLC & United Artists Corp. © 1988 Danjaq, LLC & United Artists Corp. © 1997 Danjaq, LLC & United Artists Corp. Tomorrow Never Dies 1997." ....$15-$20

Wai Lin, as portrayed by Michelle Yeoh in the film *Tomorrow Never Dies*, by Exclusive Toy Products, Inc. *Courtesy of David Spurgeon.*

INDEX

I

M

S

T